Test of Exchange Rate Determination Models

AF213330

Engin Dursun and Salih Barışık

Test of Exchange Rate Determination Models: Türkiye Application

PETER LANG
Berlin · Bruxelles · Chennai · Lausanne · New York · Oxford

Bibliographic information published by the Deutsche Nationalbibliothek.
The German National Library lists this publication in the German National Bibliography; detailed bibliographic data is available on the Internet at http://dnb.d-nb.de.

Library of Congress Cataloging-in-Publication Data
Names: Dursun, Engin, 1982- author | Barışık, Salih author
Title: Test of exchange rate determination models: TÜRKİYE application / Engin Dursun and Salih Barışık.
Description: New York : Peter Lang, [2026] | Includes bibliographical references.
Identifiers: LCCN 2025027830 (print) | LCCN 2025027831 (ebook) | ISBN 9783631933831 paperback | ISBN 9783631936771 pdf | ISBN 9783631936788 epub
Subjects: LCSH: Foreign exchange rates-Türkiye--Mathematical models
Classification: LCC HG3968.25 .D87 2025 (print) | LCC HG3968.25 (ebook) | DDC 332.4/509561--dc23/eng/20250905
LC record available at https://lccn.loc.gov/2025027830
LC ebook record available at https://lccn.loc.gov/2025027831

ISBN 978-3-631-93383-1 (Print)
ISBN 978-3-631-93677-1 (E-PDF)
ISBN 978-3-631-93678-8 (E-PUB)
DOI 10.3726/b22839

© 2026 Peter Lang Group AG, Lausanne (Switzerland)
Published by Peter Lang GmbH, Berlin (Germany)

info@peterlang.com

All rights reserved.
All parts of this publication are protected by copyright.
Any utilization outside the strict limits of the copyright law, without the permission of the publisher, is forbidden and liable to prosecution. This applies in particular to reproductions, translations, microfilming, and storage and processing in electronic retrieval systems.

This publication has been peer reviewed.

www.peterlang.com

**This book is derived from the doctoral thesis titled "Exchange Rate Determination Models: Example of TURKIYE" prepared by Dr. Engin Dursun under the supervision of Prof. Dr. Salih Barışık.*

Table of Contents

Figures

Tables

Preface

Trade in goods and services between countries, capital flows as well as many macroeconomic variables are of great importance in determining the exchange rates traded in national and international markets. It is seen that the amount of money in national and international markets, interest rates determined by central banks, growth and inflation rates affect exchange rates. There are many models developed in the literature regarding the determination of the exchange rate. The aim of the study is to investigate which of the developed models related to the determination of the exchange rate is valid for Türkiye. In the study, purchasing power parity model for Jan. 2003–Oct. 2021 period, Mundell–Flemming model for Jan. 2006–Sept. 2021 period, monetary model with flexible-price assumption for Sept. 2005–May 2021 period, and monetary hybrid model Jan. 2006–May 2021 period was analyzed for the period of Jan. 2006–May 2021. Fourier ARDL and ARDL cointegration tests were used in the analysis of the data.

As a result of the analysis, it was found that real variables did not affect the exchange rate much, the activity was mostly due to the financial system, and the change in the money supply and the interest rate affected the exchange rate. It is seen that exchange rates are affected by the exchange rate values of the past period. It has been concluded that monetarist approaches are more explanatory in explaining exchange rate changes, and even that the monetarist hybrid model has the highest explanatory power for Türkiye. As a result of the study, it was found that the exchange rate is sticky. From this point of view, it can be suggested to observe transparency during the determination and execution of exchange rate policies and to increase confidence in the Central Bank.

Keywords: Exchange Rate, PPP, Monetary Theory, ARDL, Fourier ARDL

Introduction

Today, exchange rates have become the center of attention for all segments of the economy, from commodity markets to financial markets, from public and private sector investments to individuals, and have become one of the main determinants of macroeconomic balance. The exchange rate, which is defined as the value of one country's currency against another country's currency, has become an increasingly important factor for every country engaged in economic activities with the outside world. In addition to trade in goods and services, the impact of foreign exchange transactions is increasing day by day due to their use in banking and derivative market transactions and domestic and foreign investment decisions. Due to the globalizing world economy, currencies with high convertibility such as U.S. Dollar, Euro, Sterling and Japanese Yen are more preferred due to the transaction volume in foreign currency transactions. Increasing transaction volumes increase the importance of monetary policies and exchange rate policies implemented by countries. Today, with globalization, exchange rates are affected not only by domestic dynamics but also by developments and dynamics outside the country.

There are many macroeconomic indicators that affect exchange rates. Indicators such as money supply, inflation rate, short- and long-term interest rates, GDP are among the leading dynamics affecting exchange rates. Favorable or unfavorable economic developments inside or outside the country may lead to improvement or deterioration of these indicators over time. Countries try to take measures against possible economic shocks with monetary and fiscal policies. The fact that the majority of economies have become open to foreign markets with globalization has further increased the importance of exchange rates. In this context, exchange rate stability and exchange rate determination models have become increasingly important.

In this book, exchange rate determination models are analyzed with econometric application for Türkiye. In the first chapter, the conceptual framework of exchange rate is drawn and the historical development of exchange rate, exchange rate definitions, exchange rate types and systems are explained. The reasons for the preference of exchange rate systems according to the economies of countries and the benefits and harm they will provide are mentioned. In the second part, exchange rate determination models are explained. Keynesian exchange rate determination models, purchasing power parity model, interest rate parity model, financial markets approach, speculative bubbles model, the effect of political and economic explanations on exchange rate determination, chaotic determinism and microstructure of foreign exchange markets models and their sub-expansions are explained. While analyzing these models, theoretical information on the variables that make up the models, the positive and negative aspects of the models, and the conditions under which countries can preferably use these models are presented. Although all exchange rate determination models have a theoretical framework, the variables that can test all of these models are controversial. Although there are studies that test exchange rate determination models with some data, there are successful models and models whose theory is still being studied.

The third section aims to test exchange rate determination models for Türkiye. In the section, firstly, the historical process of the exchange rate policies implemented in Türkiye will be mentioned and then a literature review on the subject will be made. In the application part, empirical studies will be conducted for the purchasing power parity model, the Mundell–Flemming model, the monetarist model with flexible-price assumption, and the monetarist hybrid model that takes into account real interest rate differentials. Purchasing power parity model will be analyzed for the period Jan. 2003–Oct. 2021, Mundell–Flemming model for the period Jan. 2006–Sept. 2021, monetarist model with flexible-price assumption for the period Sept. 2005–May 2021, and monetarist hybrid model for the period Jan. 2006–May 2021. In the analyses, Fourier ARDL cointegration tests for purchasing power parity theory, Mundell–Flemming model, monetarist model with flexible-price assumption and monetarist hybrid ARDL cointegration tests will be conducted for the model. Possible structural break tests will be applied for policy changes and economic shocks in the models.

In the Conclusion section, the findings obtained from the empirical studies will be evaluated. According to the results, the similarities and differences with the studies in literature will be discussed and some suggestions will be made.

Foreign Exchange Rate Definition, Types and Policies

1.1. Definition and Development of Exchange Rate

The issue of meeting the needs of human beings to survive and how and by which methods to do so has been one of the most important issues shaping both world history and the world economy. The behaviors of people to sustain their lives cause many economic decisions to be made, whether consciously or unconsciously. These decisions are sometimes based on desires, sometimes on necessities, and sometimes simply on the solution of a problem. However, the main problem is how many of the needs that cause these decisions to be taken are met.

The problem of scarcity, which is the fundamental problem of economics, deals with meeting unlimited human needs with scarce resources and seeks rational solutions to this problem. Considering that even the richest societies have unmet needs, the difficulty of societies to overcome this problem shapes the world economy. However, it is a fact that not all the needs of every society can be met.

In meeting unlimited needs, mankind has developed many accepted methods for centuries. In the early stages of history, the exchange system, which refers to the exchange of a certain good for another good, was used. It is seen that exchange, which has gone through a certain historical process, has evolved to another dimension with the invention of money. The invention of money by the Lydians living in Anatolia in the 7th century BC changed many phenomena in the world. It is seen that money, which has made a significant contribution to world trade and the development of civilizations since those days, is used as a means of payment for all kinds of goods and services purchased, as a unit of account, as a means of exchange, and as a means of saving (Parasız, 2009, p. 10). Before the invention of money, sometimes unfair exchanges could be made as it was necessary to exchange another good for the needed good, but with the invention of money, the obligation to exchange goods for goods has disappeared.

In the historical process, money has been transformed into commodity money, representative money, paper money, bank money (dematerialized money) and now cryptocurrencies. In its first form, the concept of commodity money refers to the exchange of another valuable commodity for a certain commodity. In the period when commodity money was accepted, grains, animals, fabrics, hides, skins, metals, etc., were accepted and exchanged for a type of commodity needed in return. In this period, unjust exchanges that did not match the severity of the need were one of the reasons that made barter difficult.

Metal money, a type of commodity money, facilitated trade after the commodity money system. Since the value of the money expressed the value of the mine in the period when the coin was used, it was one of the factors that facilitated trade for people to carry the coin instead of carrying a good in exchange for the goods they would buy in the barter process. This situation shaped the mining activities and trade of the period. Silver and gold, which were the accepted metals, ruled as single or dual metals in the periods they were used. Instability in the exchange rates due to the scarcity of gold and silver mines prepared the end of the dual metal period (Karluk, 2013, p. 700). The instability in mineral production, in turn, created a domino effect by affecting the money supply and trade in goods.

Representative money system is the system in which the habit of carrying precious metals after the commodity money system is abandoned and certificates or banknotes of the same value are used instead of coins. The system, which started in England in the 1800s, started to spread through banks (Bulut and Demirel, 2015, p. XIV). The Bank of England, one of the most important and pioneering banks of the period, tried to control the money supply by issuing banknotes against gold and silver coins. In other words, the money supply increased and decreased according to the increase in the value of goods and services, rather than depending on the demand for money, and this situation defines the classical quantity theory. Again, following the Bank of England, financial crises started to emerge due to the private banks that were opened and the valuation problem caused by the fact that each bank had its own currency. The underlying problem of these crises was the disruption of the market balance by increasing the number of banknotes printed in exchange for gold and the resulting inflation in the country (Karluk, 2013, p. 701).

The paper money system consists of the paper money used today, issued as a result of official decisions taken by governments and accepted as legal tender. Since these coins cannot be converted into precious metals, there is a danger of unlimited increase in the money supply. This danger is that the absence of the equivalent of paper money can lead to a major economic threat (Parasız, 2009, p. 34).

With today's indispensable internet network and digitalization, the banking system has not remained indifferent to these developments. The global integration process is reaching a large volume as many institutions and government agencies strengthen their digital equipment under the leadership of the private sector. As one of the requirements of the era, it is seen that people move their financial transactions from the physical environment to the virtual environment, keep their deposits in demand deposit accounts belonging to banks and/or other financial institutions rather than carrying cash with them, and make their payments with debit cards, credit cards and digital tools (Bulut & Demirel, 2015, p. XIV). For this reason, this type of money that functions as money is called bank money, also known as dematerialized money. Here, governments impose legal reserve requirements on bank deposits to limit or control the production of dematerialized money and to have the assets to transfer resources to banks when needed (Parasız, 2009, p. 36).

It is also necessary to mention the existence of cryptocurrencies, which have become widespread at the last point of the digital world. Crypto currencies can be defined as virtual currencies created with different encryption methods of digital data and used in barter transactions. In the study, which was first conducted in 2009 by a person named Satoshi Nakamoto, whose real identity is even suspicious, information was given about Bitcoin, the first and pioneer of cryptocurrencies. He prepared a technical report on Bitcoin's working principle, production, payment and transfer system (Kuzuloğlu, 2020). In general, the fact that cryptocurrencies are not linked to a central bank is an advantage for some and a disadvantage for others. While some see the independence of the country's economy from the world economy and not being affected as an advantage, others see accountability and having an interlocutor as a disadvantage. Due to this difference of opinion, the legality of these currencies is uncertain from country to country. As the cryptocurrency debate continues, some countries allow the use and trade of cryptocurrencies, while others are cautious and some prohibit them (Bitlo.com, 2021).

Almost every independent country in the world has its own financial system. While countries use the currency of their own country within their political borders, they can trade with other countries using their own currency, the currency of the country they trade with or the currency of a third country. In this case, there will be two different prices for the goods and services that countries trade.

These prices are the price of the goods and services in question in terms of foreign currency and the other is the price in terms of the home currency (Karluk, 2013, p. 591). In this case, the exchange rate is defined as the value of one country's currency in terms of another country's currency. In other words, it is the rate applied in the exchange of two different currencies (Bulut and Demirel, 2015, p. 42). The use of exchange rates has facilitated transactions in international trade, enabled the trade of more goods and services, and finally eliminated the negative effects of barter trade (Bulut, 2005, p. 7). It can also be said that the interconversion of national currencies laid the foundations of foreign exchange markets with its trade-enhancing effect.

Another effect of foreign exchange markets is that they allow price comparisons. Knowing the prices of goods and services produced in other countries leads entrepreneurs to produce many goods and services in their own countries, reduce costs and improve production techniques. Although the exchange rate is a rate, changes in the exchange rate have a deeper impact than changes in the prices of goods and services (Karluk, 2013, p. 591). Exchange rate changes have the power to affect not only the price of a good or service but also all transactions traded on the foreign exchange market.

1.1.1. Definition and Scope of Exchange Rate

Foreign currencies are generally referred to as foreign currency. For example, for Turkish citizens, Dollar, Euro, Sterling, Yuan and Yen are foreign currencies. In foreign exchange markets where all currencies of all countries are together, it is possible to exchange all foreign currencies with each other (Seyidoğlu, 2013, p. 123). This exchange is done with a coefficient that determines the exchange of two currencies and this is called the exchange rate (Eğilmez, 2013).

In its simplest definition, the exchange rate is defined as the rate of exchange between currencies. This rate is an important tool in terms of world trade, inter-country relations and domestic and foreign economic relations (Krugman et al., 2012, p. 320). The exchange rate may have positive and negative contributions to the national economy in the export of goods and services produced within the country and the import of goods and services purchased from abroad. In this sense, it is an important issue on which the exchange rate system will be built or according to which methods the exchange rate will be determined. In foreign exchange markets, foreign currencies are exchanged for their national currencies, while other currencies can be exchanged for their values through indirect methods (Bulut and Demirel, 2015, p. 42). The reason for this exchange is that all countries in the world need money for goods and services subject to trade. As long as international trade continues, these currencies will always be needed. Since there is no single currency in the world's payment systems, foreign exchange markets will continue to operate 24 hours a day, seven days a week.

The exchange rate is determined according to the exchange rate regime preferred by the country. For example, if the value of the national currency against foreign currencies is priced in the exchange rate market, the floating exchange rate regime is preferred; if the value of the national currency is priced separately for each foreign currency by the central bank, the fixed exchange rate regime is preferred (Eğilmez, 2013). Preferences and methods of determining the exchange rate vary from country to country. Since the production power, factor prices, social and political structures of each country are different from each other, countries choose the most appropriate regime for themselves according to their experiences and economic policies.

An important feature of foreign exchange markets is the difficulty of measuring the size of the market. In order to measure the size of the markets, information on market flows should be recorded instantaneously. However, while it is difficult to obtain and organize these records at the national and international level and to obtain a complete result, the main reason for this is the lack of an authority to regulate these markets (Levich, 1998, p. 68).

In addition to spot markets where financial assets are delivered instantly, forward and futures markets also exist. According to the Bank for International Settlements, the total volume of foreign exchange transactions in global markets amounted to $6,595 billion as of 2019. Of this figure, $87 billion was realized in spot markets, $999 billion in forward transactions and $297 billion in option transactions (Bank for International Settlements, 2019).

When global markets are analyzed, there are three major factors in the increase in transaction volumes. These are the introduction of the Euro as a strong player in the foreign exchange market in 2002, the increase in world trade volume, and the increase in electronic broker transactions because of bank mergers (Bulut and Demirel, 2015, p. 44). Independently of foreign exchange transactions, because of the entry of cryptocurrencies into the global market since 2009, the cryptocurrency market has reached a volume of 2.8 trillion dollars as of November 2021 (Tradingview, 2021). Although these markets are still viewed with prejudice, foreign currency inflows and outflows to and from these platforms continue from many countries around the world. When we look at the most traded currencies among all these markets, the U.S. dollar, Euro and Japanese Yen continue to dominate (Bank for International Settlements, 2021). Since foreign exchange markets are global markets, market size and market depth are increasing because transactions can be made 24/7 in every point of the world geography (Bulut & Demirel, 2015, p. 45).

1.1.2. Historical Development of the Exchange Rate

Looking at the international monetary system, it is seen that countries have tried many methods in choosing exchange rates for centuries in order to facilitate their trade relations on a common ground. Countries work on appropriate exchange rate policies by determining policies in line with their own country dynamics. In policy choices, countries focus on systems that are resilient against possible shocks, that they can intervene in response to shocks without wasting time, which reduce bureaucratic obstacles and that the parties will not suffer any victimization during these transactions. For some countries, searches and studies on the selection, implementation and sustainability of the exchange rate system are ongoing. Considering today's conditions, where instant trade of goods and services can be carried out after technological developments and world stock market movements can be evaluated instantly, studies on standard systems are being carried out in many fields in the world. In the search for systems that are understandable and usable by everyone instead of complex systems, systems that enable instant trading for stock exchange, foreign exchange and crypto assets are offered to the service of people.

Exchange rates, which express the value of foreign currencies in terms of domestic currency, are priced differently according to their current and future values in the markets where they are traded. In other words, in addition to spot and forward exchange rates, the differences between the nominal and real value of the exchange rate are also important for investors and countries. These price differences vary according to the exchange rate regimes and determinant policies of the countries. For a better understanding of exchange rate systems, it is necessary to look at the history of the international monetary system. When we look at the historical development of the international monetary system, we come across five different periods (Müslümov et al., 2002, p. 10). These periods are the dual metal standard, gold standard, gold exchange standard, flexible exchange rate systems and optimum exchange rate areas.

1.1.2.1. Dual Metal Mining Standard Era

According to the dual metal system, also called bimetallism, countries set the price of their national currencies according to the two most valuable metals (gold and silver) that were generally accepted in the world at the time. It was the dominant currency in international trade at the time of its implementation. Many countries, including the United States, China, India, Germany, France and the Netherlands, exchanged their currencies for gold or silver (Müslümov et al., 2002, p. 11). While this system facilitated international trade, it also contributed to price stability among countries. In the dual metal system, countries envisaged exchange by determining the gold and silver equivalent of their currencies. Thus, the country's currencies became convertible against gold or silver. Over time, fluctuations in the value of gold and silver made convertibility difficult. In this situation, Gresham's Law, which expresses the principle of *bad money drives good money out of the market,* emerges.

According to Gresham's Law, while the system envisaged the use of coins as a means of payment, individuals saw the coins that appreciated in value over time as a means of storage and caused price instability (Seyidoğlu, 2013, p. 48). Friedman emphasized that this system was unstable and inadequate because it envisaged a constant exchange of standards, and therefore a single metal standard was more preferable (Friedman, 1990, p. 87). As Friedman pointed out, the reason that led to the end of the double metal standard was the increase in gold production and thus the preference of gold over silver. In this process, while the gold supply increased with the discovery of gold in America in 1848, Australia in 1851 and South Africa in 1885, countries decided at the International Monetary Conference in 1867 that they would switch to a single metal standard and use only gold (Müslümov et al., 2002, p. 11). The United Kingdom enacted a law for the transition to this system long before the 1816 conference and started to implement it (Friedman, 1990, p. 97). After the conference, in the 1870s, countries such as Germany, France and the United States completed the transition to the gold standard system in turn (Friedman, 1990, p. 91).

1.1.2.2. Gold Standard Era

The gold standard system is an international monetary system in which countries defined the value of their currencies in terms of gold coins in the 1870s and which was partially applied until 1914, when World War I started, and after the war until 1929 (Karluk, 2013, pp. 701–702). With this system, it was aimed to use gold in different units in terms of weight and adjustment in domestic and foreign payments, and it was thought that the imbalance in foreign payments would be eliminated in this way in countries that advocated the freedom of foreign trade (Karluk, 2013, p. 702). Countries that adopted the system defined the currencies of their countries based on the gold price and provided convertibility to maintain parity (Müslümov et al., 2002, p. 12).

It was thought that the system would eliminate the imbalances that might occur in foreign payments during the period of its implementation. This theory is based on David Hume's price-gold money flow theory. Assume that there are two countries applying the gold standard as in Hume's classical foreign trade model. In the model, one country has a trade surplus and the other a trade deficit. Gold will flow from the country with a surplus balance of trade to the country with a deficit balance of trade as its imports exceed its exports, thus increasing the money supply, purchasing power and the general level of prices in the surplus country. The surplus country will increase its imports from the deficit country and decrease its exports as the other country's goods become more attractive. In a country with a trade deficit, gold exports will reduce the money supply, and the general level of prices will fall, leading to an increase in exports and a decrease in imports. As a result, from the countries' point of view, the picture will be reversed and a balance of payments will be achieved (Akbay, 2009).

In many studies, Mundell, Eichengreen, Obsfeld and Taylor have argued that the determination of exchange rates in international monetary systems moves together with capital markets (Karluk, 2013, p. 699). Open economies are characterized by economic welfare for the exchange rate, they strive to meet three objectives. These objectives are freedom of international capital mobility, independence of monetary policy and preference for a fixed exchange rate. However, since these three objectives cannot be realized at the same time, this situation is called a "trilemma" (Obstfeld et al., 2004, p. 76). In the impossible trilemma, it is predicted that capital mobility will occur when monetary policy independence and fixed exchange rates are realized together; fixed exchange rates cannot be implemented when capital mobility and independent monetary policy are realized together; and independent monetary policy will not work when fixed exchange rates and capital mobility are realized (Cömert, 2016, p. 121). Until 1914, when World War I broke out, more countries prioritized political independence in the period when the gold standard was applied, while fewer countries prioritized political independence in the implementation of capital mobility and fixed exchange rate systems (Obstfeld and Taylor, 2003, pp. 253–260).

The gold standard is essentially one of the fixed exchange rate systems (Karluk, 2013, p. 701). The reason why the fixed exchange rate system is compatible with the gold standard system is that the country's currency is convertible to gold. Thus, for policy purposes, it was thought that capital mobility (whether for speculative purposes or not) would ensure stability under all circumstances (Müslümov et al., 2002, p. 13).

The gold standard has contributed to an increase in trade between countries. According to López-Córdova and Meissner, while the trade volumes of countries included in a monetary union (whether other countries are members of the union or not) increased by 2.8 times, the trade of countries that adopted the gold standard with each other increased by more than 30% and these rates are statistically significant (López-Córdova and Meissner,

2003, p. 350). The adoption and spread of this standard by other countries, which started in the 1870s, increased the volume of world trade and led countries to adopt the gold standard system before World War I. Since this was a period when the free foreign trade policy was mostly adopted, it is seen that countries benefited from all the opportunities of free foreign trade, although there were interventions from time to time. It is seen that the United Kingdom, which advocated free foreign trade at that time, was the country that benefited the most from this situation, was the price determinant of many goods on the world stock exchange and was a country that shaped the capital market (Karluk, 2013, p. 702). This situation led to the strengthening of the convertible sterling.

Another feature of the gold standard is that it sets a limit on the monetary expansion of countries and the general price level is not affected by the expansion in the money supply (Krugman et al., 2012, p. 488). It is stated that the only factor that will affect the general level of prices depends on the unlimited money printing of the reserve currency country (Müslümov et al., 2002, p. 13). One of the main features of the gold standard is that the international monetary adjustment mechanism is symmetric. When a country's reserves decrease, its money supply contracts, while the money supply of countries that gain reserves increases (Krugman et al., 2012, p. 487).

The gold standard system has some disadvantages. First, it imposes restrictions on monetary policy implementations to reduce unemployment. It is stated that in times of global recession affecting the world, the problem can be overcome only if all countries raise their money supplies jointly (Krugman et al., 2012, p. 488). The second disadvantage is that since the general level of prices depends on gold reserves, the increase in gold reserves may cause price fluctuations (Müslümov et al., 2002, p. 13). The third disadvantage, again related to the previous point, is the problem of whether economic growth and gold reserves will increase in parallel. Even if countries achieve their growth targets, the absence of any gold reserves in return may cause major problems. The fourth and final disadvantage of the gold standard is that countries with gold mines have an advantage over other countries and have the power to influence the macroeconomic conditions of other countries through gold prices as they wish (Krugman et al., 2012, p. 488).

In 1914, with the outbreak of World War I, the gold standard was shelved for a while (Karluk, 2013, p. 702). In this situation, very few countries left their national currencies free floating. In the period from the war to the Great Depression of 1929, countries mostly preferred fixed exchange rates in line with the trilemma principle, only a few countries allowed capital mobility and very few preferred political independence (Obstfeld et al., 2004, p. 106). In the post-war period, until the Great Depression, countries wanted to go back to the gold standard, and the United States took the first step in 1919 by adopting the gold standard at the pre-war exchange rate (Karluk, 2013, p. 702). Following the United States, the United Kingdom and France returned to the gold standard. In the post-war period, many countries had to devalue their currencies due to the difficulty of linking their currencies to gold at the pre-war parity as a result of the increase in the amount of wartime money (Obstfeld et al., 2004, p. 87). In the post-war period, the gold standard was not as successful as in the pre-war period due to reasons such as more interventionism of states in the economy, increased protectionism in foreign trade and deterioration of price stability (Karluk, 2013, p. 702).

The fate of the gold standard, on the other hand, changed with France's massive capital inflows and its decision to use a payment instrument other than gold to pay its balance of payments surplus. France's gold imports led to deflationary pressures in the gold standard countries, especially in London, which in turn led the United Kingdom to abandon the sterling–gold parity (Eichengreen and Flandreau, 1997, p. 196). The overvaluation of national currencies due to high inflation in the post-war period made the sustainability of balance of payments deficits difficult. The Depression of 1929 marked the end of the gold standard and led to its complete abandonment in 1933 (Seyidoğlu, 2013, p. 23). It was observed that the success of gold standard practices before World War I could not continue in the post-war period. The failure of the gold standard in the post-war period led to a shift of the economic and financial center from London to New York (Obstfeld et al., 2004, p. 79).

1.1.2.3. Depression Period

The 1929 Economic Depression first started in the United States with deflation, increased unemployment and a decrease in production (Karluk, 2013, p. 703). The Smoot–Hawley Act, which was enacted in the United States in 1930 to prevent unemployment and reduce the import of agricultural products, and the increase in customs duties on industrial and agricultural products led to the collapse of foreign trade (Öz, 2009, p. 17). The law was designed to increase domestic production and reduce unemployment by raising customs duties. Nevertheless, it led to a decline in production and foreign trade in a world where balances were disrupted after World War I and its aftermath. For example, the volume of foreign trade in mid-1932 was one-third of that of 1929 (Karluk, 2013, p. 703). The closure of some banks in the United States starting in 1930 and the contraction in the money supply caused the crisis to deepen (Öz, 2009, p. 20).

The economic contraction was not limited to the United States, but almost every country raised customs tariffs with the effect of the post-war period, thus causing the revival of Mercantilism. Even the United Kingdom, one of the pioneers of free trade in the pre-war period, used the crisis as an excuse to adopt the "Preferential Tariff System" and imposed high tariffs on non-member countries (Seyidoğlu, 2015, p. 150). The implementation of protectionist policies was not limited to these two countries, and many countries adapted to this situation over time due to both political and economic conditions. The United States and the United Kingdom subsequently, for protection purposes, Germany increased customs duties by 3.75 times; Italy by 3.2 times; France and Switzerland by 2.5 times; Denmark, Czechoslovakia, Belgium and the Netherlands by 2.5 times; and India by 4 times. Not finding this sufficient, 16 European countries and France also started to apply quotas (Öz, 2009, pp. 28–29).

These policies were aimed at reducing unemployment, increasing production and exports, and cutting imports. As a result, it led to the export of political problems to neighbors with the phrase "*beggar my neighbor*," which means to put the neighbor in harm's way (Karluk, 2013, p. 703). The factor that prepared the end of the gold standard was the desire of many countries to hold on to their gold reserves through protectionist policies, as in the closed economy model, in order not to lose their gold reserves under these conditions. With the abandonment of the gold standard, there was no possibility of converting international currencies into each other, which caused countries to experience difficulties in international payments. Although some countries tried to overcome these problems through bilateral trade agreements or barter, in general, world trade and money flows declined significantly (Seyidoğlu, 2013, p. 23).

In terms of the trilemma hypothesis, the Depression period, when countries adopted protectionist policies and experienced difficulties in international payments, is the period when international capital mobility and the independence of monetary policies decreased and fixed exchange rates were preferred (Obstfeld et al., 2004, pp. 105–106).

It is also possible to say that the first monetary area was established during the Depression (Seyidoğlu, 2015, p. 150). After the United Kingdom abandoned the gold standard, the Exchange Equalization Fund was established in 1932 to prevent excessive fluctuations in sterling and to protect the value of sterling (Karluk, 2013, p. 703). Especially the fact that the former British colonial countries used the pound sterling as their national currency and made their payments in sterling caused them to experience difficulties in foreign trade. In order to overcome these problems, the United Kingdom and the colonial countries established the Sterling Area in 1938 (Seyidoğlu, 2013, p. 23).

Under the leadership of France, Switzerland, Belgium and the Netherlands formed their own union and adhered to gold in their trade and foreign exchange balances. This group of countries formed the Gold Bloc by maintaining the gold standard in return for the pound sterling area (Karluk, 2013, p. 704). The countries forming the Gold Bloc, like the countries forming the Sterling Area, resorted to measures to prevent foreign trade to keep their balance of payments strong, to prevent the decrease in gold reserves and to prevent an increase in unemployment. At this point, countries such as the United Kingdom, New Zealand, Norway, Sweden and Denmark corrected their balance of payments during the period when they did not apply the gold standard and at the same time, they applied expansionary monetary policy and cut interest rates. Considering that this was a period of limited policies, this policy partially worked. While it took three years for the industrial production of countries that preferred expansionary monetary policy to decline, it took seven years for the Gold Bloc countries that remained on the gold standard to shrink (Öz, 2009, pp. 25–26).

Germany, like many other countries in the post-World War I period, implemented a strict foreign exchange policy and abolished the convertibility of their currencies (Seyidoğlu, 2013, p. 24). Countries that maintained protectionist policies after the Depression signed very few cooperation agreements. In the period leading up to World War II, countries needed the re-liberalization of international trade and a system to regulate financial flows in order to overcome economic difficulties. The first step of the needed system was taken with the decisions taken after a series of negotiations in Bretton Woods in New Hampshire after World War II.

1.1.2.4. Bretton Woods System Period

Starting in 1929, the international monetary and payments system, which was damaged because of the Depression, had to be rebuilt. In the aftermath of the Depression, the United States began to strengthen economically as the capital and reserves of European countries shifted to the United States with the effect of World War II (Bulut and Demirel, 2015, p. 7). The need for a new international monetary and payments system and the general level of prices that could rise after the war resulted in the convening of the United Nations Monetary and Financial Conference under the leadership of the United States. The conference was held in Bretton Woods, New Hampshire, the United States, between July 1–22, 1944, 44 countries signed the Bretton Woods Agreement (Karluk, 2013, p. 705). With the decisions taken, it was decided to establish the World Bank (officially known as the International Bank for Reconstruction and Development) and the International Monetary Fund, known as the IMF. The World Bank was tasked with regulating international financial relations, while the IMF undertook the tasks of healing the wounds of the European economies destroyed in the war, the development of underdeveloped countries and providing financial aid to these countries (Seyidoğlu, 2013, p. 24).

According to the Bretton Woods System, countries that ratified the agreement are members of the IMF as per the agreement. With the agreement, the United States would become the banking country and other member countries would give their reserve gold, which they did not use except for production, to the United States at a fixed price. The United States, in turn, committed to keep this gold as a reserve and to provide access to gold only in U.S. dollars instead of direct access to gold by other member countries (Karluk, 2013, pp. 704–705). Thus, countries agreed to convert their national currencies into U.S. dollars at a fixed exchange rate and the United States agreed to convert dollars into gold. In line with this decision, the United States committed to the member countries to convert ounces of gold at a fixed price (35 dollars). The member countries also determined the price level at which their national currencies would be converted against the U.S. dollar (Bulut and Demirel, 2015, p. 8). In other words, when the United States wanted to supply the U.S. dollars held in the central banks of other member countries to the United States Federal Reserve, the FED agreed to sell these dollars at the parity of 1 ounce = $35 (Seyidoğlu, 2013, p. 24). Thus, the system was envisaged to work by linking the money of the member countries to the dollar and the dollar to gold. For this reason, this system is also called the gold exchange system (Cömert, 2016, p. 119).

IMF member countries were to decide at what price level they could convert their national currencies against the U.S. dollar. However, this did not mean that they could act with infinite freedom. The system limited the fluctuation of the dollar parity determined by other countries and allowed the parity to fluctuate only around the specified range (±1) (Seyidoğlu, 2013, p. 25). Thus, an adjustable fixed exchange rate system was adopted. Interventions outside the specified range could be made by the central banks of the member countries, but in case of large imbalances in the balance of payments, the approval of the IMF was required (Cömert, 2016, p. 119). This was considered as a precautionary measure for countries that might have problems with their balance of payments.

The Bretton Woods Conference aimed to erase the economic scars left on the world by the Depression and World War II. For this purpose, it was aimed to establish a more liberal economic order with the participation of more countries. In this context, the views of John Maynard Keynes from the United Kingdom and Harry Dexter White from the United States on the new economic process to be established were the prominent agendas of the conference. Keynes argued that for the structuring of the multilateral payments system, a clearing union should be established in international payments, countries should aim to achieve balance of payments, countries should have their own quotas, and international payments should be made through central banks with dematerialized money called "bancor" (Karluk, 2013, p. 705). In order for the Kliring system to work, countries had to offset their debts or receivables that they would announce for foreign payments in certain periods with bancor, and countries with a deficit in the balance of foreign payments were offered to provide credit support through bancor if they needed it.

White's plan aimed to overcome the difficulties experienced by countries in the aftermath of the Depression, to establish a new international payments system and to establish a more broadly participatory international financial system, and it has differences from Keynes' plan (Tekin et al., 2018, p. 151). According to White's plan, it was envisaged that a Stabilization Fund would be established on behalf of the World Bank and the United Nations, countries with difficulties in foreign payments would be supported by providing funds, and stability could be achieved by moving away from exchange controls with a fixed exchange rate system (Karluk, 2013, p. 705). White suggested that a dematerialized currency called "unitas," similar to Keynes' bancor, could be used as a dematerialized currency.

At the end of the conference, Keynes' plan was not accepted, and White's plan was accepted with a few changes. As a result, the countries that accepted the Bretton Woods System accepted the formation of two new financially powerful institutions through international financial cooperation. These institutions, known as the Bretton Woods twins, are the IMF and the World Bank. In addition to these institutions, by adopting the adjustable fixed exchange rate system, countries were able to eliminate the deterioration in the balance of payments through exchange rate adjustments by leaving exchange rates fixed in the short term. Creating the liquidity needed by the international financial system for the sustainability of the system, liberalization of trade by removing international trade barriers and finally, the convertibility of national currencies in trade between countries with the new system are the innovations brought by the system (Alper, 2016, p. 144).

The IMF's six priority objectives (De Vries, 1986, p. 14) were:

1. Promote international monetary cooperation through an institution that mechanizes consultation and cooperation on international monetary issues,
2. To facilitate the expansion and balanced growth of international trade. To make the promotion and maintenance of high levels of employment and real incomes and the development of the productive resources of all members the main objectives of economic policy,
3. To regulate foreign exchange relations among members by promoting stability in foreign exchange transactions,

4. To help eliminate foreign exchange restrictions that impede international trade by establishing a multilateral payment system for current transactions between members,
5. To enable member countries to correct any mismatches in the balance of payments without jeopardizing national or international stability by ensuring the use of IMF resources with guarantees, and
6. The objectives are to shorten the time foreseen for these transactions and to reduce the degree of imbalance in the members' balance of payments.

The IMF's role in realizing these objectives is to carry out economic supervision of the countries that use resources and to aid with the development of the production capacities of the member countries with the financial support provided. One of the most important tasks assigned to the IMF is to guide the member countries in ensuring their economic growth without destabilizing their financial stability. According to the rules of the Union, it was one of the most important issues for member countries to maintain their financial stability. The second task of the IMF was to provide assistance to member countries in need of foreign exchange in the event of a deterioration in the balance of payments in order to restore the balance of payments to provide the necessary financial support.

Thus, it was determined that the IMF would be the first organization to extend a helping hand to member countries in case of economic difficulties and crises. Finally, it was envisaged that if countries needed financial know-how and expertise in addition to direct assistance, the IMF could provide this support. Since not all member countries had the same economic infrastructure, not all of them would have the same ability to stabilize in accordance with the principles of unity. IMF undertakes to train the necessary personnel by establishing specialized institutions to determine and develop the principles of macroeconomic policies, provided that countries that may have difficulties in adaptation request it (Tekin et al., 2018, p. 152).

The Bretton Woods System initially met the needs of the period. The economic destruction of European countries due to the Depression and World War II caused the United States to emerge economically stronger from this process. Considering that European countries were war-weary at the time and Japan had not completed its economic development, the goods and technology required for the reconstruction of the destroyed economies were imported from the United States. This import intensity caused the United States to become an unrivaled power (Seyidoğlu, 2013, p. 25). The resources that these countries transferred to the United States for the transfer of goods and technology led to an increase in the United States gold stocks. It is possible to say that the idea of converting member countries' dollars into gold as a requirement of the system originated from here. The Bretton Woods System continued to function smoothly as long as the United States had sufficient gold stocks and met the liquidity needs of countries with balance of payments problems.

The United States, from which many countries in Europe and Asia imported goods such as raw materials, vehicles, machinery, equipment, etc., especially basic foodstuffs, had a surplus in foreign payments. While the United States produced and exported these needed goods, other countries had a deficit in foreign payments due to insufficient foreign exchange reserves, and importing countries suffered from dollar shortages due to the demand for dollars (Bulut and Demirel, 2015, p. 30).

In addition to this economic situation, different developments were taking place in the world. In 1947, with the Truman Doctrine, United States President Truman announced that he would provide aid to many economies affected by the war in Europe after World War II with the contribution of the threat of communism spread by Soviet Union. Within the framework of the Marshall Plan, the United States provided aid to many countries, especially Western European countries, which were experiencing liquidity shortages and were close to Soviet Union (Erhan, 1996). As a result of these aids, by the 1950s, the U.S. economy had started to run an external payments deficit, whereas European countries and countries such as Japan had run an external payment surplus since 1958. The period between 1958 and 1971 is referred to as the period of dollar abundance due to the FED's printing of dollars in excess of gold stocks, Marshall Aid, financing of the Korean and Vietnam wars, and the strengthening of European economies and foreign payments surpluses (Bulut and Demirel, 2015, p. 30).

In 1960, Belgian economist Triffin criticized the Bretton Woods System as unsustainable. This view, also known as the Triffin dilemma or the Triffin paradox, argued that for the system to continue, the United States should provide international liquidity by printing dollars, which would devalue the

dollar and damage the gold–dollar relationship of the system (Eğilmez, 2015). For this purpose, Triffin made a proposal similar to Keynes' proposal at the beginning of the Bretton Woods Conference, which was not accepted. In this proposal, he argued that the IMF should issue its own currency instead of the dollar and advocated the IMF to become the World Central Bank. In 1965, due to the increase in the U.S. current account deficit, confidence in the U.S. dollar and thus in the system was shaken. As Triffin predicted, in 1969, the IMF introduced its own currency, the Special Drawing Rights (Special Drawings Right—SDR), but this arrangement was not enough to reduce the pressure on the Bretton Woods System (Bulut and Demirel, 2015, pp. 31–32). In 1971 and 1973, two devaluations of the U.S. dollar damaged the discipline of the exchange rate system, and this negativity led to the collapse of the system by breaking the link between the dollar and gold (Karluk, 2013, p. 707).

The problems that emerged in the implementation of the Bretton Woods System prepared the end of the system. These problems can be categorized under five headings (Karluk, 2013, pp. 707–709):

1. Liquidity and confidence in reserve money,
2. The problem of external balance,
3. The problem of emission gains,
4. The problem of wasting resources, and
5. It is a question of speculation.

By linking the currencies of other member countries to the U.S. dollar, the system gave the dollar the function of being a standard of value and led to its use in all international payments. The fact that the dollar was the reserve currency in the implementation of the system facilitated foreign trade payment. However, with the onset of the liquidity problem, the attempt to overcome the problem by printing more U.S. dollars damaged the gold–dollar parity and shook the confidence in the dollar.

IMF member countries could not adjust their exchange rates frequently because of the requirement to keep their exchange rates fixed within a specified range under the adjustable fixed exchange rate regime. In cases where devaluation was necessary to eliminate balance of payments deficits, high rates of devaluation could cause imbalances in the domestic market. In the Bretton Woods System, countries with a surplus in the balance of external payments put the burden of running the system on countries with a deficit in external payments (Karluk, 2013, p. 708). This situation affected the course of foreign trade and prevented the development of developed and developing countries at the same rate.

Since the anchor currency was the U.S. dollar, the United States was entitled to seigniorage. Seigniorage or emission earnings are the difference between the economic value stated on the currency and the cost of printing the currency (Akçaba and Şafaklı, 2019, p. 19). The fact that the U.S. dollar was the international reserve instrument meant that emission gains went to the United States as required by the system. The fact that Bretton Woods member countries exported goods and services to the United States and accepted dollars in return and kept these earnings as dollar reserves meant that other countries provided interest-free loans to the United States (Seyidoğlu, 2013, p. 29). Until 1971, when the system collapsed, this interest-free loan situation was criticized by many member countries, especially France. With the dollar assuming the function of reserve currency, the dollar reserves of the member countries started to increase, and at the same time, the convertibility of dollars with gold became unsustainable as the U.S. balance of payments balance sheet ran deficits (Seyidoğlu, 2013, p. 26). As a matter of fact, the dollar reserves in other member countries exceeded the gold reserves accumulated in the United States, which prepared the end of the system. In this process, the efforts of individuals and organizations holding dollar-denominated securities to convert the securities in their portfolios into gold led to speculation and international trade and capital movements were adversely affected.

From 1969 onwards, the IMF introduced SDRs into the system, but the expected benefit from their use as international reserve currency could not be achieved. In the face of these developments, the United States, Germany, Belgium, France, the Netherlands, the Netherlands, the United Kingdom, Italy, Sweden, Japan and Canada, known as the Group of 10, came together and signed the Smithsonian Agreement in Washington in 1971 (Bulut and Demirel, 2015, p. 32). The following articles were accepted as per the agreement (Karluk, 2013, p. 713):

- The United States agreed to increase the price of 1 ounce of gold from 35 dollars to 38 dollars but abandoned the practice of converting dollars into gold. In addition, 1 SDR = 1.08571 USD, and although the gold price of the SDR was fixed, its price in dollar terms was raised.

- The currencies of participating countries other than Canada were revalued, adding 12% to the value of the dollar.
- The exchange rate of national currencies accepted in the Bretton Woods System against the dollar the fluctuation range of ±1% was increased to ±2.25%. The parity fluctuation range among currencies other than the dollar increased to 9%.

Although the Bretton Woods System ended with the Smithsonian Agreement signed in 1971, countries still continued to use the dollar as a reserve currency. The fact that countries kept the dollar as a reserve currency did not provide the desired stability in money markets, the current account deficit of the United States increased and 1 ounce of gold rose to 42.22 dollars in 1973. This rise led to an 11% devaluation of the dollar against the SDR (Karluk, 2013, p. 715). With the second devaluation of the dollar, the fixed exchange rate regime was abandoned, and the Bretton Woods System was terminated.

1.1.2.5. Flexible Exchange Rate Systems Period

In order to revise the bottlenecks of the Bretton Woods System, studies have been carried out with the relevant boards of the IMF since 1971. Three years after the Bretton Woods System was abandoned in 1973, the IMF established the Provisional Council. The Council met in Kingston, Jamaica and decided to add four articles to the IMF's founding law to contribute to the international monetary system. These decisions were adopted by the IMF Board of Governors and entered into force on April 1, 1978. With the second amendment of the IMF Agreement, three new features were added to the old agreement (Bulut and Demirel, 2015, p. 37):

1. The IMF's responsibility was expanded by giving member countries more latitude in the management of exchange rates,
2. More importance has been attached to the SDR, and
3. The IMF has been given more freedom of action in addressing the short-term balance sheet imbalances of IMF member countries.

In addition, the importance of member countries pursuing stable exchange rate policies within the IMF and among themselves was emphasized. In line with these developments, member countries could choose the exchange rate system of their choice (fixed or flexible) and these exchange rate systems were to be monitored by the IMF. The floating exchange rate system governed by the Jamaica Accords was officially recognized. Member countries were allowed to choose the exchange rate regime they wanted as long as their policies did not harm their trading partners and the world economy (Salvatore, 2013, p. 702). With the Jamaica Agreement, a floating exchange rate system was determined by reducing state interventions in the international economy. With this system, the era of exchange rate systems based on fixed exchange rates, where national currencies were linked to another country's currency or basket, began (Karluk, 2013, p. 717). The system in which the value of countries' currencies was linked to the SDR or other currency baskets was formed.

Under this system, gold, foreign exchange and SDRs held by countries are treated as reserve currencies and loans are considered as international liquidity. In other words, a country's own reserves and the reserves obtained by borrowing from other countries are all included in the international liquidity account. Liquidity has two important characteristics such as "being available" and "being acceptable" (Karluk, 2013, p. 718). International liquidity is of great importance for all countries, and they need international liquidity for development. The reserves accumulated by developing countries as well as developed countries transferring them to the market will contribute to the development of the country. Idle reserve currencies will harm the national economy by slowing down investments and growth. Countries accumulate reserves according to their own conditions in order to ensure economic stability and to fulfill their obligations to the IMF.

After the 1973 transition to the flexible exchange rate system, the demand for liquidity in international markets did not decrease and the supply of reserves increased. The ratio of IMF member countries' reserves other than gold to imports increased from 22% in the 1973–1987 period to 27% after 1987 (Karluk, 2013, p. 719). Although the SDR was created as a way to increase the IMF's resources, the share of SDRs in the international reserves of countries remained quite low. However, after 1973, currencies other than the U.S. dollar, such as the German Mark, the Japanese Yen and the Swiss Franc also became reserve currencies. Countries started to hold as reserves the currencies of economically strong countries with high interest rates, appreciating in the foreign exchange market, robust in foreign payments.

In the 1980s, the U.S. economy began to experience difficulties as the U.S. economy's budget deficits began to grow and the dollar appreciated against other currencies. Between 1980 and 1985, the trade-weighted value of the dollar against foreign currencies increased by about 90%. The U.S. real exchange rate moved strongly in the same direction and there was pressure on the U.S. Congress to implement protectionist economic policies (Eichengreen, 1994, p. 55). Although the United States was in a strong dollar position financially, it had to intervene in the strong dollar to prevent inflation from rising. After these developments, West Germany, the United Kingdom, France and Japan, the four major economies following the United States, signed the Plaza Agreement with the United States on September 22, 1985. With the agreement, it was decided to devalue the dollar to reduce the U.S. foreign trade deficit (Müslümov et al., 2002, p. 19).

Developed countries were concerned that the devalued dollar would fall further, and as a result of this concern, the Louvre Agreement was signed in Paris in 1987. With the Louvre Agreement, G7 countries decided to cooperate and coordinate for exchange rate stability. In line with the decision taken in the agreement, it was aimed at achieving more stability in exchange rates by switching to managed floating exchange rate systems. Increases in capital mobility during the 1980–1990 period made the realization of the target of adjustable exchange rates more difficult. International capital flows increased faster than economic developments, leaving governments with a difficult choice between abandoning exchange rate targets and monetary integration (Eichengreen, 1994, p. 59).

After the Bretton Woods System, the tendency toward flexible exchange rate systems increased and the number of fixed exchange rate system implementations decreased. After the 1990s, participation in flexible exchange rate systems gained momentum. Although there was a tendency toward flexible exchange rate systems after the Bretton Woods System, a system that provides exchange rate security for the whole world could not be established (Eichengreen, 1994, p. 145). As a result of the liberalization in exchange rate policies that came with the free exchange rate system, increasing capital flows since 1990 have been the cause of macroeconomic instability and financial crises for countries (Bulut and Demirel, 2015, p. 175).

1.1.2.6. Optimum Monetary Areas Period

The theory of optimal monetary areas is that the currencies of countries within the monetary union are pegged to each other at fixed exchange rates and are left to float freely against the value of the currencies of countries outside the union. The assumptions of the theory are the freedom of labor and capital movements, the diversity of products and the degree of openness (Grubel, 2000, pp. 29–30). Mundell (1961), who first introduced the theory of optimal currency areas to the literature, investigated whether the optimal boundaries for currency areas are the national borders of countries or not. He also analyzed in which cases countries should be included in monetary unions and in which cases they should have independent exchange rates policy should be abandoned. According to Mundell, when countries made their exchange rate preferences, they indicated in which area it would be in their interest to remain (Mundell, 1961, pp. 658–659).

The development of the theory of optimal monetary areas can be divided into three stages; the first one is the 1960s when the theory emerged and the criteria were determined, the second one is the 1970s when the theory was developed and the last one is the 1980s when the theory was further developed and the theory was tested through empirical studies (Özer, 2007, p. 77). In the 1960s, when the theory emerged, the mobility of factors of production, openness of the economy, product diversity, flexibility of prices and wages, level of financial integration, similarity in inflation rates and finally the necessity of political integration were emphasized (Özer, 2007, pp. 80–82). After Mundell, McKinnon stated that there should be economic openness in the monetary area and contributed to the theory by arguing that it would be more beneficial for countries that trade with each other at a similar level to establish a common monetary area (McKinnon, 1963, pp. 719–721). Kenen stated that the product diversity in the production of countries would reduce the costs of joining the optimum monetary area. He also argued that fixed exchange rates in countries with more product diversity and flexible exchange rates in countries with less product diversity would be more beneficial for countries (Kenen, 1969, p. 54).

In the formation of an optimal monetary area, the pros and cons of both flexible and fixed exchange rates should be considered together (Tower and Willet, 1976, p. 1). According to Mundell's optimal monetary area theory, not every monetary area is an optimal monetary area. A common monetary area is defined as a region where the benefit of the common currency to the country exceeds the cost to the country (Karluk, 2013, p. 734). While countries waive the use of some monetary and fiscal policies for the benefit of the monetary union, they must also consider the economic benefits that membership of the union will bring to their countries. Membership to the union has advantages such as the elimination of uncertainties in exchange rates and difficulties in the supply of different products, and the increase in trade and investments with member countries. It also has disadvantages, such as the inability of countries to take an independent monetary policy decision according to their own preferences and economic situation. According to Salvatore, countries that want to create an optimal monetary area and be successful must fulfill certain conditions (Salvatore, 2013, p. 656):

- Freedom of movement of factors of production between members,
- Countries are structurally similar, and
- They need to be willing to coordinate monetary, fiscal and other policies alike. Participating in the optimal monetary space, as it is not easy to quantify the benefits obtained, member states should aim to maximize the benefits from the optimal monetary area and minimize the costs of being part of the optimal monetary area.

Based on the optimum money area theory, the gains from the union are categorized under four headings (Özer, 2007, pp. 83–84):

1. **Improvement in microeconomic efficiency:** Due to the functions of money, it is envisaged to eliminate exchange costs, to ensure the efficiency of resource allocation as a store of value and the integration of the economy (Tower and Willet, 1976, p. 3).
2. **Increase in macroeconomic stability and growth:** It is stated that economic stability and growth will be achieved by ensuring price stability and reducing fluctuations in production and employment.
3. **Elimination of speculative capital movements:** The common currency is expected to reduce speculative flows. Depending on the stage of monetary union, the acceleration of the expectation of speculative capital flows will increase the size of capital flows (Fleming, 1971, p. 480).

4. **Saving from foreign exchange reserves:** The political policies implemented by the member states of the Union coordination will reduce the responsibility to hold foreign reserves. The foreign exchange reserves of non-member countries will be shaped according to the policies to be implemented by the union (Ishiyama, 1975, p. 363).

According to the theory of optimal monetary areas, the costs of joining the union are categorized under four headings:

1. The fact that national currencies are seen as symbols of the independence of countries may create political concerns for other member states (Demirel, 2011, p. 74).
2. With the transition to a common monetary area, monetary policies implemented by countries' own monetary authorities will be invalid. In this case, only fiscal policies will be applicable (Karluk, 2013, p. 735).
3. The common monetary policy may benefit some member countries but not others. Fiscal policy may be insufficient to increase employment in countries that do not benefit (Ishiyama, 1975, p. 366). According to Fleming, a fixed exchange rate may increase the unemployment and inflation rate (Phillips Curve) needed to keep inflation under control (Fleming, 1971, p. 469).
4. The common monetary area changes the impact of shocks for member countries. Countries that react similarly to shocks need less exchange rate changes, while countries that feel the shocks more strongly need more exchange rate changes (Tavlas, 1994, p. 216).

The most successful application of the optimal monetary areas hypothesis is the European Monetary Union. In the aftermath of World War II, European countries came together to end their conflicts among themselves and to ensure their economic development. European countries first established the European Coal and Steel Community (ECSC) in 1951, the European Economic Community (EEC) and the European Atomic Energy Community (EURATOM) in 1957. They aimed to ensure resource allocation, development and nuclear research in Europe. In 1965, the ECSC, EEC and EURATOM were united under one roof with the Brussels Treaty and became the European Communities (EC). The EC pegged its currencies to the U.S. dollar during the period when the Bretton Woods System was in force.

For the Community to pursue an independent monetary policy, it had to get rid of the Bretton Woods System and the U.S. dollar. In this context, a working group was established under the chairmanship of Prime Minister Werner of Luxembourg to introduce a special monetary and exchange rate policy for the Community. In 1969, the Werner Plan for the establishment of the European Economic and Monetary Union was presented to the Commission. Adopted in 1970, the Werner Plan consisted of three stages. In the first stage, exchange rate movements were to be limited, and the members were to coordinate their monetary and fiscal policies. In the second stage, the adjustment process would be checked to see whether the implementation was feasible. In the third stage, it was planned to transition to full monetary union by irreversibly switching to a fixed exchange rate and establishing a decision-making center where economic policies were determined on a community basis (Chown, 2003, p. 200).

In the first phase of the Werner Plan, they minimized exchange rate movements in order to minimize the fluctuations of European currencies among themselves and to ensure exchange rate stability. On the other hand, they preferred to leave the U.S. dollar to float freely within the band range determined by the Bretton Woods System. This system is called the "Snake in the Tunnel" or the "European Monetary Snake." According to the system, the European Community countries allowed their currencies to fluctuate ± 2.5% among themselves, and they called this margin the snake. Since the band range envisaged by the Bretton Woods System fluctuated freely against the dollar, this band range was called the tunnel (Bulut and Demirel, 2015, p. 225).

In 1971, after the Bretton Woods System became obsolete, it was agreed by the Smithsonian Agreement signed in 1972 that the snake range of European countries would be ± 2.25% and the tunnel range ± 4.5% (Müslümov et al., 2002, p. 20). In 1973, with the accession of the United Kingom, Denmark and Ireland, the area of application of the EC and the Snake in the Tunnel system expanded. The 1973 Oil Crisis and related foreign trade problems were among the challenges faced by the Snake in the Tunnel system. In 1976, the process came to an end when the United Kingdom, France, Italy and Ireland, which had difficulty in coping with these problems, left the system (Bulut and Demirel, 2015, p. 225). Following these developments, the EC member states, led by Germany and France, came together in 1979 and established the European Monetary System (EMS) with a fluctuation margin of ±2.25% to advance the Werner Plan and to prevent the integration process from being left unfinished (Chown, 2003, p. 203). For the European Monetary System to be fully effective, it had to complete three stages (Bulut and Demirel, 2015, p. 226):

- Creation of the European Currency Unit (ECU)
- Exchange rate mechanism (ERM I)
- Creation of the European Monetary Fund

In 1979, the European Currency Unit (ECU) was defined as the official currency of the union, and the value of the currency was established according to the currency basket technique, which was determined according to the economic weights of the member countries. For example, the German mark had a 30% weight in the basket, while the French franc had a 20% weight (Seyidoğlu, 2013, p. 33). The existence of the ECU ended with the introduction of the Euro on January 1, 1999. However, there were some problems regarding the functioning of the exchange rate mechanism. At the time, high inflation in countries such as France, Italy and Ireland were the biggest threat to the functioning of the system. The ECU and the ERM I system had to be followed without compromise. The insistence on this issue ensured that the average inflation rate of 12% in the EC member states in 1980 dropped to 5% in 1985 (Bulut and Demirel, 2015, p. 228).

The ECU was to be issued by the European Monetary Cooperation Fund (EMCF), an important step in the European Monetary System, and 20% of each of the dollar and gold reserves of the member countries were transferred to the fund on condition that they were kept in ECU (Seyidoğlu, 2013, p. 34).

In 1986, the European Single Act was signed, which would transform the EC into a single market. With this signature, it was aimed to adopt free trade among the members, to remove the conditions preventing free trade and to increase harmonization among the members. Moreover, Jacques Delors' Report on Economic and Monetary Union, which prepared the Single European Act, laid the groundwork for the Maastricht Treaty to be signed in 1992. As a result of this step, the basis for negotiations on the establishment of a single currency and a European Central Bank was laid (Apel, 2003, p. 2).

The Maastricht Treaty (Maastricht Treaty) was signed on February 7, 1992, which was the most important agreement to realize the economic and monetary union of the EC on the way to becoming the European Union (EU). In the Maastricht Treaty, the free movement of goods, services, labor and capital among member states and the use of a single currency within the union were accepted. The Euro was adopted as the single currency and the start of implementation was set for January 1, 1999. Thus, the EC member states irrevocably converted their national currencies into Euro and as of that date, the assets accepted as ECU were calculated as 1 ECU=1 Euro. The Euro was used as dematerialized money in banks and payment systems as of January 1, 1999, and became a physical currency as of January 1, 2002 (Seyidoğlu, 2013, pp. 34–35).

The Maastricht Criteria was adopted for the harmonization of the monetary and fiscal policies of the EC members and for economic convergence among countries. These criteria (Karluk, 2013, pp. 742–743) were as follows:

- The 12-month average of the 12-month inflation in the member countries, the lowest inflation rate in the member countries. The maximum inflation rate will be 1.5% above the average inflation rate of the three countries with the highest inflation rate.
- In member states, government debt cannot exceed 60% of GDP.
- Member states' budget deficit cannot be more than 3% of GDP.
- Member countries' 12-month long-term interest rates can be at most 2% higher than the interest rates of the three members with the best interest rate performance.
- The currency of the member countries must not have been devalued against the currency of another country in the last 2 years.

Members' unrealistic statements on price stability, budget discipline and balance of payments accounts led to criticism of the Maastricht Criteria (Bulut and Demirel, 2015, pp. 240–243). European countries' efforts to create a monetary area was appreciated. On the other hand, it was criticized that the monetary area-like practices of the United States and the United Kingdom did not impose restrictions like the Maastricht Criteria (Moss and Michie, 1998, p. 42). The ERM I exchange rate system implemented by the community during this period was shaken by the currency crisis in 1992–1993. As a result,

ERM II was established as a new exchange rate system and it was decided to apply the rules set out in Maastricht. The aim of ERM II is primarily to ensure exchange rate stability and to increase the efforts of countries that are members of the monetary union or aspiring to become members to meet the convergence criteria. In this context, it has been of great importance to determine the exchange rate target of the member country and the fluctuation band after joining the union. Band ranges may vary depending on the situation of the countries (Bulut and Demirel, 2015, pp. 249, 250). The aim of the Eurozone is to overcome the impossible trilateration problem for the member countries by using a single currency. In this way, member countries will be stabilized with the Euro, while countries outside the union will have an independent monetary policy with a flexible exchange rate system and will be able to apply for it. Mongelli conveyed this situation in Figure 1 (Mongelli, 2008, p. 13).

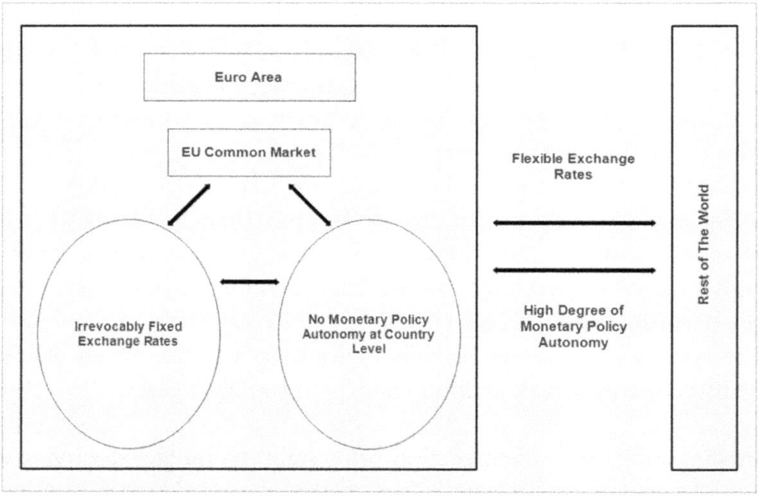

Figure 1: Solving the impossible trilemma in the Euro Area
Source: (Mongelli, 2008, p. 13)

As a result, with the introduction of the Euro system, the debt structures of the countries have improved, the exchange rate risk has decreased, and economic stability has been achieved. This stability reduced the additional

bond interest rates of the member countries and affected the strong entry of the Euro against the dollar (Bulut and Demirel, 2015, p. 256). The fact that the Euro system led to a decline in short and long-term interest rates shows that the monetary policies implemented by the European Central Bank were successful (Fagan and Gaspar, 2007, p. 5).

1.2. Foreign Exchange Rate Types

In international trade, the currencies of the trading parties are used because buyers and sellers are citizens or companies of different countries. Trade may sometimes be in the currencies of the trading parties, but in most cases, it may be in the currency of a third country that is not a party to the trade. One of the most important factors is that the price to be paid for the goods and services subject to trade should be paid in a convertible currency. In addition to commercial matters, international investments and services also require the currency of one-party country to be converted into the currency of the other party country. In order to complete these transactions, these currencies, which can be converted into each other, have a price or rate among themselves, which we define as the exchange rate. The exchange rate is the rate at which two national currencies exchange with each other (Karluk, 2013, p. 591).

Exchange rates are one of the indispensable components of international trade. In international trade, exchange rate differences, customs duties, trade facilities or barriers cause the prices of goods and services to differ from country to country. Since not all countries use the same or the same factors of production in the production of goods and services, price differences will occur between countries. These price differences will help price and cost comparisons across countries. Another feature of exchange rates is that exchange rate changes affect the prices of internationally traded goods. In this context, all imported and exported products subject to international trade are closely related to the exchange rate. Changes in exchange rates affect the prices of these products and the demand for them in the international market.

There is a risk that exchange rates may not reflect their real value in the event of instantaneous changes in foreign currencies traded in the foreign exchange market and if they turn into open positions for speculation. The value differences that may occur between exchange rates cause the national currency to lose its value against another country's currency, in other words, the country transfers its resources to foreign countries at a cheaper price. When the classification of exchange rates according to their value is examined, it is seen that the exchange rate is divided into two as nominal and real value. According to this classification, nominal and real exchange rates can be expressed as follows.

1.2.1. Nominal Exchange Rate

The nominal exchange rate is defined as the value of one unit of foreign currency in terms of national currency and the determined exchange rate is a nominal value (Seyidoğlu, 2013, p. 168). The nominal exchange rate does not show the real value of the national currency in countries outside the country or in the foreign exchange market. The amount of goods and services that a currency can purchase can change with fluctuations in the foreign exchange market. Since the nominal exchange rate is expressed in current prices, it includes inflation effects. For a real exchange rate, the exchange rate needs to be adjusted for the effects of inflation.

Purchasing power parity envisages a change in exchange rates to compensate for domestic and international inflation differences (Baillie and McMahon, 1990, p. 17). Thus, the change in prices due to the exchange rate differential means that the real value of the exchange rate remains constant. This does not cause a change in the external competitiveness of the country (Seyidoğlu, 2013, p. 168).

The exchange rate is of great importance in comparing the strength of countries in foreign trade. For example, a fall in the real effective exchange rate increases the country's competitiveness in exports. On the contrary, a rise in the real effective exchange rate means that the exchange rate has increased more than the real exchange rate and the national currency has a value below its real value. This situation reduces the external competitiveness of the country (Krugman et al., 2012, p. 324). Real exchange rates are reached by adding the inflation rates of countries to the exchange rate calculations and the real purchasing power of the national currency to the measurement.

1.2.2. Real Exchange Rate

A real exchange rate is a type of exchange rate in which the nominal exchange rate is calculated by considering the inflation differences between countries. The real exchange rate is also defined as the nominal exchange rate adjusted for domestic and international price levels (Hsieh, 1982, p. 355). The real exchange rate is calculated as follows (Seyidoğlu, 2013, p. 169).

$$R_{er} = N_{er} \frac{P_f}{P_d} \tag{1.1}$$

According to the formula, R_{er} is the real exchange rate, N_{er} is the nominal exchange rate, P_f is the foreign inflation rate and P_d is the domestic inflation rate. As can be seen from the formula, a fall in domestic inflation leads to an increase in the real exchange rate, while a rise in domestic inflation leads to a fall in the real exchange rate.

A rise in the real exchange rate is called real appreciation. When real appreciation occurs, the prices of domestically produced goods become relatively more expensive than the prices of goods produced in foreign countries. This leads to a fall in foreign demand for domestically produced goods and a decrease in exports. Moreover, the preference for imported goods over relatively more expensive domestic goods leads to an increase in imports. Thus, a real appreciation will reduce net exports, which is the difference between exports and imports (Krugman et al. 2012, p. 322). A fall in the real exchange rate is also called real depreciation. In real depreciation, domestically produced goods will become cheaper than goods produced in foreign countries. With real depreciation, foreign demand for domestic goods that becomes cheaper compared to foreign goods will lead to an increase in exports and a decrease in imports. In sum, net exports will increase (Krugman et. all., 2012, pp. 322–323,424).

If domestic inflation is higher than foreign inflation, the real exchange rate should be higher than the nominal exchange rate. A rise in real exchange rates can be a harbinger of a possible devaluation. Changes in the real exchange rate help countries to compare their competitiveness in foreign trade.

1.2.2.1. Bilateral Real Exchange Rate

The real exchange rate is obtained by multiplying nominal exchange rates by the inflation rates of countries. Bilateral real exchange rates are constructed with the prices of representative baskets of goods at home and abroad. It is the exchange rate calculated by converting into the currency of one of the trading countries. The bilateral real exchange rate is calculated as follows.

$$RER = \left(ulusal\ para\ /\ P^d\right) / \left(yabanc1 para\ /\ P^f\right) = ER\frac{P^f}{P^d} \qquad (1.2)$$

According to Formula 1.2, *ER* is the bilateral nominal exchange rate, ^{pd} is the domestic price level, ^{pf} indicates the foreign price level. PPI, CPI, GDP deflator, import and export price indices can be used as deflators (Yıldırım et al., 2016, p. 76). An increase in the bilateral real exchange rate implies that goods produced abroad are more expensive than goods produced at home. With the depreciation of the national currency, the country's international competitiveness will increase as domestic production costs and prices of goods and services fall compared to prices abroad (Ünsal, 2009, p. 116).

1.2.2.2. Real Effective Exchange Rate

The effective real exchange rate, which is similar to the bilateral real exchange rate, is the exchange rate calculated with the country's trading partners. In the calculation, which includes countries with which a country has intensive foreign trade, an index determined according to the volume of trade activities with countries is used. This index is obtained by weighting the trade volumes with countries (Ünsal, 2009, p. 117).

In the real effective exchange rate formula, the weights to be assigned to each country's currency are determined as (*wi*). While these weights are determined according to the weights of countries in imports and exports, bilateral exchange rates with *n* countries are included in the basket, with the sum of these weights being equal to one. The formula for the real effective exchange rate is as in 1.3 (Yıldırım et al., 2016, p. 77).

$$REER = \sum_{i=1}^{n} w_i\ RER_i \qquad (1.3)$$

The real effective exchange rate can also be calculated as an arithmetic average. However, the arithmetic index, which shows the percentage change in the index between the specified dates, depends on the choice of base year. Since the choice of base year with geometric mean does not affect the index, the results will be symmetric and consistent (Özkan, 2003, p. 7). A decrease in the index of the real effective exchange rate compared to the previous year means that the national currency used domestically has appreciated in real terms compared to the currencies of other countries. It also means that local goods have become more expensive compared to the goods of trading partners (Yıldırım et al., 2016, p. 78).

In real life, the calculation of the real effective exchange rate utilizes a basket of goods rather than a single commodity. For this reason, while domestic and international price indices are used, it is possible to use producer or consumer price indices. In the formula, the *pf/pd* ratio can be interpreted as the ratio of the general level of prices in the foreign country to the national general level of prices or the terms of trade. This ratio helps both to measure the competitiveness of countries and to compare domestic and foreign labor costs (Ünsal, 2009, p. 117).

1.3. Exchange Rate Systems

Exchange rate systems help explain the conditions under which exchange rates are determined, the characteristics of the system and the decision makers of the system (Bulut and Demirel, 2015, p. 68). The main objective of exchange rate systems is to achieve economic stability by preferring an exchange rate system that stabilizes the balance of payments rather than by whom or how exchange rates are determined (Calvo et al., 1995).

Many exchange rate systems have been implemented until today. However, while the flexible exchange rate system, which is determined according to market conditions, is rarely applied, fixed and mixed exchange rate systems are preferred. With the Bretton Woods System (1944–1971), an adjustable fixed exchange rate system was used, but the system was terminated in 1971 with the abolition of the convertibility of the U.S. dollar to gold. A report was prepared by the IMF in 1976 to create an alternative system to the adjustable fixed exchange rate system applied in the 1944–1971 period. As a result of this report, a supervised floating system was adopted with the Jamaica Agreement agreed by its members (Krugman et al., 2012, p. 463).

Exchange rate systems basically consist of a fixed exchange rate system and a flexible exchange rate system. There are many mixed exchange rate systems in the fixed exchange rate system. In a fixed exchange rate system, exchange rates are kept at a fixed price, while in a flexible exchange rate system, exchange rates are set according to which supply and demand in the foreign exchange market are determined. Mixed exchange rate systems fall between fixed and flexible exchange rate systems but are considered as fixed exchange rate systems.

Exchange rate systems classified by the IMF can be divided into four main categories. According to the IMF, this classification is categorized as a fully fixed exchange rate system, semi-fixed exchange rate system, freely floating exchange rate system and other exchange rate systems. According to the IMF classification, exchange rate practices are as follows (IMF, 2019, p. 17);

- **Fully Fixed Exchange Rate Systems:** The category of countries that do not have a separate national currency and currency board arrangements,
- **Semi-Fixed Exchange Rate Systems:** Traditional fixed exchange rate arrangements, creeping parity arrangements, creeping parity-like arrangements, and fixed exchange rate systems within a horizontal band,
- **Floating Exchange Rate Regimes:** Floating exchange rate system, free floating exchange rate system, other managed floating systems, and
- **Other Exchange Rate Systems:** According to the IMF, the similarities and differences in the exchange rate systems adopted by countries are reflected in their monetary policies. In addition, there may be countries with different exchange rate policies but similar monetary policies. The three factors that frame countries' monetary policies are exchange rate anchors, aggregate supply targeting and inflation targeting (IMF, 2019).
- ***Exchange Rate Anchors:*** The monetary authority buys and sells foreign exchange to maintain a predetermined exchange rate at a certain level or range. Since monetary policy is linked to the exchange rate, this policy is called exchange rate anchoring. This practice is seen in currency board and traditional fixed exchange rate systems where there is no national currency.
- ***Aggregate Money Supply Target:*** The monetary authority endeavors to realize the targeted growth in the money supply with the instruments at its disposal.
- ***Inflation Targeting:*** The monetary authority continuously informs the public about the policy it will implement to realize the targeted or publicly announced inflation target and takes responsibility for it. If inflation

deviates from the target, monetary policy decisions can be changed to achieve the targeted rate.

Exchange rate systems mentioned in the IMF exchange rate classification and in the literature will be analyzed under subheadings.

1.3.1. Fixed Exchange Rate Systems

A fixed exchange rate system is a system determined by the official authority without taking market conditions into account. The authority, which may be different official institutions depending on the country, aims to keep the exchange rate in a permanent and stable equilibrium through policy instruments. In a fixed exchange rate system, the authority relinquishes its authority to implement monetary policy, while fiscal policy becomes a more important tool in growth and employment policy (Krugman et al., 2012, p. 472). In fixed exchange rate systems, the official authority intervenes in the market as a buyer or seller to ensure exchange rate stability (Ünsal, 2009, p. 117).

In fixed exchange rate systems, inflation plays an important role in keeping the parity at the same value. Inflation that may occur in a country with a fixed exchange rate system will lead to depreciation of the national currency, an increase in imports, decrease in exports and consequently deterioration in the balance of payments. In this system, the devaluation of the national currency by the authority is called devaluation and the increase of the value of the national currency is called revaluation. In flexible exchange rate systems, the appreciation and depreciation of the exchange rate depends on market conditions (Bulut and Demirel, 2015, p. 74).

In a fixed exchange rate system, the official authority may have to devalue when the balance of payments deteriorates (Parasız, 2009, p. 10). In fixed exchange rate systems, there are countries that peg the national currency to a single currency such as dollar, Euro and sterling, as well as countries that peg the national currency to a basket such as SDR (Seyidoğlu, 2013, pp. 42–43).

Advantages of fixed exchange rate systems (Parasız, 2009, pp. 613–614);

- The reduction of uncertainty in a fixed exchange rate system will allow citizens, companies and banks to look to the future with more confidence and to act more comfortably in all kinds of commercial activities,

- Economic destabilization through speculation will be greatly reduced.
- Price discipline will be ensured, and inflation will be prevented. Disadvantages of fixed exchange rate systems (Bulut and Demirel, 2015, pp. 73–74).
- It can lead to balance of payments deficits. Therefore, countries may prefer devaluation.
- Official authorities need foreign exchange reserves to intervene in the foreign exchange market when necessary. Therefore, the problem of inefficient use of resources may arise as the foreign exchange held as reserves sits idle.

The fixed exchange rate system is divided into full fixed exchange rate and semi-fixed exchange rate. Then, the fully fixed exchange rate system is divided into the currency board and the common currency, and the semi-fixed flexible exchange rate system is divided into fixed pegs and flexible pegs. Semi-fixed exchange rates will be discussed in the following sections. The fixed exchange rate system classification is shown in Figure 2 (Karluk, 2013, p. 602).

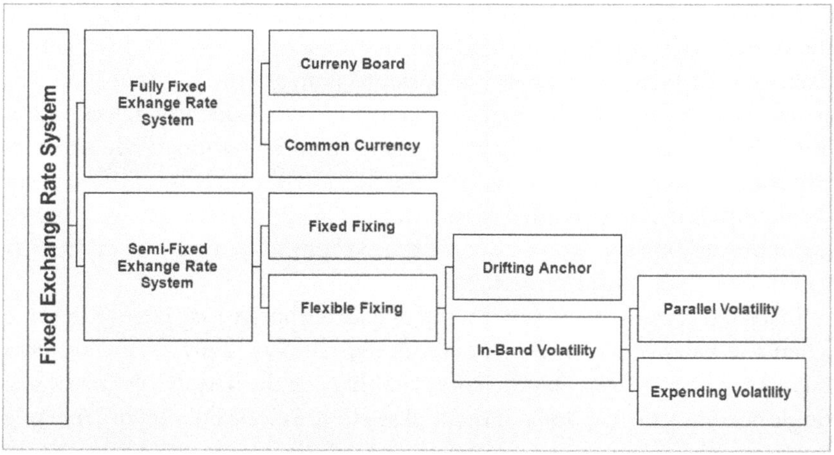

Figure 2: Fixed exchange rate systems
Source: (Karluk, 2013, p. 602)

In a fixed exchange rate system, the monetary board is a system in which monetary policy is strictly implemented and these rules are determined by law. According to the system, the national currency is pegged to a strong currency or a basket of currencies (Barışık, 2001, p. 51). The system aims to provide political stability and credibility without being affected by real exchange rate volatility. For the system to work, the central bank must have foreign currency equivalent to the national currency and print the national currency against the foreign currency. While the system fails in countries such as Argentina due to its vulnerability to external shocks, it seems possible to implement the system in countries where capital movements are not liberalized and have a rigid regime (Karluk, 2013, p. 602).

In fixed exchange rate systems, the most important example of a common currency system is the European Union (EU), where countries agree to be governed by a single currency and central bank. EU countries use the official currency, the Euro, under the control of the European Central Bank. The system is based on the consistency of predetermined target policies and exchange rate advantages, such as reduced volatility, can make capital flows and investments attractive for the region. The disadvantage of the system is that member countries cannot determine independent policies. The success of the system can be ensured through coordination among the members (Bulut and Demirel, 2015, p. 69).

There are sub-divisions of fixed exchange rate systems in the literature and these sub-divisions have been mentioned earlier. However, the distinctions under these headings will be explained in the following sections.

1.3.2. Flexible Exchange Rate Systems

A flexible exchange rate system is a system in which changes in the supply and demand for foreign exchange in the foreign exchange market change the exchange rate and is also called floating exchange rate and floating exchange rate (Karluk, 2013, p. 606). An increase in the exchange rate will lead to a depreciation of the national currency and an increase in the domestic prices of imported goods. On the other hand, a fall in the exchange rate will cause the national currency to appreciate and the prices of imported goods to fall and may change the balance of trade. In this system, monetary policy and exchange rate policies are separated from each other and monetary policy becomes an independent policy (Müslümov et al., 2002, p. 19).

In this system, the national currency value is determined according to the balance of supply and demand in international markets, providing economic stability, which has four benefits for the country (Krugman et al., 2012, p. 529):

- ***Autonomous Monetary Policy:*** Central banks will be able to use monetary policy to stabilize domestic and foreign markets without having to intervene in foreign exchange markets to fix exchange rates. While countries in the Bretton Woods System import U.S. inflation through fixed exchange rates, they can avoid importing inflation in the flexible exchange rate system.
- ***Symmetry***: In the Bretton Woods System, the U.S. dollar has a high power to influence monetary conditions due to its weight in the system. Due to this feature, flexible exchange rate systems allow the U.S. dollar to have the same weight as other member countries by reducing its weight. Thus, since each country has the authority to regulate the conditions of its own currency, it eliminates the power of other countries to influence the monetary conditions of its own country.
- ***Exchange Rates as Automatic Stabilizers:*** Even if countries do not have an active monetary policy, a flexible exchange rate system helps to maintain internal and external balance in the face of changes in aggregate demand. In the Bretton Woods System, adjustments in exchange rates were subject to certain rules. The difficulties encountered in determining the ideal exchange rate are eliminated in the flexible exchange rate system without the need to make any adjustments and relieve the hands of the government-central banks.
- ***Exchange Rates and External Balance:*** Exchange rates determined under market conditions will act automatically to prevent countries from running large current account deficits and surpluses, which will be advantageous for policymakers. Although flexible exchange rate systems are generally accepted after the Bretton Woods System, there are also disadvantages in its implementation (Seyidoğlu, 2013, pp. 15–18).
- ***Deterring Trade and Financial Flows:*** Uncertainties arising from changes in exchange rates discourage trade and financial flows. Central bank interventions due to exchange rate adjustments lead to interest rate changes. Increased exchange rate risk has a restrictive effect on world trade and such situations harm the economy.

- ***Inflationary Characteristics of the System:*** Exchange rate increases in flexible exchange rate systems first of all, the prices of raw materials, basic food, machinery and equipment, etc., increase. These increases are followed by increases in wages, which increase the costs of industrial products, leading to an inflationary process.
- ***Distorting Budget Discipline and Loosening Control on Inflation:*** In flexible exchange rate systems, in case of balance of payments deficits, exchange rates change automatically, and the deficit can be eliminated immediately. Due to the automatic equalizing feature of the system, the public authority may disrupt budget discipline by not paying the necessary attention to monetary and fiscal policies.
- ***Low Elasticities:*** In order for small changes in exchange rates to balance the balance of payments, the elasticities of foreign exchange supply and demand should be large enough. Otherwise, it is stated that large exchange rate changes are needed.
- ***Destabilizing Speculation:*** There is a possibility that a flexible exchange rate system may lead to destabilizing speculation and that larger fluctuations in the exchange rate may devalue the national currency. It is important to determine whether these fluctuations are aimed at stabilizing or destabilizing the exchange rate.
- ***"Overshooting" in Short-Term Exchange Rate Changes:*** The concept of overshooting is defined as an excessive rise or fall in exchange rates following unexpected and sudden developments. Since commodity markets cannot react instantly to such exogenous effects, reactions to exchange rate changes will be slow and economic losses will occur.

Flexible exchange rates are divided into free floating and supervised floating according to the degree of fluctuation. The flexible exchange rate system is presented in Figure 3 (Karluk, 2013, p. 608).

The free exchange rate is determined without the intervention of any authority. Supervised floating is divided into clean and dirty floating in terms of its purpose. Clean floating exchange rates are intervened to prevent short-term fluctuations, while dirty floating exchange rates are monitored and intervened to prevent the country from losing its competitiveness. Exchange rate surveillance and audit practices are divided into three categories: decisions of governments, international agreements and decisions of international authorities (Karluk, 2013, p. 608).

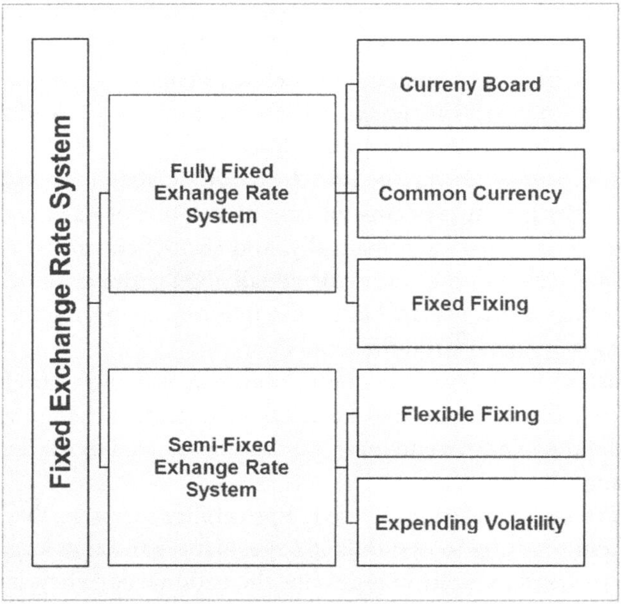

Figure 3: Flexible exchange rate systems
Source: (Karluk, 2013, p. 608)

In the flexible exchange rate system, there are cases where central banks intervene in the market by buying and selling foreign exchange when deemed necessary. Supervised fluctuations are more common in practice due to the interventions made by the official authority to prevent excessive fluctuations in the exchange rate (Ünsal, 2009, p. 118).

1.3.3. Mixed Systems

If we compare exchange rate systems to a spectrum, fixed and flexible exchange rate systems constitute the two ends of the spectrum. The other systems mentioned in this section will cover the other intermediate exchange rate systems between these two ends (Seyidoğlu, 2013, p. 42). In practice, it is possible to say that not all of these systems have common features. According to Article 4 of the IMF's Articles of Association, governments can determine the exchange rate system they wish for the balance of external payments (Parasız, 2009, pp. 638–639). Therefore, countries aim to determine the most appropriate exchange rate system for their countries according to their market structures and the political position of the monetary authority.

In the literature, there are studies that classify exchange rate systems in different ways. The pioneers of these studies can be classified as Edwards and Savastano (1999), Ghosh et al. (2002), Müslümov et al. (2003) and IMF (2019). In the classifications, each exchange rate regime is referred to by similar or different names. The classifications are compiled from the referenced studies and presented in Figure 4 (Ghosh et al., 2002; IMF, 2019).

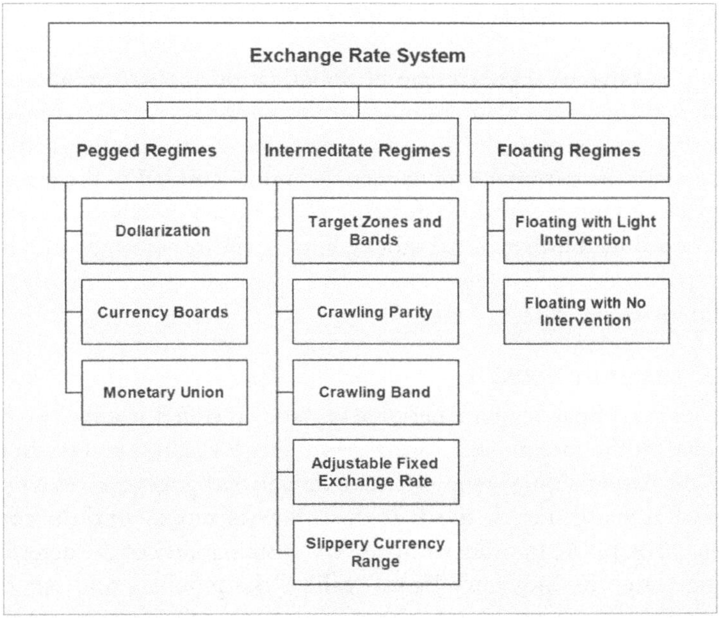

Figure 4: Exchange rate systems
Source: (Ghosh et al., 2002; IMF, 2019)

1.3.3.1. Full Currency Substitution

In a dollarized exchange rate system, another country's currency is used instead of the country's own national currency. Although coins continue to be minted in the country, a foreign currency is used as legal tender

(Ghosh et al., 2002, p. 40). One of the important elements of the system is which country's currency will be substituted for the national currency. The reserve currency country should be a country with which it has good trade relations (if possible, a regional country), a neighboring country or a country with which it has cyclical similarities. In the country where the system is in effect, independent monetary policy instruments cease to be valid, leaving only fiscal policy instruments in the hands of the government implementing the system. In the dollarization system, the inflation rate is important for the system. A low inflation rate stabilizes the system and prolongs investment periods. With the system, there are advantages such as the elimination of risks arising from the exchange rate and the decrease in capital costs (Müslümov et al., 2002, p. 6).

The first obvious disadvantage of dollarization is that the question of sovereignty due to the abandonment of the national currency can lead to political crises. Second, the loss of seigniorage revenues between the cost of producing the currency and its intrinsic value is added to the income of the reserve country. Third, dysfunctional monetary policy can make the economy vulnerable to external shocks. Finally, the loss of the central bank's role as the lender of last resort may cause problems in the banking sector (Müslümov et al., 2002, p. 7).

1.3.3.2. Monetary Board

In the currency board system, national currency is issued at a fixed exchange rate equal to the foreign exchange reserves (Karluk, 2013, p. 603). In other words, the national money supply tied to foreign exchange reserves is printed at a fixed exchange rate as much as the inflow of money into the country (Gözen, 2018, p. 16). In order to ensure the sustainability of the determined exchange rate, the Monetary Board realizes the purchase and sale of the money selected as reserves within the framework of the determined legislation. However, although the Monetary Board is structurally similar to the central bank, its most important difference from the central bank is that it is politically independent and can operate independently without being affected by political populism (Barışık, 2001, p. 54).

One of the most important features of the system is the obligation of the board to hold as much foreign exchange as the amount of money available in the economy. For the system to work, the country should not face a shortage of foreign currency. Since the currency board system prevents the financing of budget deficits by printing money, it has become a reliable instrument. In inflationary countries, it allows investments to increase and expectations to become positive by establishing confidence in a short time (Karluk, 2013, p. 605).

The advantage of the system is that it is not affected by exchange rate volatility. Ensuring stability in economic policies increases credibility and has a positive impact on the banking sector. In addition to lowering interest rates and inflation, it also has a mitigating effect on potential crisis risks. It has advantages that give confidence to the public authority in ensuring the balance of payments and fiscal discipline (Barışık, 2001, pp. 55–57).

One of the disadvantages of the system is that it becomes vulnerable to external shocks. There is a risk that the central bank loses its role as the lender of last resort and the resulting increase in interest rates on domestic borrowing increases the debt burden. Moreover, it has effects such as pacification of monetary policy instruments, increasing dependence between the currency board country and the reserve country, and reducing the flexibility of wages (Barışık, 2001, pp. 57–59). The deprivation of seigniorage revenues by countries that prefer a currency board is another drawback of the system disadvantage (Gözen, 2018, p. 16).

1.3.3.3. Monetary Union

A currency union exchange rate regime is an exchange rate regime in which a country uses a common currency with other countries or is a member of a union that uses a common currency. The success of the system depends on the compatibility of the monetary and fiscal policies of the member countries, the political and economic understanding of the member countries and the degree of liberalization of labor-capital movements (Bulut and Demirel, 2015, p. 69). The system is based on the application of the "Optimum Exchange Rate Areas" theory first developed by Mundell (Mundell, 1961). McKinnon and Kenen contributed to the theory and stated that four basic factors are needed for the success of the system (McKinnon, 1963; Kenen, 1969):

5. Free movement of factors of production within the Union,
6. Members of the Union have intensive commercial relations,
7. Harmony among members, and

8. If the first three conditions are not met, financial assistance should be provided from developed to less developed regions.

The advantages of the monetary union system are listed as follows (Müslümov et al., 2002, p. 10):

- Failure to adopt foreign monetary policy,
- Reduced costs arising from foreign exchange transactions,
- Reduced interest expenses,
- Reduced nominal exchange rate risk, and
- Sharing of emission gains by member states.

The monetary union has the disadvantages of not being able to implement independent macroeconomic policies and the inability of member developing countries to make competitive devaluations.

One of the requirements of the system is the application of a fixed exchange rate among the member countries of the union. After this process, a single currency and a single central bank are needed to control this system (Bulut and Demirel, 2015, p. 74). The best example of this system in practice is the transition of the member countries to the Euro as the common currency at the end of the development process of the European Union and the establishment of the European Central Bank as the central bank.

1.3.3.4. Target Zones and Bands

The target zone and exchange rate band system is one of the alternative exchange rate systems that countries established to reduce the effects of fluctuating exchange rates after the collapse of the Bretton Woods System in 1973. According to the system, the range within which the nominal exchange rate will fluctuate is determined and the exchange rate is allowed to fluctuate within this range (Edwards and Savastano, 1999, p. 6). The fact that the lower and upper bounds of the band are fixed and the exchange rate fluctuates within the specified range protects the system against external volatility (Ghosh et al., 2002, p. 41). Moreover, the flexibility of the exchange rate is determined by the width of the exchange rate band or the targeted zone. While the widening of the fluctuation range of exchange rates brings the system closer to the flexible exchange rate system, the decrease in the fluctuation range brings the system closer to the fixed exchange rate system (Gözen, 2018, p. 14).

The system combines the benefits of flexibility arising from exchange rate fluctuations within the band with the band system combines a certain amount of credibility and helps to mitigate the effects of shocks by providing the monetary authority with a certain intervention flexibility against possible exogenous shocks. The banding system has the disadvantage of exposing the exchange rate to speculative attacks and the inability to maintain a stable exchange rate policy due to speculative attacks (Edwards and Savastano, 1999, p. 6).

The exchange rate mechanism (ERM) implemented by the European Monetary System is an example of this system. The ERM system caused the 1992–1993 crises due to the exposure of the system to speculative pressures, currency mismatches and the hesitation of central banks to maintain the bands (Edwards and Savastano, 1999, p. 6). As a result of the crisis, the ERM was revised as ERM II for EU countries that are not members of the European Monetary System. ERM II sets out broad exchange rate zones against the euro and intervention methods to support the zones. In order for EU members outside the Euro Area to avoid competitive devaluations against the euro, Maastricht Treaty criteria were introduced for candidates to enter the union (Krugman et al., 2012, p. 566).

1.3.3.5. Crawling Parity

In the creeping parity system, the exchange rate is determined periodically at a predetermined rate or depending on deviations from inflation (Ghosh et al., 2002, p. 41). In the system, the value of the country's currency is initially fixed, and exchange rates are changed periodically until they reach the equilibrium exchange rate (Bulut and Demirel, 2015, pp. 81–82). The initial range determines whether the system will resemble a fixed or a flexible exchange rate. The advantages of the system are that it prevents overvaluation of the country's currency in countries with high inflation and prevents larger imbalances by making small devaluations at the predetermined exchange rate. However, adjustments based on past inflation differentials lead to the problem of inflation inertia.

The system was first implemented in Latin American countries struggling with high inflation. It was implemented in Chile, Colombia and Brazil in the

1960s and 1970s, in Mexico in the 1980s, in Indonesia before the 1997 Asian Crisis and finally in Türkiye before the 2001 crisis. The implementations resulted in failures. It is observed that the countries that abandoned the system preferred rigid fixed exchange rate or flexible exchange rate systems (Bulut and Demirel, 2015, p. 72).

1.3.3.6. Crawling Band

In a crawling band system, the exchange rate is fixed within a certain band and the exchange rate is allowed to fluctuate within this band. The determined parity is changed over time by taking inflation differences into account. The crawling band is divided into two according to actual and expected inflation (Edwards and Savastano, 1999, p. 6). The advantage of the system over other band systems is that it provides more flexibility to the implementation system. The system helps countries with high inflation to implement the parity without the need to constantly change the parity and helps countries to be unaffected by exchange rate changes against external shocks (Müslümov et al., 2002, p. 17).

The main disadvantage of the system is whether the pre-selected parity will be determined according to past or future inflation. Since past inflation differentials are taken into account in past exchange rate adjustments, an inflationary process may occur. In the case of forward-looking exchange rate adjustment, on the other hand, since the expectation of inflation differences is taken into account, a speculative pressure process may occur by appreciating the national currency in case the inflation targets are not met (Bulut and Demirel, 2015, p. 72). The system has been implemented in Israel, Chile, Italy, Malaysia and Thailand (Edwards and Savastano, 1999, p. 6).

1.3.3.7. Adjustable Fixed Exchange Rate

In an adjustable fixed exchange rate system, the national currency is the national currency of another country currency, a basket of several internationally strong national currencies, gold or the SDR (Gözen, 2018, p. 16). This exchange rate system first reached its maximum level of applicability with the Bretton Woods System, and after the collapse of the Bretton Woods System, there are developed countries that apply the system. In the system, the nominal exchange rate is fixed, but since the central bank is not obliged to maintain parity indefinitely, the central bank can pursue different monetary and fiscal policies to maintain parity. The most powerful policy tool available to the monetary authority is devaluation (Edwards and Savastano, 1999, p. 7).

The most important benefit of the system is to reduce exchange rate uncertainties. In addition to contributing to the country's foreign trade and exchange rate stability, the reduction of uncertainties helps countries to achieve macroeconomic discipline. When implemented correctly, the adjustable fixed exchange rate system contributes positively to the balance of payments of many countries (Salvatore, 2013, p. 668). The biggest dilemma of the system is that if the devaluation authority given to the monetary authority is applied at high rates, uncertainties may be created in the system again and macroeconomic stability may be disrupted.

1.3.3.8. Slippery Currency Range

The slippery range exchange rate system is a system in which the exchange rate fluctuates within a certain range and a central parity is set within this range. The system is stabilizing in protecting the exchange rate against speculation in countries with high inflation (Gözen, 2018, p. 15). However, as in other band systems, the lack of clarity in determining the parity and the range may cause uncertainty in the markets and adversely affect macroeconomic indicators. Moreover, the uncertainty about the timing of the parity change may lead to high exchange rate volatility as an element of uncertainty. A similar system was implemented in Israel only in 1989–1991. After the uncertainty and exchange rate volatility caused by the system, the crawling band system came to the fore (Edwards and Savastano, 1999, p. 6).

1.3.3.9. Managed Volatility

In a managed floating exchange rate system, the monetary authority determines the exchange rate by directly or indirectly intervening in the market without being tied to any parity. The absence of restrictions on the monetary authority's monetary policy implementation increases economic resilience to external shocks (Müslümov et al., 2002, p. 20). The monetary authority has a view on the targeted level and progress of the exchange rate. Therefore, it can intervene in the exchange rate when necessary and use a separate nominal anchor such as the inflation target (Ghosh et al., 2002, p. 41). One of the advantages of the system is that it does not require high reserves against exogenous shocks, while the monetary authority intervenes through the use of central bank reserves or interest rate changes (Edwards and Savastano, 1999, 6). By empowering the monetary authority to intervene in exchange rates, the system can prevent excessive volatility in exchange rates.

The fact that the system does not have an explicit exchange rate policy has the disadvantage of causing uncertainty in foreign trade and exchange rate volatility, while causing trust problems in the monetary authority (Müslümov et al., 2002, p. 20). The system has been implemented in Canada, Australia and Mexico.

1.3.3.10. Fully Flexible Exchange Rate

A fully flexible exchange rate system is one in which the exchange rate is determined by supply and demand in the foreign exchange market and the monetary authority does not intervene. The exchange rate automatically adjusts to possible internal and external shocks and there is no need for large foreign exchange reserves (Edwards and Savastano, 1999, p. 6). The system imposes no restrictions on monetary policy, which generally uses inflation targeting (Ghosh et al., 2002, p. 41).

In addition to these advantages, the system also has disadvantages. Inflationary pressures may arise with the end of the nominal anchor feature of the exchange rate. Inflationary pressures may lead to the need to stabilize the system through other policies (Bulut and Demirel, 2015, p. 70). Thus, in case of a credibility problem, currency substitution will tend to increase (Gözen, 2018, p. 13). High nominal exchange rate volatility may distort resource allocation. The inflation caused by the system and its costs cause central banks to abandon the system and adopt low inflation and exchange rate stability policies again (Bordo and Schwartz, 1997, pp. 22–23). It is observed that the system has not been fully implemented in any country and the closest implementations are in countries such as the United States, Germany, Switzerland and Japan (Edwards and Savastano, 1999, p. 6).

Exchange Rate Determination Models and Factors Affecting Exchange Rates

An analysis of the studies in the field of international economics reveals that the problems arising from the economic interaction between economically powerful countries are addressed. The topics of these studies are generally evaluated under headings such as revenues from trade, trade models, protectionism, balance of payments, exchange rate determination, political coordination and the international capital market (Krugman et al., 2012, p. 3). In addition, the determination of exchange rates is also an important topic in international economics.

In addition to endogenous factors such as the amount of money, interest rates, inflation and growth, exogenous factors such as goods and capital flows are also effective in the formation of exchange rates. In addition to these variables, political, social and many other economic factors that structurally affect exchange rates and determine exchange rates have led to the formation of new approaches to the determination of exchange rates (Öztürk and Bayraktar, 2010, p. 157). In each of these approaches, models are constructed with different theories and variables related to the established models are selected and analyzed to determine exchange rates.

In the literature, models that try to explain the determination of exchange rates are divided into traditional models and newly developed models, as in Öztürk and Bayraktar's (2010) study. Without making such a distinction, theories such as purchasing power parity, balance of payments and portfolio balance based on the monetary approach have been produced (Salvatore, 2013). While some of these models are supported by applied analyses with theoretically determined variables, some models provide theoretical explanations without applied analyses or without the need for them.

This part of the book includes main topics such as exchange rate determination models, Keynesian models, purchasing power parity theory, interest rate theory, financial approaches theory, speculative bubbles theory, chaotic determinism, microstructure of foreign exchange markets and the impact of economic and political explanations on exchange rate determination. The analysis of these models will be evaluated in the last chapter of the book.

2.1. Keynesian Exchange Rate Determination Models

Although the Keynesian model can be considered as a model first developed by John Maynard Keynes, the models to be discussed under this heading are based on Keynes' income-expenditure model. This model was developed by Metzler, Lerner, Laursen, Alexander and Machlup after World War II. Keynesian models are based on the adaptation of the income-expenditure model mentioned by Keynes in his General Theory to open economies. In addition, the flexibility approach is handled with three different models: the income-expenditure approach and the Mundell–Fleming Model (Bulut and Demirel, 2015, pp. 90–91).

The model, also known as the balance of payments approach theory in the literature, is based on the principle of making exchange rate forecasts by recording the transactions based on foreign exchange demand and supply of countries in a certain period in the balance of payments (Seyidoğlu, 2015, p. 889). While foreign resources provide foreign exchange inflows to the national economy, goods and services purchased by residents and firms from abroad cause foreign exchange outflows. These transactions constitute the foreign exchange supply and demand of countries. Since the transactions that determine the supply and demand of foreign exchange are variable, countries will have a balance of payments deficit or surplus. Hence, the national currencies of countries with balance of payments surpluses while the national currencies of countries with balance of payments deficits will depreciate against foreign currencies (Tunca and Tunalı, 2007, p. 5).

In periods of increased inflows of foreign currency from foreign countries, the demand for imported goods and services will increase as increases in the supply of foreign currency will make the national currency more valuable. If these goods are intermediate or investment goods, they will increase the country's supply of goods and services in the future, which will positively affect the country's economy. If these goods are consumption goods, the country's economy will be negatively affected (Ulusoy and Karakurt, 2004, p. 112).

Countries need to achieve five basic goals for economic success. These goals are economic internal balance, external balance, reasonable growth rate, fair income distribution and sustainable environment. There are three main policy instruments that countries apply to achieve these goals. These instruments are demand policies, spending modification policies and direct intervention mechanisms (Salvatore, 2013, p. 573). Expenditure modifying policies include both fiscal and monetary policies. Fiscal policies include public expenditures, taxes, borrowing policy or a mix of these policies. Increasing public expenditures or reducing taxes are expansionary in terms of fiscal policy. These instruments lead to an increase in domestic production through the multiplier effect, leading to an expansion of income and an increase in imports. Contractionary fiscal policy means that domestic production will decline, imports will fall due to lower income, public expenditures will decrease, and taxes will increase.

According to Keynes, movements in the goods market are more important than movements in the money market in determining exchange rates. In the elasticity approach, trade in goods and services between countries plays an important role in the determination of exchange rates. While countries produce the goods they need for their domestic markets, they earn foreign exchange income by exporting goods in excess of their needs to other countries. Countries meet the needs of society by importing from other countries the products that they cannot produce in line with their needs or that they cannot meet their domestic demand. For these transactions, they make payments to other countries in foreign currency. In the Keynesian approach, exchange rates will depend on the supply and demand for foreign currency because of exports and imports of goods and services.

In this approach, since changes in exchange rates depend on the elasticity of demand for imported and exported goods, the sum of the domestic elasticity of demand for imported goods and the foreign elasticity of demand for exported goods must be equal to or greater than 1 for changes in exchange rates to lead to trade balance. This is the elasticity condition known as the Marshall–Lerner condition (Müslümov et al., 2002, p. 48). According to the Marshall–Lerner condition, $em + ex \geq 1$ under the assumption that export goods can be produced domestically and imported goods can be produced in other countries without any problem and production can be increased at any moment. It is stated that an increase in the exchange rate will reduce the foreign trade deficit and, on the contrary, a decrease in the exchange rate will reduce the foreign trade surplus (Seyidoğlu, 2015, p. 488). In a fixed exchange rate system, raising the official exchange rate is called devaluation and lowering it is called revaluation. In free exchange rate systems, changing exchange rates and changing them by governments have the same effects (Seyidoğlu, 2015, pp. 492–493). This situation disrupts the balance foreign trade creates.

It is predicted that a devaluation that disrupts the balance of trade and a rise in the exchange rate will first negatively and then positively affect the balance of trade. The fact that the balance of payments, which starts to run a deficit as a result of devaluation, then recovers and runs a surplus is called the "J Curve Effect" since its graphic representation resembles the letter "J" (Salvatore, 2013, p. 576). This effect arises due to low elasticities of demand in the short run.

In the income-expenditure approach, unlike the elasticity model, the exchange rate is developed in conjunction with the demand for goods and services and income. In the model, which excludes money and asset markets as well as public expenditures and capital movements, the equilibrating effects of devaluation are explained through national income. The condition for achieving equilibrium is based on the equality of production and consumption in the country (Bulut and Demirel, 2015, p. 92).

Since international capital movements, which determine exchange rates, are not included in the elasticity and income-expenditure models, the Keynesian model is based on current account transactions. With the models developed by Robert Mundell and J. Marcus Fleming, a new model that does not include capital movements has emerged. This model is called an advanced version of the Keynesian income-expenditure model that includes capital movements.

In this model, the main instruments for achieving macroeconomic economic balance are public expenditures, fiscal policy based on taxation and monetary policy based on the central bank's money supply. In order to achieve macroeconomic equilibrium, it is assumed that equilibrium must be achieved in three main markets: the goods market equilibrium, the money market equilibrium and the balance of payments. If these three equilibria are analyzed with a graph, they are shown in Figure 5 with the IS-LM-BP curves. Various combinations of interest rates and national income that achieve equilibrium in all three markets can be seen (Melvin and Norrbin, 2013, p. 246).

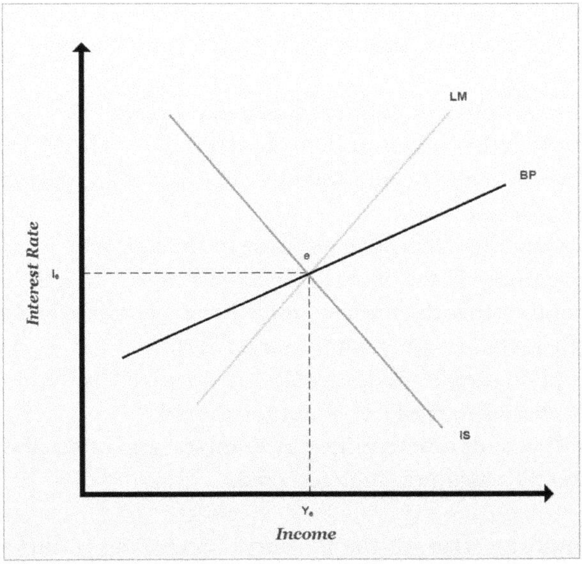

Figure 5: Goods market (IS), money market (LM) and balance of payments balance (BP)

The IS-LM-BP model differs from previous models in that capital movements are considered for the first time, and therefore capital movements have an important place in today's world. While the fact that the model takes into account capital and asset movements is seen as an important contribution to the theory, the fact that it does not take into account the effect of interest rate differentials on the asset market is seen among the main shortcomings of the model (Taylor, 1995, p. 21).

According to the Mundell–Fleming model, the goods market, the money market and the balance of payments must be in equilibrium to achieve economic equilibrium. This equilibrium occurs at the intersection of the *IS*, *LM* and *BP* curves, where the interest rate and income are in common equilibrium. At point *e* in Figure 5, i_e is the equilibrium interest rate and Y_e *is* the equilibrium income level. Until a change occurs that shifts one of the curves, the *IS-LM-BP* equilibrium shows investment-savings equilibrium, money demand-money supply equilibrium and a current account surplus equal to a capital account deficit with a zero balance.

The Mundell–Fleming model treats exchange rate changes in real terms. Considering the assumptions of the model (Dornbusch, 1980, p. 194):

- Assumption of constant nominal wages and prices.
- The assumption that aggregate demand is positively related to government expenditures, foreign income and exchange rate and negatively related to the domestic interest rate.
- Money demand has a negative response to the domestic interest rate and a positive response in the domestic income level is a directional function.
- The assumption that the money supply has a negative effect on the deviation of the exchange rate from its target level.
- The assumption that the trade account is determined by the level of domestic output relative to the level of output abroad.
- The capital account is determined by domestic and international interest rate differentials assumption is accepted.

Figure 6 shows the states of the BP curves according to different capital movements. When the BP curve is parallel to the interest rate axis (becomes steep), it indicates that capital mobility is not allowed. Parallel to the income axis (becoming horizontal) indicates that full capital mobility is allowed. Different slopes other than these angles indicate that there is no full capital mobility (Seyidoğlu, 2015, p. 892).

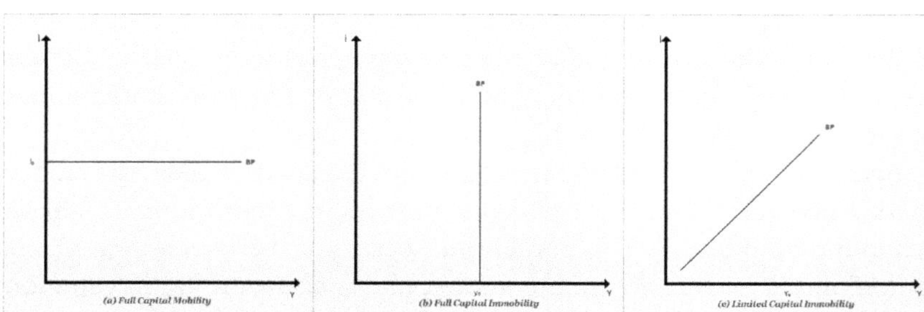

Figure 6: BP curves for different capital flows

In constructing the BP curve, it is assumed that higher interest rates will attract foreign investors and reduce the capital account deficit. Under the assumption of full capital mobility, the deviation of the domestic interest rate from the international interest rate will encourage investors to hold higher yielding assets. Therefore, the BP curve becomes flat when capital movements are free. The more the restricted capital flows are, the steeper the BP curve becomes (Melvin and Norrbin, 2013, p. 252).

Figure 7 shows a horizontal BP curve and a positively sloping BP curve.

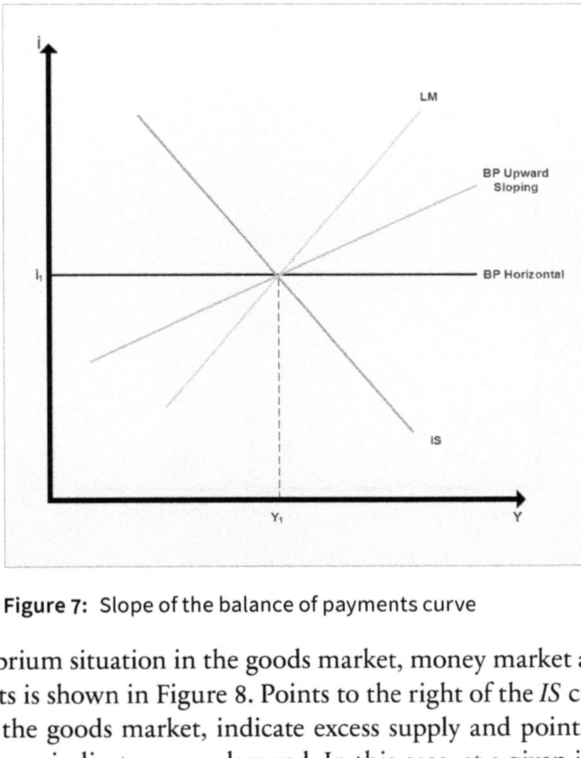

Figure 7: Slope of the balance of payments curve

The equilibrium situation in the goods market, money market and balance of payments is shown in Figure 8. Points to the right of the *IS* curve, which represents the goods market, indicate excess supply and points to the left of the IS curve indicate excess demand. In this case, at a given interest rate, the points to the right of the *IS* curve indicate that the supply in the goods market is greater than the demand for goods, while the points to the left of the *IS* curve indicate that the supply in the goods market is less than the demand for goods.

Points to the right of the *LM* curve, which represents the money market, indicate excess money demand, while points to the left indicate excess money supply. A shift of the *BP* curve to the right indicates a balance of payments deficit, while a shift to the left indicates a balance of payments surplus. Even with capital inflows at a given interest rate, a balance of payments deficit implies a higher level of domestic income and a larger trade deficit. A balance of payments surplus implies a higher level of domestic income and a larger trade surplus (Uçan, 2011, pp. 31–32).

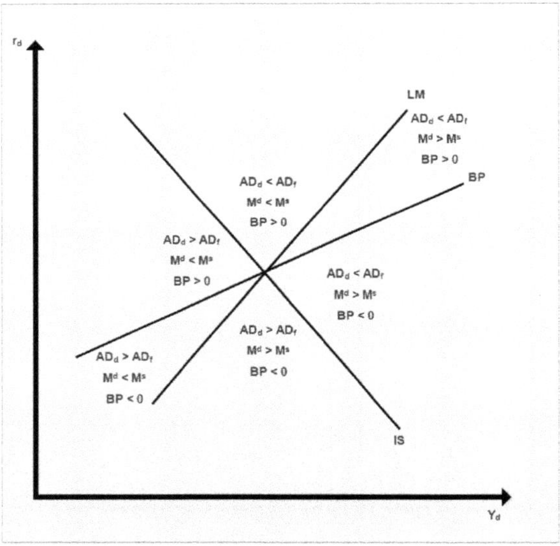

Figure 8: Internal and external balance in open economies
Source: Hossain and Chowdhurry (2001) as cited in (Uçan, 2011, p. 44)

Capital flows are an important instrument in the valuation of the national currency. Therefore, when capital leaves the country, the national currency depreciates, whereas when capital inflows occur, the national currency depreciates money appreciates in value. Reasons such as the profitability of investment arguments in the country, the increase in interest rates, and the decrease in risks in the country lead to an increase in capital inflows, while the opposite situation leads to an increase in capital outflows (Güven and Ekmen Özçelik, 2020, p. 19).

The Mundell–Fleming model is generally divided into fixed and flexible exchange rate systems. Since the model treats goods, mone and foreign exchange markets separately, the structure of capital flows and exchange rate systems play an important role in the determination of the exchange rate.

In fixed exchange rate systems, exchange rates are determined by national monetary authorities. While national central banks are usually the decision makers, in some countries the government is the decision maker. Together with the Mundell–Fleming model, the main determinant of the exchange rate is the freedom of capital movements.

In fixed exchange rate systems, the central bank does not have the freedom to conduct monetary policy independently of foreign markets. In the case of perfect substitution between domestic and foreign assets, the assets should provide the same return to all investors. In this case, it becomes impossible for central banks to conduct an independent monetary policy in fixed exchange rate systems (Melvin and Norrbin, 2013, p. 253). In the case of perfect substitution of all assets, capital inflows to the country with a higher local interest rate will increase, while capital outflows from the country with a lower local interest rate will increase.

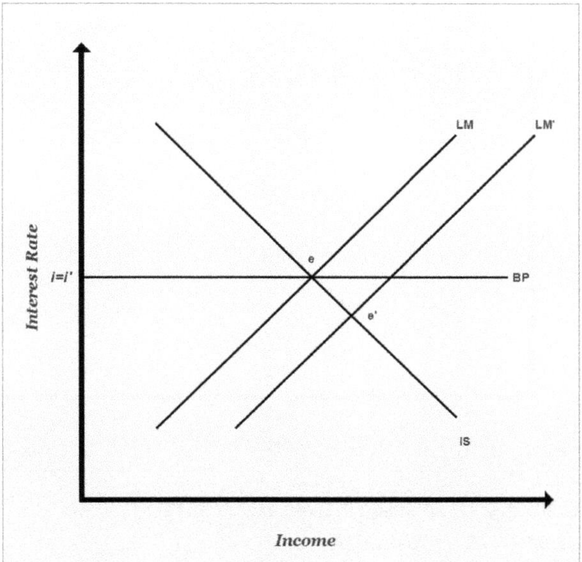

Figure 9: Monetary expansion in fixed exchange rate systems
Source: (Melvin & Norrbin, 2013, p. 254)

If the central bank increases the money supply, the IS-LM equilibrium will deteriorate, and the interest rate will fall below its initial equilibrium level. This would lead to a balance of payments deficit with capital outflow out of the country. In case of a depreciation of the national currency, the central bank must sell foreign exchange to the market to buy the national currency from the market to maintain a fixed exchange rate. Figure 9 shows that when the national money supply decreases, the initial equilibrium will be restored.

In the case of full capital mobility, the IS-LM-BP equilibrium will not change due to the prediction that the central bank and the market will react instantaneously. With full capital mobility, the new equilibrium state will change instantly, and no movement will be observed at the equilibrium point.

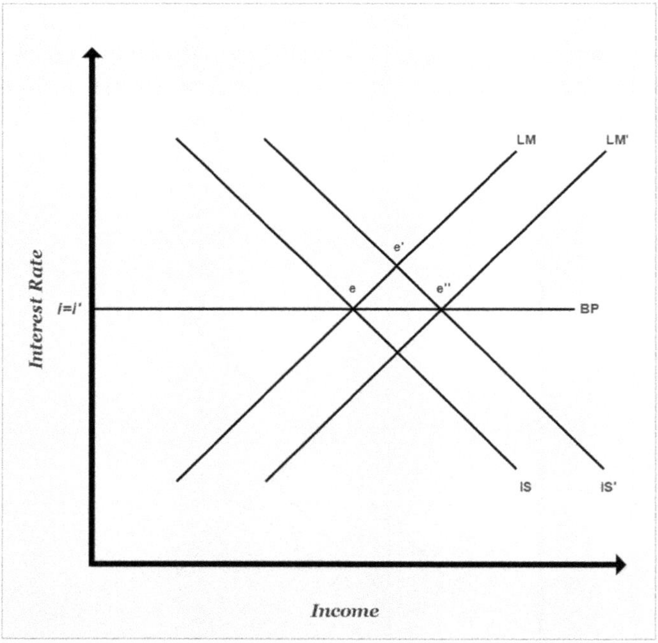

Figure 10: Fiscal expansion in fixed exchange rate systems
Source: (Melvin & Norrbin, 2013, p. 255)

Expansionary fiscal policy changes, such as public spending or tax increases, will shift the IS curve to the right. The new equilibrium is characterized by a higher interest rate and more income point in the balance of payments. Since the new equilibrium will be at a point above the BP curve, a higher domestic interest rate will be reached, and the balance of payments will start to run a surplus as capital inflows increase. In this situation, the central bank needs to increase the money supply and buy foreign exchange with the national currency to prevent the depreciation of the national currency. With the increase in money supply, the LM curve will shift to the right and reach the interest rate point at the initial equilibrium and income will increase. This is illustrated in Figure 10.

The important difference between this situation and the expansionary monetary policy in fixed exchange rate systems is that in fixed exchange rate systems and full capital mobility, monetary policy is effective in changing the level of income. This is because with a fixed exchange rate, independent monetary policy cannot be implemented, while fiscal policy increases domestic production through its income-enhancing effect (Melvin and Norrbin, 2013, pp. 254–255).

In a flexible exchange rate system, the exchange rate is determined by changes in the supply and demand for foreign exchange. Changes in the supply and demand for foreign exchange are immediately reflected in the exchange rates, thus achieving internal equilibrium in the foreign exchange market. External balance depends on exchange rate changes. In a flexible exchange rate system, a possible balance of payments surplus causes the exchange rate to fall, while a balance of payments deficit causes the exchange rate to rise. In this case, the central bank has no responsibility for the exchange rate and balance of payments and the system balances itself automatically (Uçan, 2011, p. 38).

In practice, in the flexible exchange rate regimes implemented around the world, the exchange rate is either completely determined by supply and demand in the market or there are interventionist exchange rate regimes in which the central bank intervenes periodically in the exchange rate determined by supply and demand in the market (Eğilmez, 2013).

In a fixed exchange rate system where capital movements are completely free, it is not possible to implement monetary policies independently, and monetary policies will be shaped according to capital movements and the exchange rate. However, if capital movements are subject to controls, a fixed exchange rate regime and independent monetary policy can be implemented together. This is called the impossible trilemma hypothesis in the literature (Aydın Y., 2014, p. 2).

2.2. Exchange Rate Determination Models According to Purchasing Power Parity Theory

Purchasing power parity is conceptually similar to the application of the single price law in foreign exchange markets (Seyidoğlu, 2015, p. 455). According to the law of one price, a market is a market with a large number of buyers and sellers, where free competition prevails, and market information is available at small costs. In environments where these markets work effectively, the prices of tradable goods should be the same all over the world. Although there may be exchange rate differences between countries, price differences should at most not exceed transportation costs. In efficient markets, buyers will tend toward low prices and sellers will tend toward high prices. Naturally, the market will come to equilibrium on its own.

The law of one price is realized through arbitrage activities in international markets. Arbitrage is the process of making profit by taking advantage of price differences between markets without incurring risk. Arbitrageurs make profits by selling the goods they find at low prices in markets where they can sell them at higher prices. Arbitrageurs' profit-making activities will reduce the price differences between countries over time. Prices will start to fall in the country where the relatively expensive product is sold, and prices in the country where it is sold relatively cheaply will start to rise. The law of one price is characterized by the fact that fluctuating prices in international markets can stabilize before too long. The law of one price is valid not only in goods and services markets but also in foreign exchange and capital markets (Seyidoğlu, 2015, p. 456).

According to the purchasing power parity theory, the nominal exchange rate is obtained by the ratio of domestic and foreign price levels (Lothian and Taylor, 1996, p. 491). The theoretical debate, which started during the World War I period, gained a solid foundation when Gustav Cassel added the concepts of absolute purchasing power and relative purchasing power to the theory (Krugman et al., 2012, p. 386). Thus, the concept of purchasing power in the determination of exchange rates has been divided into two categories: absolute and relative purchasing power parity method.

2.2.1. Exchange Rate Determination Model According to Absolute Purchasing Power Parity

In the absolute purchasing power parity method, the ratio of the general price levels of two countries is equal to the exchange rate between these countries. Absolute purchasing power parity assumes that the law of one price applies to all goods. Baskets of certain goods or groups of goods are expected to have the same value in all parts of the world. In other words, it is argued that goods purchased with a given amount of national currency in a given country should be the same as goods purchased in a foreign country with the foreign currency equivalent of the same amount of national currency.

In the absolute purchasing power parity exchange rate determination model, it is argued that the exchange rate is equal to the ratio of the domestic consumer price index and the foreign price index (Öztürk and Bayraktar, 2010, p. 162). In the absolute purchasing power parity theory, the law of one price should be extended to all goods in the country and price indices should be used. One of the important points in the theory is that the indices used should cover the same period (same month, quarter, six months or year). When the domestic price index is denoted *by Pd*, the foreign price index by *Pf* and the exchange rate by *ER*, absolute purchasing power parity is expressed in equation (2.1) (Seyidoğlu, 2015, p. 456).

$$P_d = \mathrm{ER} \times P_f \tag{2.1}$$

Based on this equation, it is possible to find the exchange rate by summing the indices on one side of the equation. Therefore, absolute purchasing power parity is considered as one of the important indicators in determining exchange rates. This is shown in equation (2.2) (Karluk, 2013, p. 622).

$$\mathrm{ER} = P_d \,/\, P_f \tag{2.2}$$

Purchasing power parity theory is particularly favorable in the long run-in environments of high inflation, high levels of growth and supply shocks (Enders, 1987, p. 1).

In addition to economists who think that absolute purchasing power parity theory is a determinant of exchange rates, there are also economists who think that it is not completely determinant. In particular, the single price law is criticized for not being a complete price index since it covers goods traded between countries and does not cover all goods used in countries. Today, countries use different price indices, use different baskets of goods even if they use the same indices, or weight goods differently in baskets of goods. Due to the inhomogeneity of the goods compared in purchasing power parity, there are criticisms that the theory cannot provide reliable results in exchange rate forecasting (Bulut and Demirel, 2015, p. 97).

Another criticism of the absolute purchasing power parity theory is that it focuses only on trade in goods and services and ignores capital flows. In addition to tradable goods and services, international capital flows can also cause balance of payments surpluses or deficits (Seyidoğlu, 2015, p. 457). Another criticism of the theory is that it ignores customs tariffs in foreign trade, as freight and transportation costs create barriers to trade (Krugman et al., 2012, p. 395). In addition, another criticism of the theory is that it does not consider cross-country efficiency (Bulut and Demirel, 2015, p. 98).

2.2.2. Exchange Rate Determination Model According to Relative Purchasing Power Parity

In the theory of relative purchasing power parity, the change in exchange rates depends on the inflation rates of the countries being compared. As in absolute purchasing power parity, the inflation rates of the countries are compared on the basis of a certain period. According to the theory, in the two-country model, the higher the domestic inflation rate compared to the foreign country, the higher the exchange rate of the country. The lower the domestic inflation compared to the foreign country, the lower the exchange rate of the country (Seyidoğlu, 2015, p. 460).

The relative purchasing power parity theory differs from the absolute purchasing power parity theory in that it takes into account the relative differences of these factors rather than the absolute differences in prices and exchange rates. According to the theory of relative purchasing power parity, we can express change in terms of an equation like (2.3). In the equation, the beginning of the period is 0, the end of the period is 1, inflation rates are denoted *by P*, the domestic economy is denoted *by d* and the economy of the foreign country is denoted by *f* (Krugman et al., 2012, p. 387).

$$\frac{ER_1 - ER_0}{ER_0} = P_d - P_f \tag{2.3}$$

The equation expresses the percentage change in exchange rates equal to the percentage change in the countries' general level of prices. Relative purchasing power parity can also be obtained by taking the logarithms of the two sides of the equation as expressed in the absolute purchasing power parity equation in equation (2.2). In this case, the equation is written in first differences as in equation (2.4) (Bulut and Demirel, 2015, pp. 96–97).

$$\Delta Ln\ ER = \Delta\ Ln\ _{Pd} - \Delta\ Ln\ _{Pf} \tag{2.4}$$

As in the absolute purchasing power parity theory, there are some theoretical problems in the relative purchasing power parity theory. To summarize these problems under general headings; trade barriers and non-tradable goods and services, monopolies and oligopolies in goods markets that prevent free competition in different countries practices and differences in consumption patterns and inflation measurement across countries (Krugman et al., 2012, pp. 396–400).

According to the purchasing power parity theory, it is also possible to obtain misleading results in the calculations. Deviations in calculations are expressed in two ways. One of them is categorized as structural deviations that cause relative price changes, and the other is categorized as temporary deviations arising from the difference in the speed of adjustment of pricing in goods and asset markets. The reasons for these deviations can be categorized under headings such as changes in the terms of trade, interactions in the relative prices of domestic and foreign goods as a result of economic development, late reflection of changes in money supply and exchange rates on prices and wages, which are rigid in the short run (Bulut and Demirel, 2015, pp. 98–99).

2.3. Exchange Rate Determination Models According to Interest Rate Parity Theory

Apart from internationally traded goods, transfers of financial assets between countries play an important role in determining exchange rates. The theory of interest rate parity attempts to explain the relationship between the returns on bond investments between two countries. Since interest rate parity theory is largely driven by profit arbitrage, it is also referred to as the interest rate arbitrage approach in the literature. The general characteristic of asset markets is that asset owners seek the maximum return they can obtain. As in asset markets, participants in the foreign exchange market act by comparing the expected returns between different currencies. To compare different returns on deposits, participants must calculate how the monetary value of deposits will change. To compare rates of return measured in different currencies, they need to know how exchange rates will change (Krugman et al., 2012, p. 332).

According to the theory of interest rate parity, it is necessary to relate the exchange rate traded in spot and futures markets to the interest rates of that country. In this relationship, similar to the purchasing power parity theory, it is assumed that domestic and foreign financial assets are perfect substitutes without any restrictions and therefore the rates of return on assets will be equalized (Claassen, 1996, p. 39).

Investors' expectations of future returns on their deposits are important when choosing between asset returns. If there is an expectation that the return on domestic deposits in the country will be higher than the return on foreign deposits, the demand for the national currency should be higher than the demand for foreign currencies. The remarkable point here is the change in the demand for national and foreign currencies. In this context, the expected returns on national and foreign currencies should be compared. Citizens of the country are based on the return they expect from their own currencies, while foreigners are based on the return they expect to obtain from foreign currencies (Karluk, 2013, pp. 615–616). Investors generally want to obtain maximum return with minimum risk. In these transactions, investors assume the risk of the future value of exchange rates. While it is possible to make a profit from exchange rate forecasting, it is also possible to make a loss (Bulut & Demirel, 2015, p. 104).

Suppose we have a deposit account between citizens living in Türkiye and the United States and we are comparing the returns in these countries. Assume that the interest rate on deposits in the United States is $_{i\$}$, the interest rate on deposits in Türkiye is $_{itl}$, the forward rate on the U.S. dollar in Türkiye is $_{Fer}$ and the spot rate on the U.S. dollar in Türkiye is $_{Eer}$. For assets with interest rates and forward rates of the same maturity, investors in the United States earn \$10 + $_{i\$}$ for a \$10 investment. Alternatively, the U.S. investor can convert the dollar into Turkish lira and invest in Türkiye in

Turkish lira. In Türkiye, the exchange rate of $_{10/Eer}$ by investing in Turkish lira, it will increase its money to $(10 + _{itl})_{/Eer}$. This is the Turkish lira equivalent of \$10 and will be converted back into U.S. dollars at the end of the period. Thus, the investment entering the market as $_{10/Eer}$ will become $(10 + _{itl})_{/Eer}$ at the end of the period and the U.S. investor will convert his investment into dollars at the end of the period.

Given the lack of certainty in future spot rates, U.S. investors can hedge their Turkish lira deposits with a forward contract at $(10 + _{itl})_{/Eer}$. Thus, the investor secures the Turkish lira investment opportunity corresponding to (10 + *itl*) *Fer/Eer* dollars. In sum, the U.S. investor will earn \$10 + $_{i\$}$ in his/her home country or $(10 + _{itl})\ _{Fer/Eer}$ dollars in Türkiye (Melvin and Norrbin, 2013, pp. 115–116). Hence, the investment opportunities between the two investments are shown in equations (2.5) and (2.6). Subtracting 1 from both sides of equation (2.6) yields equation (2.7).

$$10 +_{i\$} = (10 +_{itl})_{Fer} \,/\, _{Eer} \tag{2.5}$$

$$(10 +_{i\$}) / (10 +_{itl}) =_{Fer} \,/\, _{Eer} \tag{2.6}$$

$$(_{i\$} -_{itl}) / (10 +_{itl}) = (_{Fer} -_{Eer}) / _{Eer} \tag{2.7}$$

An approximation can be made by assuming that the denominator on the left-hand side of equation (2.7) is approximately one. Assuming that the denominator is equal to 1, approximate interest rate parity is expressed by equation (2.8).

$$(_{i\$} -_{itl}) = (_{Fer} -_{Eer}) \,/\, _{Eer} \tag{2.8}$$

The smaller the value of the Turkish deposit rate, $_{itl}$, the larger the convergence between equations (2.8) and (2.7). Equation (2.8) shows that the interest rate spread between the United States and Turkish investment is equal to the term premium or discount on the Turkish lira (Melvin and Norrbin, 2013, p. 116). It should be noted that this is not always the case and there are exceptions. There are also cases where the interest rate cannot always equalize the spot and forward exchange rate and there are deviations from the theory of interest rate parity. Theory sons for deviations from the theory can be listed as transaction costs, risk premiums, restrictions on capital movements and differences in tax practices in the countries of investment (Bulut and Demirel, 2015, p. 105).

Investors who have deposits and want to earn higher income through arbitrage can convert their money back into Turkish lira at the spot rate and invest Turkish lira against the dollar at the forward rate. The forward price of the Turkish lira is expected to be higher than the interest rate parity return. Since the future earnings from these transactions will be equal to the interest income spread, this transaction will have the effect of increasing the spot rate and decreasing the forward rate. At the same time, deposit interest rates are also volatile. The reallocation of investment funds into Turkish lira will lower the interest rate on Turkish lira deposits, while the reallocation of U.S. dollar investments out of the country will raise the interest rate on U.S. dollar deposits (Melvin and Norrbin, 2013, p. 117). Since the return on deposits is not only the interest rate return, the exchange rate return is also added.

The explanations we have given under the heading of interest rate parity theory are referred to as assured interest rate parity theory in some publications. Since exchange rate movements are subject to future uncertainties, it is natural for investors to assume minimum risk and seek maximum gains. Despite this behavior, in some cases, investors may ignore the risks they take depending on the size of the gains they can obtain.

Such investors make decisions based on the financial performance of countries under the assumption that markets operate efficiently. Since investors are more interested in return than risk, they may prefer to remain indifferent to the future level of spot exchange rates. This theory of exchange rate determination is referred to in the literature as the theory of precarious interest rate parity.

The most important argument in the theory of precarious interest rate parity is the existence of an efficient market. What is meant by an efficient market is a perfectly competitive market in which all economic agents in the market act rationally and aim for maximum profit. The model including expectations can be analyzed in three ways according to the efficiency of the markets (Yörük, 2000, pp. 7–8):

- Weak markets taking into account past prices and earnings.
- Semi-strong markets that take into account past prices and earnings as well as current information.

- A distinction is made between publicly disclosed and non-disclosed markets and strong markets where all private information is reflected.

For the precarious interest rate parity theory to be valid, investments within the country should have the same risk as investments outside the country. A general comparison between the secured and unsecured interest rate parity theories suggests that while the secured interest rate parity theory is supported by empirical studies, there is no empirical evidence for the unsecured interest rate parity theory (Bulut and Demirel, 2015, p. 108). The theory of precarious interest rate parity is logically consistent, and the predictions of the model are consistent with real life. In addition, more factors affecting foreign exchange behavior should be added to the modeling of the precarious interest rate parity theory (Husted and Melvin, 2013, p. 296).

2.4. Financial Markets Approach

In the financial markets approach, it is emphasized that monitoring changes in the general level of prices and current account transactions in the models examined so far is not sufficient to explain the determinants of exchange rates. It is stated that exchange rates are traded as a financial asset and expectations are also important (Woo, 1985, pp. 1–2). It is emphasized that the most important factors that become difficult to predict in the model with the inclusion of expectations in the model are the supply and demand quantities of national and foreign currencies. Considering the common assumptions of the model, national and foreign currencies are considered as financial assets and capital mobility is assumed to be complete. International demand for national assets should be taken into account when determining the exchange rate.

It is also possible to divide the financial markets approach into three. Therefore, the financial markets approach will be analyzed under three headings: monetary model, money substitution model and portfolio balance model.

2.4.1. Monetarist Model Approach

In the monetarist model approach, the relative price of the national currency is determined by the supply and demand of the foreign currency and the national currency. Although the model is similar to the classical model, the model assumes full capital mobility and no transaction costs or barriers to transactions. In line with these assumptions, portfolios are expected to be in equilibrium thanks to fully substitutable national and foreign investment instruments and only national and foreign currency markets are expected to be effective in determining the exchange rate (Taşkın, 1995, pp. 41–42). In essence, after the fluctuations in exchange rate systems following the Bretton Woods System, the exchange rate determination has been a price determination model.

In the classical monetary model, monetary variables and policies affect real variables.

In quantity theory, the money stock is denoted by M, the velocity of circulation of money *by* V, the general level of prices *by* P and the level of output by Y and formulated as in equation (2.9).

$$M.V = P.Y \tag{2.9}$$

The classical quantity theory of money emerges with the assumption that both V, the income rate of money, and Y, the output level, are constant. With the assumption that the economy is at full employment, it is assumed that the real output level is constant, and the velocity of circulation will not change much. Although the validity of these assumptions in practice is low, the assumption that V and Y are constant implies that the general price level is proportional to the money stock. This result shows that the classical quantity theory is also an inflation theory (Dornbusch et al., 2017, p. 402).

Since the value of money depends on the quantity of money in the economy, the theory predicts that it will be priced according to the law of supply and demand. Increases in money supply increase the general level of prices and at the same time changes in money supply and demand affect exchange rates. Thus, an increase in the money supply is expected to increase the general level of prices and a decrease in the money supply is expected to decrease the general level of prices. Thus, a decrease in the money supply is expected to lead to an appreciation of the exchange rate at the same rate, while an increase in the money supply is expected to lead to a depreciation of the exchange rate at the same rate. For this reason, the role of purchasing power parity is not ignored in the classical monetarist approach. In the analysis of monetarist models, a distinction is made according to price elasticity, and they are analyzed under two headings: the flexible-price monetarist model and the rigid-price monetarist model.

2.4.1.1. Flexible-Priced Monetarist Approach

With the development of the classical monetarist theory, significant progress has been made in the literature. In addition to the commodity markets mentioned in the classical theory, an important stage has been reached in the determination of the exchange rate with the inclusion of bond markets and expectations in the theory. In addition to the classical theory, interest rate differentials between countries are added to the model in determining the exchange rate (Müslümov et al., 2002, p. 49).

The monetarist model of exchange rate determination is derived from a basic model of money demand. Assuming purchasing power parity, the equilibrium exchange rate can be determined by trends in relative money supply growth, relative GDP growth and relative interest rate differentials. In the monetarist model, a relative increase in domestic monetary growth is expected to lead to a relative decrease in domestic GDP growth and a relative increase in domestic interest rates (Rosenberg and Folkerts-Landau, 2002, p. 104). Moreover, according to the monetarist approach, an increase in money supply leads to an increase in the general level of prices rather than a direct activity-enhancing effect in the real sector. Increases in activity lead to an appreciation of the national currency against foreign currencies by increasing production. With the increase in income in real terms, the demand for the domestic money stock will increase and the interest in foreign currencies will relatively decrease (Bilson J., 1978, p. 53).

The difference in interest rates applied by countries gives the proportional holding cost of financial assets. With the addition of expectations to the model, earnings from financial assets are equalized. At this point, it can be said that the Fisher condition holds, the nominal interest rate is equal to the sum of real interest rates and expected inflation. Assuming that real interest rates equalize ($r - r^* = 0$), equation (2.11) is obtained (Bulut and Demirel, 2015, p. 112).

$$i = r + Ep \text{ and } i^* = r^* + Ep^* \qquad (2.10)$$

$$i - i^* = (r - r^*) + (Ep - Ep^*) \qquad (2.10a)$$

$$i - i^* = (Ep - Ep^*) \tag{2.11}$$

As domestic prices increase due to the rise in domestic inflation, this increases nominal interest rates on financial assets, which in turn increases the exchange rate due to the fall in the demand for national currency. According to the flexible-price monetarist model of exchange rate determination, in addition to the balance of money supply and demand, real incomes and expectations should be added to the model (Frenkel and Mussa, 1984, pp. 48–52).

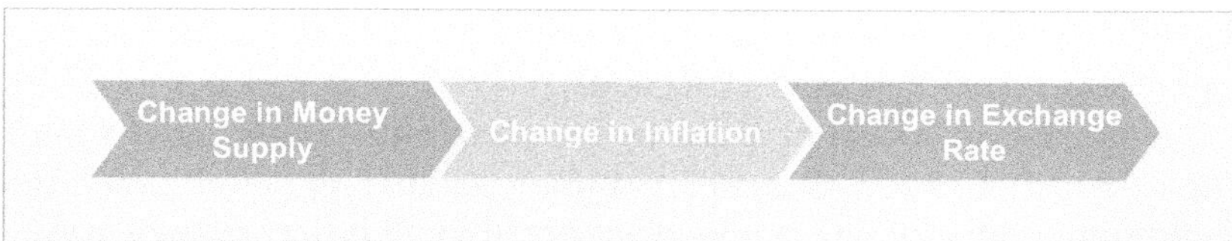

Figure 11: Direct effect of money supply changes on the exchange rate in the flexible-price money model of exchange rate determination

Source: (Rosenberg and Folkerts-Landau, 2002, p. 104)

According to Figure 11, a change in money supply leads to a change in the general level of prices and a change in the general level of prices leads to a change in purchasing power parity and exchange rate.

The effect of real economic activity on the exchange rate is schematized by Rosenberg in Figure 12 within the framework of the monetary model. Accordingly, a real increase in national income is expected to lead to a higher demand for national currency and, assuming that the existing money stock remains unchanged, the increased demand for national currency is expected to lower prices in relative terms. Relative decreases in the domestic price level

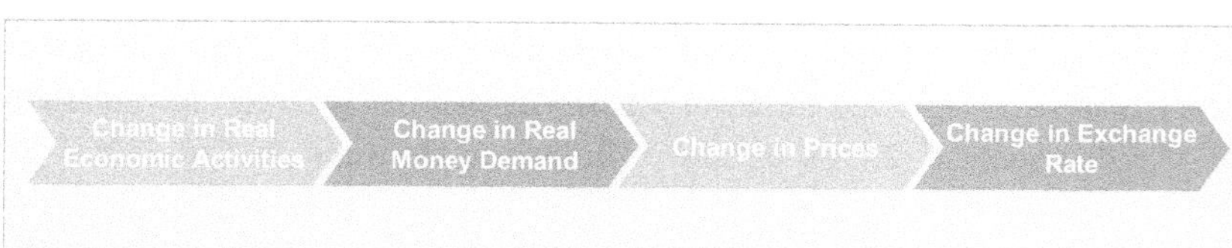

Figure 12: Direct effect of money supply changes on the exchange rate in the flexible monetary model

Source: (Rosenberg and Folkerts-Landau, 2002, p. 104)

at purchasing power parity also lead to appreciation of the national currency (Bulut and Demirel, 2015, p. 113).

According to the model, an increase in interest rates is expected to increase the value of the national currency by increasing capital flows (Dornbusch, 1976, p. 1171). However, in periods of hyperinflation, due to the monetary nature of the problem, it is argued that expectations will suppress the liquidity effect and there will be a positive relationship between interest rates and exchange rates. In sum, high interest rates are caused by monetary expansion due to inflation expectations (Frenkel, 1976, p. 210). Increases in interest rates lead to an increase in inflation expectations and depreciation of the national currency in anticipation of monetary expansion.

The monetary policy implemented by the monetary authorities of countries and the trust in these authorities are of great importance in determining the exchange rate. According to the model, the reason for the success of stable and tight monetary policy is trust in authority (Bulut and Demirel, 2015, p. 114). The decisions of credible monetary authorities to change the money supply will be reflected in the changes in the national currency and exchange rate. At this point, the effects of changes in the money supply on the exchange rate can be divided into direct and indirect effects.

According to Rosenberg in Figure 13, while the direct change in money supply affects the exchange rate, its indirect effect affects the future money supply and inflation expectations by adding expectations to the model. After this effect, the inflation expectation affects the change in money supply in the long run, the change in money supply affects the change in real money demand and finally the change in money demand affects the exchange rate.

The contribution of the model is the addition of stock variables and flow variables to the factors affecting the money supply. While stock variables represent the instantaneous stock of money in a given period, flow variables take into account the values of imports, exports, production and consumption in certain periods. In the determination of exchange rates, the monetarist model states that an increase in national income and the volume of transactions will cause citizens to demand more money and the value of the national currency will increase. However, in the Keynesian model, this situation is stated that the import multiplier will be affected when the national income level and exchange rate increase (Bulut and Demirel, 2015, p. 117).

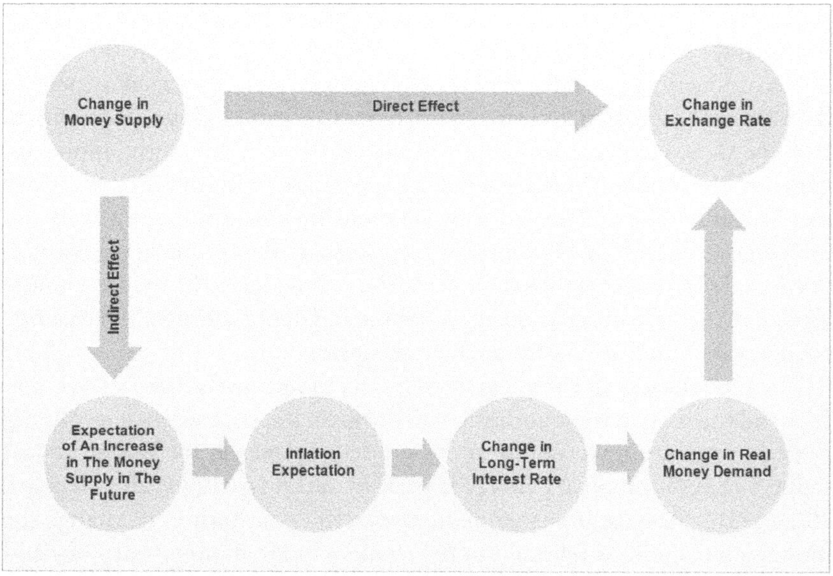

Figure 13: Direct and indirect effects of inflation expectations on exchange rate in the flexible monetary model
Source: (Rosenberg M. R., 1996, p. 147)

2.4.1.2. Strict Price Monetarist Approach

One of the major criticisms of the flexible-price monetarist model is the assumption that purchasing power parity is always valid. However, empirical studies have found that purchasing power parity is not valid in the short run. In order to overcome this problem, Dornbusch has developed a model similar to the flexible-price monetarist approach, but with the assumption that purchasing power parity is valid in the long run (Dornbusch, 1976). The Dornbusch model assumes that prices are rigid in the short run in case of possible monetary shocks since goods markets react later than financial markets. According to the model, an increase in nominal money supply due to rigid prices in the short run leads to an increase in real money supply and leads to a fall in interest rates due to the liquidity effect. The initial monetary increase not only leads to an equivalent depreciation of the exchange rate, but also to a further depreciation of the exchange rate by causing domestic interest rates to fall and hence capital outflows abroad. Thus, the exchange rate rises above the long-run purchasing power parity level in the short run.

In the flexibly priced monetarist approach, domestic monetary expansion causes the general level of prices to rise and the exchange rate to depreciate at the same rate through the purchasing power parity method. At this point, the difference between the rigidly priced monetarist approach and the flexibly priced monetarist approach is that in the flexibly priced model, monetary expansion affects the exchange rate at the rate of increase in money supply. However, in the rigidly priced model, the direct effect of the interest rate change is accompanied by the overshooting effect, which causes the exchange rate to rise further (Demiray, 1998, p. 54).

The cross-border effect arises when capital flows are complete. Exchange rate volatility has increased because of increased capital flows in the world, especially after the collapse of the Bretton Woods System. The increase in capital flows in the short run due to increased exchange rate volatility has caused economic crises in many countries. Eichengreen et al. (1995, pp. 163–166) proposed the idea that a Global Transactions Tax could be introduced to restrict capital flows in the short run and to prevent economic downturns in countries (Eichengreen et al., 1995, pp. 163–166). The aim here is for countries to achieve stability in the monetary policies they implement according to their own macroeconomic conditions. This mechanism is illustrated in Figure 14.

In the flexible-priced monetarist model, the interest rate differential is expected to increase inflation, whereas in the rigid-priced model, this relationship is reversed. This relationship assumes that there will be deviations from purchasing power in the short run, and monetary policy cannot be effective in the long run in the rigidly priced monetarist model (Copeland, 2014, p. 202).

The differences of the rigidly priced monetarist model from other exchange rate models are that it is more dynamic than the Mundell–Fleming model, quantity theory and purchasing power parity are valid in the long run, interest rate parity is valid in the short and long run, and expectations are included in the model (Bulut and Demirel, 2015, p. 120).

2.4.2. Money Substitution Model

Monetarist models generally assume that countries' own national currencies are effective in exchange rate formation. However, in practice, economic

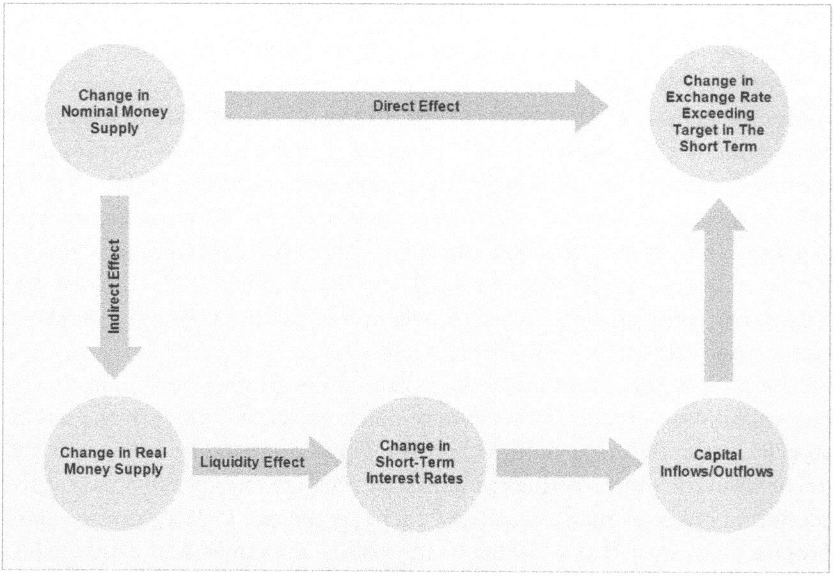

Figure 14: Effects of money supply changes on the exchange rate in the monetary model with strict prices
Source: *(Rosenberg M. R., 1996, p. 149)*

agents in countries do not transact only in national currency. Therefore, the currency substitution approach uses the assumption that citizens living in a country hold not only financial instruments such as bonds and bills for their investments but also their own and foreign currencies. In addition to citizens making transactions, multinational and international corporations, arbitrageurs and speculators also generate foreign currency demand. Therefore, economic agents in the country form portfolios of financial instruments, national currencies and foreign currencies (Müslümov et al., 2002, p. 54).

The currency substitution model assumes that citizens and economic agents living in a country hold both national and foreign currencies, while foreign citizens and economic agents living in foreign countries hold both national and foreign currencies. This model is not opposed to the monetarist and portfolio equilibrium models of exchange rate determination that we will discuss next, but it modifies some of their assumptions (He and Sharma,

1997, p. 327). When we look at the money substitution model, it is possible to write the money demand functions as equation (2.12) for domestic countries and equation (2.13) for foreign countries (He and Sharma, 1997, p. 328). In the equations, *m* is the money supply of the domestic country, p is the general level of prices of the domestic country, *y* is the output level of the domestic country and *r* is the interest rate of the domestic country; m^* is the money supply of the foreign country, p^* is the general level of prices of the foreign country, y^* is the output level of the foreign country and r^* is the interest rate of the foreign country demand, *k* income elasticities, λ interest rate elasticities.

$$m = {}_{m1^*} + p + ky - \lambda r \tag{2.12}$$

$$m^* = {}_{m1} + p^* + ky^* - \lambda r \tag{2.13}$$

When the spot exchange rate in the domestic country is denoted by *s*, the assumption of long-run purchasing power parity is given by equation (2.14).

$$s = p - p^* \tag{2.14}$$

When the money demand functions are re-adjusted using the purchasing power parity equation, equation (2.15) is obtained. This equation is a modified long-run flexible-price exchange rate model of the Frenkel–Bilson model. The model is based on Dornbusch (1976) and Frankel (1979) added rigidity of domestic prices and deviations from purchasing power parity, and Frankel (1979) transformed equation (2.16) with the assumption that augmented regressive expectations are rational (Uçan, 2011, p. 73).

$$s^1 = m - m^* + m_1 - m_1^* - k(y - y^*) + \lambda(r - r^*) \tag{2.15}$$

$$s^e_{t+1} - s_t = \theta\ (s^1 - s)_t + (\pi^e - \pi^{*e})_t \tag{2.16}$$

In equation (2.16), s^e t+1 denotes the expected future exchange rate $(\pi^e - \pi^{*e})t$ denotes the expected inflation differentials and θ denotes the adjustment parameter. With these assumptions, the precarious interest rate is provided, and equation (2.17) is obtained, and equation (2.15) and equation (2.17) yield equation (2.18) (Meese and Rogoff, 1983, p. 5). In order to include expectations in the model, the model is completed by inserting inflation differentials into equation (2.18).

$$s^e\ t{+}1 - {}_{st} = r - r^* \tag{2.17}$$

$$s = m - m^* + {}_{m1} - m1^* - k(y - y^*) + (\lambda - 1/\theta)(r - r^*) + 1/\theta\ (\pi^e - \pi^*\ )^e \tag{2.18}$$

Two different results are obtained from the currency substitution approach. The first one is that the instabilities that cause currency substitution cause changes in the exchange rate and in this case, the limits of exchange rate changes are unpredictable. The second result of the approach is that exchange rate uncertainty due to money demand persists when currencies between countries are perfect substitutes (Girton and Roper, 1981, p. 26).

2.4.3. Portfolio Balance Approach

The portfolio balance approach is based on the work of Markowitz and Tobin on portfolio theory and the demand for money (Pentecost, 1993, p. 151). In the money substitution model, a model is developed based on the possibility that changes in the real sector may take time to be reflected in financial markets. The portfolio balance approach, on the other hand, accepts this assumption but draws a different road map starting from the implicit interest rate point. In the portfolio balance approach, investors' risk aversion motive in choosing between domestic and foreign products is based on the idea that the implicit interest rate parity will lead to risks that are too large to work. Thus, the portfolio balance approach tries to ensure that decisions are made based on the results of risk premium analysis of the exchange rate (Copeland, 2014, p. 220).

The portfolio balance approach considers cash, assets and bonds held by individuals and private firms as their wealth. Asset demands are determined not only by rates of return but also by the returns of other assets. In this approach, investors seek to diversify their holdings according to their risk structures, and portfolio allocations are created that increase as the returns on assets increase relative to other assets not in the portfolio. Moreover, since assets are denominated in different currencies, they are no longer considered to be perfect substitutes (Müslümov et al., 2002, p. 56). According to the approach, investors should be willing to accept transaction costs when exchanging between assets. The assets that make up the portfolio are not perfect substitutes since investors who are willing to bear the costs assume a risk premium.

The portfolio balance approach differs from other exchange rate determination models, The financial sector is discussed in detail. A broader and more detailed model is obtained by adding short and long-run savings to the model. Savings are treated as the accumulation of foreign assets and are reflected in surplus or deficit accounts in the balance of payments depending on the floating exchange rate (Copeland, 2014, pp. 220–221).

The portfolio balance approach is a more general and adaptive model in the sense that it combines the capital mobility assumption of the Mundell–Fleming model and the slow adjustment of the general level of prices of the Dornbusch model. In other words, it has similar features in terms of exchange rate determination and its consequences in terms of combining two different schools of thought. However, the most important difference between the monetary approach and the portfolio balance approach is that the monetary approach remains risk neutral. Since the monetary approach ignores expectations in exchange rates, this deficiency is completed in the portfolio balance approach. For this reason, economic agents aim to allocate and minimize risks through the portfolio approach in order not to be adversely affected by exchange rates in the future (Bulut and Demirel, 2015, p. 121).

According to the portfolio balance approach model, economic agents want to hold risk-free domestic assets and risky foreign assets in their portfolios in order to maximize returns by avoiding risk. The necessary factor for economic agents' gains is the condition that the expected return on foreign assets is higher than the expected return on domestic assets (Claassen, 1996, p. 60). According to the model, exchange rates ensure that domestic and foreign assets come to equilibrium in financial markets, while interest rates applied by countries are another instrument that helps to stabilize financial markets. Exchange rates are determined by factors such as interest rates and changes in money supply, which affect the supply and demand of monetary and financial assets (Bulut and Demirel, 2015, p. 123).

According to the portfolio balance approach, economic agents adjust the assets in their portfolios according to changes in rates of return. In the model, the net financial wealth of the public and private sector is assumed to consist of three parts. Total nominal wealth is denoted by W, money by

M, domestic financial instruments denominated in domestic currency by *B* and foreign financial instruments denominated in foreign currency held by residents by *SB** to form the following equations. In equation (2.19), *S* denotes the nominal exchange rate. Total nominal wealth is equal to the sum of domestic currency anchors, domestic financial instruments and foreign currency denominated financial instruments (Müslümov et al., 2002, p. 56).

$$W=M+B+SB^{*} \tag{2.19}$$

Since the asset market equilibrium is determined by domestic and foreign rates of return, this phenomenon is expressed as in equation (2.20). In the equation, the domestic interest rate is denoted *by i*, the foreign interest rate by i^{*} and the expected depreciation of the national currency by $\hat{S}e$ (Gözen, 2018, p. 53).

$$M= M(i,i^{*}+\hat{S}e)W \qquad M1<0,\ M2<0 \tag{2.20}$$

$$B= B(i,i^{*}+ \hat{S}e)W \qquad B1>0,\ B2>0 \tag{2.21}$$

$$SB^{*}= B(i,i^{*}+\hat{S}e)W \qquad B1^{*}<0,\ B2^{*}>0 \tag{2.22}$$

$$B^{*}= T(S/P)+i^{*}B^{*} \qquad T1>0 \tag{2.23}$$

Equations (2.20), (2.21) and (2.22) standard asset demand equations. They are also goods prices are not deterministic in the models. According to the equations, the demand for money moves in the opposite direction to changes in the interest rates of domestic and foreign financial assets. The demand for domestic and foreign financial assets varies in the right direction with the interest rates of the country in which they are located and in the opposite direction with the rate of return on financial assets of the other country (Müslümov et al., 2002, p. 57). In equation (2.23), B^{*} is the rate of change in foreign financial instruments. According to the model, since the current account and the capital account should be equal, the trade balance has a positive direct effect on the real exchange rate (Sarno and Taylor, 2003, p. 116).

Finally, it should be noted that exchange rates are also affected by the "safe haven effect" in the portfolio balance approach. This is because the returns on financial assets are affected by countries' new taxation policies, political decisions, political developments and economic destabilizing factors such as war and terrorist incidents. In such cases, investors shift their investments to countries that are safe for them, usually developed economies, due to the increase in risk premiums in risky countries (Bulut and Demirel, 2015, pp. 124–125). This situation, which causes capital mobility in countries, causes the national currency to depreciate in the countries where the funds leave and the national currency to appreciate in the countries where the funds are invested (Öztürk and Bayraktar, 2010, p. 184).

In sum, the portfolio balance approach establishes a relationship between exchange rates and the current account balance, rejects the validity of implicit interest rate parity and emphasizes the existence of a risk premium instead.

2.5. Speculative Bubbles Theory

The idea that macroeconomic variables generally affect exchange rates in exchange rate determination models has been found to have failed empirically after the 1970s, especially in the determination of short-term exchange rate movements (De Grauwe, 2005, p. 125). The divergence of empirical results from the theory has been interpreted in two different ways in the literature. The first one is that the differences in short-run results may be due to technology, tastes and preferences, and the second one is interpreted as the speculative bubbles theory (De Grauwe et al. 1995, p. 317).

The speculative bubble theory assumes that market expectations, rather than macroeconomic variables, are the cause of exchange rate changes. Speculation is a profit-making process by taking positions against future risks. If speculators believe that a foreign currency will appreciate in the future as a result of forecasts, speculators take a position by buying the foreign currency at the point when its value is low. A rise in the value of the foreign currency in the future as a result of forecasts will profit speculators, while a fall in the value of the foreign currency in the future as a result of forecasts will cause speculators to incur losses. In currencies whose value is expected to fall, speculators exhibit the opposite behavior model (Seyidoğlu, 2015, p. 438).

Since speculation is a transaction that aims to gain profit by assuming risk, the greater the risk taken, naturally the greater the gains and losses to be obtained from the transaction. Moreover, the theory accepts exchange rate movements that occur outside macroeconomic variables as the effect of speculative behavior (Bulut and Demirel, 2015, p. 130). In foreign exchange speculation, speculators can trade in three different types of markets. These are spot markets where they can trade instantly, forward markets where they can trade futures and future markets where they can trade in the future. In spot markets, speculation is carried out on currencies that are traded instantaneously, while in forward markets, speculation is carried out by predicting the value of the exchange rate in the future. A speculator who decides to trade in forward markets decides between the spot market value and the value he will receive in futures transactions. If he finds this forward transaction profitable, he enters a forward purchase and sale contract for the future (Karluk, 2013, p.566).

Speculative bubbles theory, spot in the market transaction seeing foreign currency dry and the expected exchange rate based on macroeconomic variables. This difference is characterized in the literature as a speculative bubble, since it is likened to a bubble, first growing and then rapidly disappearing (Philon, 1995, p. 72). Speculative bubbles are divided into two categories: endogenous bubbles and exogenous bubbles. Internal bubbles are stated to be caused from fundamental macroeconomic variables and target region applications, while external bubbles are stated to be due to external factors independent of macroeconomic variables (Froot and Obstfeld, 1989).

It is argued that exchange rate targeting makes countries vulnerable to speculative attacks against the exchange rate (Obstfeld and Rogoff, 1995, p. 77). Targeted countries may suffer losses at home against shocks that may occur in foreign countries. Speculators may also prefer to take positions in foreign currencies by reviewing the exchange rate policies of countries. Thus, there may be pressure on the exchange rate and depreciation of the national currency (Müslümov et al., 2002, p. 68).

The theory generally emphasizes that individuals act according to expectations rather than macroeconomic variables. Individuals who act according to macroeconomic variables and have rational expectations may have more robust forecasts. In addition, people who predict that a currency will appreciate without any macroeconomic variables increase the demand for money more than they should, causing the exchange rate to rise. In some cases, these predictions are spread by word of mouth and may even lead to individuals imitating each other without questioning the information.

When calculations based on basic macroeconomic data replace the forecasts, most of the forecasts turn out to be false and the bubbles burst (Öztürk and Bayraktar, 2010, p. 184).

2.6. The Impact of Political and Economic Announcements on Exchange Rate Determinations

When we look at the exchange rate determination models, we see that exchange rates are affected by many macroeconomic variables, models are constructed with these variables and empirical studies are conducted on them. However, it is observed that some of the empirical studies have yielded negative results due to factors that are excluded from the model (Seyidoğlu, 2013, p. 209). Globalizing economies, sudden developments in the world and economic shocks related to these developments affect exchange rates. An unexpected event, disaster, news and announcement increases the volatility in exchange rates traded in spot markets, especially in the short term, and enables economic agents to reposition in exchange rate transactions in forward markets.

The most important feature of the model that distinguishes it from other models is that it considers the possibility of error even in models based on basic macroeconomic variables and states that unexpected events can cause fluctuations even in stable economies (Bulut and Demirel, 2015, p. 133).

Among the reasons that increase exchange rate instability and fluctuations in national and global contexts, it is stated that the expectations of economic agents and changes due to new news are effective (Bonser-Neal, 1996, p. 797). While exchange rates are immediately affected positively or negatively by new news, the time it takes for this to be reflected on prices in goods and services markets may cause deviations from purchasing power parities of countries (Karfakis and Kim, 1995, pp. 575–576).

Changes in the policy decisions of governments or policy makers also affect spot and forward foreign exchange markets (Öztürk and Bayraktar, 2010, pp. 182–183). Unexpected announcements and news will affect both current and future exchange rates because they affect expectations as in financial asset approaches. For example, the possibility of a change in the monetary and fiscal policies that may be implemented in the country following a situation such as the resignation or death of a high-level official such as a head of state, prime minister, minister, government official, etc. will cause a depreciation of the national currency by creating doubts in countries that follow a successful policy. Especially in countries with unsuccessful policies, the new administration may be seen as a beacon of hope and may cause the national currency to appreciate as it gives confidence to the market (Seyidoğlu, 2013, pp. 209–210).

Political stability of countries is an important variable for the model. Political crises in countries bring along economic instability, and the environment of mistrust toward political authorities causes exchange rates to fluctuate (Öztürk and Bayraktar, 2010, p. 183). In addition to the fact that exchange rate volatility is caused by unexpected events and news, oil prices, uncertainties, new information and rumors also affect exchange rate volatility (Baillie and McMahon, 1989, pp. 190–192). Among the factors affecting exchange rate volatility, the impact of terrorist incidents as well as wars cannot be denied (Seki and Akyıldız, 2018; Alp, 2013).

There are many indicators that are used to predict the economic situation and exchange rates of countries. The data shared monthly, quarterly, semi-annually and annually by the official institutions of the countries are interpreted by the governments or policy makers and new decisions are made in accordance with the economic trend. Accordingly, they decide to implement new policies or not to make any changes in their policies. For example, current account balance sheets, foreign trade statistics, interest rates set by central banks, foreign exchange reserves of central banks, consumer and producer price indices, etc. Since such indicators have high news quality, governments develop policies accordingly (Seyidoğlu, 2013, p. 210). In addition to these data, the credit ratings of countries by expert organizations affect foreign exchange inflows and outflows and exchange rates as they affect the confidence and investments in countries in international markets.

2.7. Chaotic Determinism

Although many theories have been developed for exchange rate determination models, the difficulty of forecasting exchange rates has created a driving force for the development of new methods on the subject. As a result of the spread of flexible exchange rate systems after the Bretton Woods System, the volatility of exchange rates has increased, and different models have tried to explain the reasons for this volatility. Chaotic determinism provides an opportunity to develop a more complex view of the role of news in the foreign exchange market. The news paradigm in the foreign exchange market treats exchange rate changes as news. Market observers identify some random events that can be blamed for the incomprehensible movement of the exchange rate. At this point, speculators could generate complex dynamics using different pieces of information. Although news remains important in decision making, it is not possible to explain every observed movement of the exchange rate. Speculations are unrelated to the occurrence of news and follow uncertain dynamics. For this reason, the exchange rate news model can guide exchange rate movements through speculative dynamics (Grauwe and Dewatcher, 1993, pp. 375–376).

In the chaotic determinism approach, estimation methods are generally divided into two differentiated. The first method makes forecasts by taking into account macroeconomic variables as in the previous models. The second one tries to make forecasts by analyzing the movements of exchange rates over time through graphs (Frankel, 1993, pp. 73–75). In the literature, those who make forecasts by taking macroeconomic variables into account are called "*fundamentalists*," while those who make forecasts by analyzing graphs are called "*chartists*."

Fundamentalists try to determine an equilibrium exchange rate by assuming that variables such as money supply, inflation rate, GDP and benchmark interest rate determine the exchange rate. They act on the assumption that movements above the equilibrium exchange rate will lower the exchange rate and movements below the equilibrium exchange rate will raise the exchange rate.

Although chartists do not give priority to changes in macroeconomic fundamentals, they emphasize the need to examine past movements of exchange rates in order to predict future movements. These examinations are more of a visual examination and are aimed at fitting the past data of exchange rates into a behavioral model or developing a new model with a new pattern. Based on exchange rate movements, chartists make forecasts to create indicators, limits and patterns to predict future movements of the exchange rate.

De Grauwe and Dewatcher compared the forecasting work of fundamentalists and chartists with the addition of speculative dynamics to a monetary model. By adding forecasting rules on speculation to the monetary model, they computed a moving average procedure for chartists and purchasing power parity for fundamentalists. As a result, they concluded that even the monetary model's own variables create a chaotic environment (Grauwe and Dewatcher, 1993, p. 375).

The main point that fundamentalists and chartists want to achieve in their work is to make a consistent forecast for the future with the available data. Both research groups first test the consistency of the data and then try to find the characteristic pattern of exchange rate movements by examining the trends, if any, in the series of variables they use. However, the biggest factor that deteriorates the reliability of the series is the shocks that may be observed in the series. This is because in the analyzed series, different reactions of the series are observed against the shocks and the patterns formed are disrupted. This is an indication of the irregular and cyclical nature of the series (Frankel, 1993, p. 73). Some, if not all, movements in exchange rates do not seem to be easily explained by observable news. In his study, Goodhart found that in analyzing high-frequency exchange rate data, exchange rates do not respond to observable news very often and that many exchange rate movements cannot be attributed to news (Goodhart, 1990).

In explaining chaos theory, it is necessary to mention two basic properties such as *sensitive dependence on initial state* and *non-randomness* (Gleick, 2000, p. 679). The property of sensitive dependence on the initial state is that in complex systems, an event that is too small and insignificant to be taken into account can lead to a situation with major consequences. This property is also known as *the butterfly effect.* The non-randomness property emphasizes that many events, although seemingly complex, actually have an order within themselves. This feature states that chaotic structures, which are a dynamic process, actually have a harmony even within the parts that seem to be irregular (Biçici, 2016, pp. 30–31).

In the empirical studies on exchange rates, it is thought that the shocks in the series do not allow the formation of certain patterns in the series, and therefore, the approach that can be explained by the characteristics of chaos theory has emerged. Based on the theory, exchange rate forecasting is difficult, and all series have their own characteristics markets have been attempted to provide an explanation. However, it is emphasized that stability in foreign exchange markets and determination of the equilibrium exchange rate is an impossible endeavor, and it is difficult to establish a specific model or pattern in exchange rate series (Bulut and Demirel, 2015, pp. 136–137). The reason for this is that there are countries with different exchange rate systems in the world and political and economic shocks prevent the characterization of these models (Frankel, 1993, pp. 73–74).

Another empirical study of exchange rate price dynamics compares stochastic and chaotic systems. These systems have a completely different forecasting potential. While stochastic processes are intrinsically unpredictable, chaotic models are found to be predictable in the short run. An important parameter for price forecasting is that the more accurate the information is, the longer the forecast times (Grauwe and Dewatcher, 1993, p. 376).

2.8. Microstructure of Foreign Exchange Markets

The models mentioned so far in the analysis of exchange rate determination models are based on the view that exchange rates are determined by macroeconomic variables. Empirical studies with models based on macroeconomic variables have found that the effects of variables in foreign exchange markets are negative in the short run, but positive results can be achieved in the long run. Moreover, the inconsistency between exchange rate changes and changes in macroeconomic variables in empirical studies has led to criticism of the models. Due to the criticism of macro models, studies on the microstructure approach have been conducted since the 1990s (Chionis and MacDonald, 1997).

According to the microstructure approach of foreign exchange markets, rather than the macroeconomic variables used in previous models, the volumes of transactions in foreign exchange markets, the transparency of transactions, the risks and uncertainties of the market, the behavior of economic decision makers trading in the market, symmetric and asymmetric information play a role in the determination of exchange rates (Bulut and Demirel, 2015, p. 137). In the microstructure approach, the behavior of individual decision makers affects other institutional and collective structures and thus plays an important role in the determination of exchange rates (Öztürk and Bayraktar, 2010, p. 185).

Due to the partial success of models based on macroeconomic variables and their failure in the short run, interest in the microstructure approach has increased since the 1990s. In particular, the effect of speculation on short-run exchange rate fluctuations has been the subject of many empirical studies and has led to an increase in studies on microstructure (Flood and Taylor, 1996, pp. 286–287).

In the microstructure approach, it is emphasized that foreign exchange buying and selling transactions determine the exchange rate rather than the variables used in macro models to explain short-run exchange rate transactions (Berke, 2014, p. 30). Studies on microstructure reject three assumptions of other exchange rate determination models. These assumptions (Galac et al., 2006, p. 3) are as follows:

1. Microstructure, according to information, everyone by in hand which is one is asymmetric because it has no properties.
2. Market actors may have the power to change prices, indicating that the market has a heterogeneous structure.
3. Institutions can influence prices, albeit in different ways.

The microstructure approach focuses on information, market participants and institutions in asset markets. Since access to information in foreign exchange markets is not homogeneous for all participants, market participants and institutions also affect exchange rates (Berke, 2014, p. 31). Market participants evaluate every piece of information they obtain about the market. They seek to maximize their profits and, in positions where they cannot make a profit, at least not to make a loss or to make a small loss.

One of the most important criticisms of the microstructure approach to macro models is the absence of market participants and their behavior in macro models. According to macro models, there is an idea that all participants in the market should or must react in the same way to economic developments. This idea is not appropriate for real life conditions, and for this reason, the microstructure approach accepts the idea that market participants react heterogeneously to economic developments. It is not realistic to expect all people to react in the same way to events. It is also possible for people to have different interpretations of the information they receive. Information can be interpreted differently by different participants and different reactions can be given (Bulut & Demirel, 2015, p. 139).

The microstructure approach assumes imperfect competition in the markets due to the presence of asymmetric information. Participants have the power to influence the market due to imperfect competition and asymmetric information in foreign exchange markets. Moreover, due to these conditions, accurate and real information is both costly and not accessible to everyone (Öztürk and Bayraktar, 2010, p. 186). For these assumed reasons, the existence of heterogeneous information structure in shaping foreign exchange market transactions shows that micro transactions are more effective on the market than macro models.

A feature of microstructure analyses is the existence of non-rational transactions that do not exist in macro models. One of the results of empirical studies is that although the long-run effects of macroeconomic variables in exchange rate models are high, more variables need to be added to the model in the short run. Another one of these results is irrational foreign exchange transactions. Flood and Taylor call irrational foreign exchange transactions as *noise* and conclude that these transactions prevent the effects of macroeconomic variables in the short run (Flood and Taylor, 1996, p. 287). Participants in foreign exchange markets use information to maximize their profits. However, *noise* transactions refuse to use this information. They do not even accept the monetary and fiscal policies accepted in macroeconomics. It is also difficult to make large profits with irrational trades, but these trades are important to maintain trading volume in liquid markets (Bulut and Demirel, 2015, p. 155).

Noise transactions approach is one of the alternative approaches to the efficient market hypothesis (Menkhoff, 1998, p. 547). According to this approach, there are two main groups of irrational traders. The first group is the rational group that trades based on analysis, such as fundamentalists, and the second group is the irrational group that trades with different analysis methods. The main difference between these groups is the difference in rationality when evaluating transactions (Menkhoff, 1998, pp. 550–551).

Another effect of irrational foreign exchange transactions is that they may cause shocks such as crises in the markets as a result of the intensification of transactions. This is because irrational foreign exchange transactions in periods when markets are open to speculation and trading transactions are carried out without taking macroeconomic data into account prepare the ground for crises and even cause crises.

The idea that macro models are incomplete due to the large transaction volumes in exchange rate transactions and therefore the inability to make precise calculations has been tried to be explained by the existence of speculative movements (Bulut and Demirel, 2015, p.140). Two issues that are not clear in foreign exchange markets are how exchange rates are determined and exchange rate volatility. The microstructure approach argues that the uncertainty in exchange rates depends on the buy and sell orders placed in foreign exchange markets (Berke, 2014, pp. 34–35). Frankel and Froot, as a different feature from macro models, argue that in the microstructure approach, exchange rates are determined by transactions. They found a bidirectional causality relationship between trading volumes and exchange rate volatility. They found a positive relationship between trading volumes and exchange rate volatility and concluded that both variables mutually affect each other (Frankel and Froot, 1990, p. 183).

Foreign exchange markets are divided into two categories. The first is the interbank market with market makers, or in other words, the interbank market, and the second is the retail foreign exchange market. The interbank market is open 24 hours a day, 7 days a week and is a continuously traded market and operates with interconnected systems through computers that allow instantaneous data monitoring at the globalized world level. Since these systems provide instantaneous data flow at the global level, market makers see the buy and sell orders, quotation increases and decreases, and, in short, all the movements of all participants in the market and take positions according to the size of these movements (Bulut and Demirel, 2015, p. 145). In retail foreign exchange markets, transactions are carried out on a smaller scale. However, regardless of the market, in a foreign exchange market with asymmetric information, those with the most accurate information are the ones who win the most

Another important issue for foreign exchange markets in microstructure analysis is the bid-ask spreads between the buy and sell orders of market participants and the bid-ask spreads between buy and sell orders. These orders create buying or selling pressure on the market and prices may also increase in response to these pressures (Evans and Lyons, 1999, p. 2).

Testing Exchange Rate Determination Models: Application to Türkiye

The Republic of Türkiye, which is now in the group of developing countries, has undergone many economic, legal, social and political transformations since its establishment. When the production factors of Türkiye are evaluated with the technological developments of our age, it is seen that Türkiye has a greater production potential than its current situation. In the transformation process that Türkiye has undergone until today, there have been periods when production has increased, unemployment has decreased, inflation has fallen, and high growth rates have been achieved. On the other hand, there have also been periods of economic crisis. Türkiye has economic, commercial and political cooperation with many countries around the world. These collaborations are increasing day by day due to technological developments and globalization. This situation leads to an increase in the trade network between countries, economic and political partnerships, more investments and capital movements. In these international activities, foreign exchange earnings and foreign exchange reserves of countries are of great importance. The determination of exchange rates is influenced not only by national policies and transactions but also by many developments abroad. This study will investigate which factors are effective in determining the exchange rate in Türkiye and to what extent.

In this section of the study, the empirical analyses and results of the exchange rate determination models mentioned in the second section will be presented. Although there are many determination methods for exchange rate determination models, the models that are suitable for empirical analysis will be selected. The necessary data on these models will be obtained from the CBRT and St. Louis Federal Reserve Bank database and subjected to analysis.

Before proceeding with the results of the analysis, it is necessary to investigate the historical development of Türkiye's exchange rate policies. In order to shed light on recent history, the process starting from the pre-1980 period until today will be discussed.

3.1. Historical Process of Exchange Rate Policies in Türkiye

Different exchange rate systems have been preferred in Türkiye over different periods. The subject of our study is the exchange rate determination methods in Türkiye. For this reason, since the fixed exchange rate regime was applied in Türkiye in the pre-1980 period, it is deemed appropriate to start from the 1980 period for the history of exchange rate policies. Prior to 1980, the Turkish economy was affected by rising oil prices due to the Arab–Israeli War in 1973, the Cyprus Peace Operation in 1974 and the embargo imposed afterwards, and experienced foreign payment difficulties due to foreign exchange shortages (Büyükkantarcı Tolgay, 2019, p. 127). After this process, inflation increased rapidly, the Turkish lira depreciated in real terms, and economic and political instability coupled with foreign exchange shortages created an environment of recession in the country. On January 24, 1980, a stabilization program was prepared to overcome the crisis in the economy.

On January 24, 1980, the most important feature of the Stability Program announced was the desire to shift from import-substitution policies to an outward-oriented and export-oriented economic model. This brought about a structural transformation for financial markets and a transition to a flexible exchange rate system. As of December 29, 1983, the exchange rate, which was left to float within the range determined by the CBRT, was left freer than before with the Decree No. 30 as of July 7, 1984 (Toprak, 2008, p. 317). In 1980–1989, there was a period of transition from a fixed exchange rate regime to flexible exchange rate regime and frequent devaluations were made. Between 1989 and 1999, the controlled free exchange rate regime continued (Barışık and Demircioğlu, 2006, p. 72).

In 1989, with the Decree No. 32 on the Protection of the Value of Turkish Currency, the Turkish lira became convertible and foreign capital was liberalized (Parasız, 2004, p. 345). Increased foreign capital inflows because of the exchange rate change being lower than interest rates made the Turkish lira overvalued, increased imports and decreased exports. Imbalances were created in the balance of payments and interest rates kept low despite public deficits increasing the demand for foreign exchange. As a result of the depressing effect of the pressure on exchange rates on foreign exchange reserves, the 1994 Crisis occurred (Hepaktan et al., 2011, p. 65).

In 1994, the government announced a new program known as the "April 5 Decisions." According to the program, it primarily aimed to reduce high inflation, devalue the Turkish lira, reduce domestic demand and increase exports. Thanks to the decisions, the expected increase in exports was achieved, but the Turkish lira continued to depreciate (Gözen, 2018, p. 18). In 1995, a stand-by agreement was signed with the IMF and the CBRT allowed forward transactions. This helped to curb devaluation expectations in the markets (CBRT, 1996, p. 78). In 1996, the CBRT revised its exchange rate policies again, which reduced exchange rate fluctuations and increased the real value of the Turkish lira. Between 1995 and 1998, growth and expenditure-oriented policies increased the value of the Turkish lira and led to an increase in imports (Gül and Ekinci, 2006, p. 166).

While a controlled flexible exchange rate system was applied in the 1989–1999 period, a daily fixed exchange rate system was applied in the 2000–2001 period. As of 2001, the flexible exchange rate system, in which CBRT interventions were limited, was adopted (Barışık and Demircioğlu, 2006, p. 72). In the early 2000s, it was decided to implement the "Disinflation Program." This period should be handled in two stages. In the first 18-month period, daily exchange rate adjustments were made according to the inflation target in accordance with the exchange rate policy implemented by the CBRT. In the second 18-month period, it was stated that the band system would be gradually adopted (Hepaktan et al., 2011, p. 66). Although it was thought that the program would be successful, the exchange rate increased below the expected inflation rate despite high inflation. The program was not successful due to reasons such as the fall in exports and the rise in imports with the appreciation of the Turkish lira (Büyükkantarcı and Tolgay, 2019, p. 131).

In the aftermath of the crisis in November 2000, there was an imbalance in the balance of payments due to the increase in the demand for foreign exchange stemming from the liquidity needs in the financial markets. In order to prevent further adverse effects on banking systems, the Turkish lira was floated on February 22, 2001. The markets reacted by raising the exchange rate. In the fight against high inflation, the monetary anchors in the early 1990s and the exchange rate anchors in the Stabilization Programs of 1994 and 2000 were not successful in practice (Hepaktan et al., 2011, p. 67). The weak capital structure, open accounts of the banking sector, current account deficit and overvaluation of the Turkish lira were effective in the failure of the program (Yıldırım O., 2002, p. 109).

On April 14, 2001, with the Transition to a Strong Economy program, the CBRT's "implicit inflation targeting" policy was adopted and it was stated that the CBRT intended to switch to "explicit inflation targeting" when appropriate conditions arose (CBRT, 2003, p. 15). In addition to inflation targeting, it was aimed to achieve exchange rate stability by adapting to the flexible exchange rate system and to reorganize the public administration by reducing the increasing public debt (Yıldırım O., 2002, p. 109). From 2002 onwards, the flexible exchange rate system continued to be applied, and as a result of the achievement of inflation targets between 2002 and 2005, "explicit inflation targeting" was introduced in 2006 (Büyükkantarcı and Tolgay, 2019, p. 131).

In the last quarter of 2007, the housing crisis, which started in the United States, affected all countries around the world in 2008. Although the crisis affected the real sector and consumption due to the high interest rate and low exchange rate policy implemented in Türkiye, it made Türkiye an attractive country for foreign investments (Hepaktan et al., 2011, pp. 67–68). To this end, the CBRT held foreign exchange selling auctions totaling USD 900 million in 2009 and released foreign exchange reserves to the market through the banking sector (Bozdağlıoğlu and Yılmaz, 2017, p. 4). Starting in November 2008, the CBRT embarked on a monetary easing process and managed to reduce policy rates by 1025 basis points until September 2012. In this period of overvaluation of the Turkish lira and credit abundance, the current account deficit increased. In a healthier process in April 2010, short-term interest rates were lowered, and banks' reserve requirement ratios were increased. This prevented short-term speculative capital inflows, and the current account deficit and credit growth yielded positive results (Delice, 2015, pp. 43–44).

Since 2013, global balances have started to change, and the policies implemented by countries have started to vary due to their different growth performances. For example, while the European Central Bank lowered policy rates, the U.S. Federal Reserve stopped its asset purchases and the Bank of Japan increased its asset purchases (Gözen, 2018, p. 22). This situation caused countries to price financial assets and increased capital flows between countries. In this period, the CBRT preferred to overcome these problems by changing the interest rate corridor, repo rates and reserve requirement ratios and pursuing an active monetary policy, and achieved price stability and financial stability (CBRT, 2016, p. 37).

In 2016, the global recession, terrorist incidents and the attempted coup reduced Türkiye's growth rate to 3.2%. As of 2017, the CBRT decided to implement a tight monetary policy due to the increase in exchange rate volatility and inflation (CBRT, 2018, pp. 18–19). In 2018, the tight monetary policy continued to be implemented, while the protectionist policy tendencies of developed countries increased exchange rate volatility in financial markets, leading to an increase in risk premiums in emerging economies. Türkiye was similarly adversely affected by portfolio flows (CBRT, 2019, pp. 17–18). In 2019, the moderate recovery achieved at the beginning of the period thanks to the tight monetary policy measures taken in 2018 continued to spread across all sectors until the end of the year. The CBRT kept the policy rate unchanged at 24% in the first half of 2019 and lowered it to 12% in the second half of the year due to the improvement in the inflation indicator. However, investments did not reach the desired level due to high-risk premiums and financial tightness (CBRT, 2020, p. 17). In 2019, exchange rates continued to be volatile due to the changes in interest rates in global markets.

In 2020, the CBRT's policy rate cuts continued and a rapid decline in inflation was achieved. The COVID-19 pandemic, which started in China in 2019 and affected the whole world with the emergence of cases in Türkiye in 2020, had an impact on the Turkish economy along with global effects. The depreciation of the Turkish lira as well as the decline in international commodity prices had a positive impact on the inflation outlook. In this period, comprehensive measures were taken to curb the negative effects of the pandemic. In 2020, the impact of the pandemic, expectations regarding vaccines and medicines, declining economic activity, rising debts and the profitability of the banking sector were factors that reduced financial stability (CBRT, 2021, p. 36). In this period, domestic banks' swap transactions with foreign banks increased and reached a volume of USD 2.7 billion at the end of the year (CBRT, 2021, p. 30). Inflation was the leading macroeconomic balance that deteriorated in 2021 due to the ongoing pandemic. The inflation outlook reached 35% due to increases in prices of basic goods, food and energy. One reason for the high inflation in these sectors was the increase in international prices due to exchange rate pass-through and exchange rate volatility (CBRT, 2022, p. 21). In the same year, the CBRT first raised the policy rate from 17% to 19%, then kept it unchanged at 19%, and then lowered it to 16% in anticipation of an increase in inflation expectations by continuing to implement a tight monetary policy. Following the rate changes, in December 2021, the CBRT intervened in the foreign exchange market and sold a total of USD 7.2 billion worth of foreign exchange in four sales (CBRT, 2022, s. 29).

In sum, flexible exchange rates are determined by the supply and demand for foreign exchange, and the supply and demand for foreign exchange are determined by monetary and fiscal policies, international developments and expectations (Büyükkantarcı and Tolgay, 2019, p. 135). Economic and political crises increase exchange rate volatility by causing foreign exchange inflows and outflows. Liquidity imbalances and the CBRT's market interventions had a destabilizing effect on economic stability with exchange rate volatility (Gözen, 2018, p. 23).

3.2. Literature Review

Forecasting exchange rate fluctuations is important for the economic behavior of both households and the public sector. Although exchange rate movements are difficult to predict, many models and hypotheses have been put forward to explain exchange rate movements and many studies in the literature have tried to predict the underlying causes of exchange rate fluctuations. In this section of the chapter, national and international studies for each model will be reviewed and summarized.

It would be appropriate to examine the purchasing power parity model in the first place. This is because most of the studies on exchange rate determination in the economic literature test the validity of purchasing power parity. For this reason, more studies that test purchasing power parity are included in the literature review. Information will be given in date order without making any distinction between national or international studies. After summarizing all the studies, the results will be compared. In addition, in order to see methodological innovations, recent studies are included as much as possible.

Seyrek (2003) analyzed the Turkish economy for the period 1972–2011 using cointegration methodology and tested nominal exchange rate and consumer price index data and concluded that the purchasing power hypothesis is valid for the period analyzed.

Çağlayan and Saçaklı (2006) tested Türkiye and the United Kingdom in terms of purchasing power parity for the post-1994 period. Using PP, ERS, KPSS and ADF tests, the authors conclude that absolute purchasing power parity is not valid in both countries using real and nominal exchange rates and relative prices.

Aslan and Kanbur (2007) analyzed the Turkish economy using monthly data for the 1982–2005 period. They analyzed purchasing power parity with unit root tests and cointegration tests. The authors concluded that purchasing power parity was invalid during the period under consideration.

Kalyoncu et al. (2010) tested purchasing power parity with data from Algeria, Egypt, Iran, Iraq, Israel, Jordan, Lebanon, Libya, Morocco, Saudi Arabia, Syria, Tunisia and Türkiye between 1970 and 1998. The authors used the LM unit root test method and included real exchange rate and nominal exchange rate data in the model. According to the results of the analysis, they concluded that purchasing power parity is valid for both real and nominal exchange rates in ten of the 13 countries.

Abumustafa and Feridun (2010) analyzed Egypt, Jordan and Türkiye for the period 1976–2000. They tested purchasing power parity using ADF, PP and KPSS unit root tests. They included exchange rate fluctuations, interest rate, general level of prices, wages and unemployment in the model. As a result of ADF and PP tests, they found that purchasing power parity fails in all countries. Only in the trended model of the KPSS test, they found a valid result for three countries. As a result, they emphasized that the validity of purchasing power parity varies according to the method.

Kum (2012) tested whether purchasing power parity is valid in the Turkish economy between 1953 and 2009. Using ADF, DF-GLS and Zivot–Andrews and LM tests considering structural breaks, the author tested nominal exchange rate and consumer price index data. The results of the ADF and structural break unit root tests suggest that the purchasing power parity is valid, while the DF-GLS test concludes that it is not valid.

Yıldırım et al. (2013) tested the validity of purchasing power parity for different country groups. They tested purchasing power parity for the period 1960–2012 for EU-15, G-8, EU-27, OECD countries and Türkiye. Using ADF-PP unit root tests, Lee–Strazicich unit root test, Carrion-i-Silvestre et al. unit root test with structural breaks and CADF panel unit root tests, the authors concluded that purchasing power parity is not valid for Türkiye, while it is valid for EU-27, EU-15, OECD, and G-8 countries.

Ağazade (2014) analyzed the validity of purchasing power parity in the Russian economy for the period 1993–2013 with the help of nonlinear unit root tests. Analyzing the parity with the real effective exchange rate, the author concluded that the parity is valid in the Russian economy since the unit root tests reach the results related to the stationarity of the ruble.

Özdamarlar (2014) tested the validity of purchasing power parity using the data of the Organization for Economic Cooperation and Development member countries for the period 1990–2013. Using nonlinear unit root tests, the author used real exchange rate data in the analysis. The results indicate that the purchasing power hypothesis is not valid for the member countries of the union. Comparing the results of linear and nonlinear unit root tests, it is observed that the nonlinear unit root tests give results that indicate invalidity, while the linear ones provide more support for validity.

Haji-Othman and Yahaya (2015) analyzed the economies of Chile, Uruguay, Sierra Leone, Suriname, Mexico, Malaysia, Singapore, the Netherlands, Switzerland and Türkiye for the period 1973–1996. In their analysis, they tested exchange rate data using DF and ADF unit root tests. They concluded that purchasing power parity is valid only in Mexico and Sierra Leone among the countries with high inflation rates and that there is no cointegration especially in Türkiye. In countries with low inflation rates, purchasing power parity is not valid. Based on these results, they infer that the higher the inflation rate, the higher the probability that purchasing power parity is valid.

Şener et al. (2015) analyzed the Turkish economy in the 1980–2012 period within the scope of purchasing power parity. In doing so, they analyzed the real exchange rate data with unit root tests and concluded that purchasing power parity is not valid for the Turkish economy and purchasing power parity with break-trend-bounded is valid.

Ceviş and Ceylan (2015) tested the validity of purchasing power parity in the "Fragile Five" countries (India, Brazil, Indonesia, Türkiye, South Africa).

Using the nominal exchange rate and consumer price index, the authors concluded that the series are stationary, that is, purchasing power parity is valid for the period 2003–2013.

Özmen and Şanlı (2015) tested the validity of the parity with a larger group of countries. Using country data for Brazil, India, Indonesia, South Korea, Mexico, Türkiye, Russia, South Africa, Türkiye, Russia and South Africa for the period 1997–2014, the authors used unit root tests and HRGY regression analysis methods. Taking nominal exchange rates into account within the scope of flexible exchange rate strategy, the authors concluded that purchasing power parity will be invalid in countries with flexible exchange rate strategy.

Akçay and Erataş (2015) analyzed G-7 countries for the period 1995–2012. Using first- and second-generation panel unit root tests, the authors analyzed real exchange rate data. With the second-generation unit root tests, they concluded that the series contains a unit root, that is, purchasing power parity is not valid in G-7 countries.

Yalçınkaya (2016) used the nominal exchange rate for the validity of purchasing power parity in G-20 countries for the period 1994–2015. According to the results of the panel CADF test, purchasing power parity is valid in 7 G-20 countries in the long run, and according to the results of the panel KPSS unit root test, purchasing power parity is valid in all G-20 countries in the long run.

Topal (2016) used unit root and cointegration tests with structural breaks to test whether purchasing power parity is valid in BRICS countries. Using exchange rate and consumer price index data, the author concluded that purchasing power parity is valid in the long run when structural break is not considered, but not when structural break is taken into account.

Karagöz and Saraç (2016) analyzed the Turkish economy for the period 2003–2014 and used the nonlinear unit root test method. Using exchange rate and consumer price index data, the authors conclude that purchasing power parity is not valid.

Destek and Okumuş (2016) used ADF, KSS, Fourier KSS unit root test and Fourier ADF unit root tests to test purchasing power parity for OECD countries. According to the results of the nonlinear unit root test, the series are stationary in 14 OECD countries and purchasing power parity is valid.

Güriş et al. (2016) analyzed Türkiye with 1992–2015 data. Harvey and Leybourne (2007) and Harvey et al. (2008) used linearity tests to test the nonlinearity of the series in Türkiye and Kapetanios et al. (2003) and Kruse (2011) used nonlinear unit root tests to test the real exchange rate. In both unit root tests, they concluded that purchasing power parity is valid for the mean-adjusted and trend-adjusted series.

Gedik and Karaer (2017) analyzed the 1983–2011 period for Türkiye using Granger causality test, LM test and ADF unit root test. Including export, import, foreign trade volume, foreign trade balance and exchange rate data in the model, the authors concluded that there is no causality between the variables. This supports the invalidity of purchasing power parity.

Burgaç Çil and Dülger (2017) used the cointegration tests of Maki (2012) and Kejriwal (2018) in their study analyzing the Turkish economy for the period 2001–2016. They tested the relationship with real exchange rate data and did not find strong evidence supporting the hypothesis for the Turkish economy for the post-2001 period when the purchasing power parity flexible exchange rate was applied.

Aliyeva and Hüseynov (2017) analyzed the Azerbaijani economy for the period 2000–2015 and used ADF unit root test, Johansen cointegration test and error correction model. While including exchange rate and consumer price index variables in the model, they found a long-run relationship between the series and concluded that purchasing power parity is valid.

Sağlam and Erataş Dönmez (2017) used panel data unit root and cointegration tests to analyze the BRIC-T countries (Brazil, Russia, India, China and Türkiye). According to the results of the analysis using nominal exchange rate and consumer price index data, they concluded that purchasing power parity is not valid.

Bilgin (2018) tested purchasing power parity in the Turkish economy for the period 1986–2017. According to the results of unit root and cointegration tests using exchange rate and inflation data, he concluded that absolute purchasing power parity is not valid while relative purchasing power parity is valid.

Aydın (2018) analyzed OECD countries for the period 2007–2017 and tested purchasing power parity using RALS-EG and RALS-ARDL cointegration tests with nominal exchange rates and domestic relative prices data. RALS_EG according to the cointegration test, it is concluded that purchasing power parity is valid for Iceland, Japan and Norway. According to the RALS_ADL cointegration test, purchasing power parity is valid for Japan and Iceland. For Türkiye, the tests show that purchasing power parity is not valid.

Nakıpoğlu, Özsoy and Özpolat (2018) tested MIST countries for the period 1990–2016 using CIPS unit root test, Pedroni cointegration test, Westerlund cointegration test and FMOLS and DOLS tests with CPI and GDP data. Pedroni cointegration test rejected the existence of cointegration, while Westerlung cointegration test accepted the existence of cointegration. According to the result of cointegration coefficient estimation, it is concluded that purchasing power parity is valid in the countries examined.

Kaya and Çelik (2018) analyzed the Turkish economy for the period 2002–2017. They tested U.S. dollar and Euro exchange rate data using ADF, PP, KPSS unit root tests. The analysis concluded that purchasing power parity is valid in Türkiye.

Şeker and Şimdi (2018) used ADF unit root test, Zivot and Andrews unit root test with one structural break and Kapetanios unit root test for the Turkish economy. Using the exchange rate and domestic consumer price indices, the authors concluded that there is a long-run relationship between the variables.

Yıldırım et al. (2019) analyzed real exchange rate data for ASEAN countries for the period 1995–2017 using panel data, unit root and LM tests. Panel LM test results show that the purchasing power hypothesis is valid.

Büyükkantarcı and Tolgay (2019) tested the Turkish economy for the period 2003–2017 using ADF, PP and Lee–Strazizich unit root tests. The test results indicate that purchasing power parity is valid.

Hatipoğlu (2019) analyzed the economies of Morocco, United Arab Emirates, Malaysia and Indonesia in the context of purchasing power parity using ADF unit root test, ARCH and LM tests. Analyzing the regime change, the authors find that purchasing power parity is valid in Malaysia and Indonesia. They obtained opposite results in Morocco and the United Arab Emirates.

Zümbül (2020) used ADF, PP, KPSS, Zivot Andrews unit root tests, LM unit root and M-KSS tests to test the real effective exchange rate, inflation rate, changes in money supply, capital flows and differences in price level measurement for Türkiye. The results show that purchasing power parity is not valid in Türkiye.

Yılmaz and Özcan (2020) tested purchasing power parity in the economies of Bulgaria, Canada, Czechia, Denmark, Denmark, the United Kingdom, Croatia, Hungary, Romania, Russia, Sweden, Türkiye and the United States for the period 2000–2017. The regression results show that purchasing power parity is more significant in Russia and Canada.

Aytemiz et al. (2021) tested the validity of purchasing power parity by using RALS-LM Unit Root Test and RALS_ADF Unit Root Test in their study analyzing the Turkish economy. The results of the analysis showed that purchasing power parity is not valid.

Ergün and Tatar (2021) analyzed NAFTA, MERCOSUR, EU-15 and selected OECD countries for a long period of 1960–2019 and analyzed the validity of purchasing power parity with fractional frequency Fourier ADF test and conventional ADF tests. Using real exchange rate data, the authors conclude that purchasing power parity is valid in all country groups except MERCOSUR countries.

When the domestic and foreign applied literature on the subject is analyzed, there is no common conclusion on the subject. Although the studies conducted for Türkiye generally show that purchasing power parity is not valid, there are also a few studies to the contrary are available.

In the second stage, studies examining the Mundell–Flemming model will be examined. However, when the literature on the subject is examined, it is seen that there are few of them. One of them belongs to Kesbic and Çevik (2007). In their study, in which they analyzed the economies of Argentina, Brazil, Israel and Türkiye using VAR method, the authors analyzed the consumer price index, interest rate, money supply and nominal exchange rate variables for the period 1990–2004. According to the results of the analysis, a significant portion of the inflation in the Turkish economy is due to past inflation rates (Kesbic and Çevik, 2007).

Another approach that tries to answer the question of what factors determine the exchange rate is the flexible and fixed-price models. Econometric analyses have been conducted by adding data other than exchange rates of countries to the model. This section summarizes these studies.

Ersöz (2006) analyzed the determinants of the real exchange rate for the Turkish economy for the period 1995–2005 within the monetarist approach. Using an autoregressive model in his analysis, the author extended the model by including the ISE index. The findings of the study reveal that the real exchange rate index has a strong link to its past values. This is because the series has its own memory, that is, its relationship with its own past values. This is evident from the results of both variance decomposition and impulse response analysis.

Uz and Dalan Bildir (2009) tested the flexible-price model for the period 1986–2006 in their model for determining the exchange rate in developing countries including Türkiye. Using both time series and panel data approaches in their study, the authors analyzed the existence of cointegration among the variables in the long run with panel data tests. The results obtained from time series analysis were found to support the model only for Türkiye, Brazil and Argentina.

Uz and Ketenci (2009) analyzed 11 countries including Türkiye for the period 1993–2005. Using the fixed-price model, the authors analyzed the relationship between exchange rate and monetary variables using a cointegration test. No cointegration was found between the variables. This result implies that the model is invalid in the long run.

Kardaşlar (2013) analyzed macroeconomic variables in explaining the exchange rate within the framework of the model. Evaluating the Turkish economy for the period 2003–2012 within the framework of unit root and autoregressive methods, the author observed that there are movements in exchange rates that cannot be explained by macroeconomic factors. This situation, which is called the deviation of the exchange rate from fundamental variables, expresses the conclusion that it is due to the microstructure of the foreign exchange market.

Finally, the studies analyzing the monetarist hybrid model, also known as the real interest rate differentials model, are summarized in the following text. These studies generally analyze country groups. However, there are also studies that include Türkiye in country groups.

Taşkın (1995), using monthly data for the period 1988–1993, tried to explain the determinants of the value of the Turkish lira against the U.S. dollar and the German mark within the scope of the monetarist hybrid model and used the cointegration analysis method. The results of the analysis show that income and interest rate variables are effective in the relationship between the German mark and the Turkish lira. This result is not valid for the U.S. dollar exchange rate.

Another study evaluating this model belongs to Dülger and Cin (2002). Dülger and Cin (2002) analyzed the Turkish economy with monthly data for the period 1986–1999. They added relative money supply, relative income level, relative interest rate and relative price variables. They found a long-run relationship in their models as a result of cointegration analysis. As a result of their analysis, they determined that the variables are insufficient to explain the change in exchange rate. Instead, they concluded that purchasing power parity is more explanatory in the unit root analysis.

Civcir (2004) tested the determinants of exchange rate in the Turkish economy with the Johansen cointegration model. Using data for the 1987–2000 period, he emphasized that the main determinants of exchange rates are monetary variables.

Öruç (2016) analyzed the factors affecting the exchange rate in his study on the Turkish economy. In his analysis, he used relative income, relative interest rate, relative money supply and relative inflation rate variables within the monetarist hybrid approach. The results of unit root and cointegration analysis show that there is cointegration between the variables and relative income is very effective in explaining the exchange rate.

To summarize the entire literature review, there are still important questions about the validity of purchasing power parity. However, when the literature on other models is analyzed, it is possible to conclude that monetarist models are more valid.

3.3. Empirical Application of Exchange Rate Determination Models in Türkiye

In this section, the validity of different models for determining the exchange rate in the Turkish economy is tested with different and advanced econometric methods. In this context, the "Purchasing Power Parity (PPP) Model," the Keynesian exchange rate determination model known as the "Mundell–Flemming Model," the "Monetarist Model with Flexible Prices" and the "Monetarist Hybrid Model" known as the real interest rate differentials model are tested with appropriate econometric models.

Firstly, information on the national and international literature where each model is tested will be provided. The main findings in the literature will be grouped and compared with the empirical findings obtained at the end of the analysis. In the following part of the section, each model will be tested, and the results will be presented in graphs and tables.

3.4. Application Results

The results obtained from the empirical analysis of which exchange rate modeling is appropriate for the exchange rate system implemented in Türkiye are presented in the following text. The variables and data used in each model are defined at the beginning of each model.

The model to be used in the first analysis with purchasing power parity theory is derived from the model used in Frenkel (1976) (Frenkel, 1976). The model will utilize data on the Turkish nominal exchange rate, the Turkish consumer price index (CPI) and the U.S. consumer price index. Data for Türkiye are obtained from the CBRT EDS and data for the United States are obtained from the Federal Reserve Bank of St. Louis. Data are in monthly frequency form. Due to the differences in the start and end dates of the data, the common period Jan 2003:Oct 2021 is used in the analysis.

The second analysis, in which the Mundell–Fleming model will be tested, is inspired by the model used by Hsing (2009) (Hsing, 2009). According to the model, nominal exchange rate, money supply (M2), consumer price index (CPI), public expenditures, tax revenues, industrial production index, 2-year bond interest rate and expected inflation data will be used. Relevant data are obtained from the CBRT EDS. Data are obtained with monthly frequency. Due to the differences in the start and end dates of the data, the common period Jan 2006–Sept 2021 is used in the analysis.

In the third analysis, where the theory of the flexible-price monetarist assumption will be tested, the model used by MacDonald and Taylor (1994) is preferred (MacDonald and Taylor, 1994). In the model, Türkiye nominal exchange rate, Türkiye money supply (M2), U.S. money supply (M2), Türkiye industrial production index, U.S. industrial production index, Türkiye 2-year bond interest rate and U.S. 2-year bond interest rate data will be used. Data for Türkiye are obtained from the CBRT EDS and data for the United States are obtained from the Federal Reserve Bank of St. Louis. Data is obtained monthly frequency. Due to the differences in the start and end dates of the data, the common period Sept. 2005–May 2021 is used in the analysis.

The fourth analysis, which tests the monetarist hybrid model, is inspired by the models in Frankel (1979) and Pilbeam (2006) (Frankel, 1979, Pilbeam, 2006). According to the model, Türkiye's nominal exchange rate, Türkiye's money supply (M2), U.S. money supply (M2), Türkiye's industrial production index, U.S. industrial production index, Türkiye's 2-year bond interest rate, U.S. 2-year bond interest rate, Türkiye's expected inflation rate and United States expected inflation data will be used. Data for Türkiye are obtained from the CBRT EDS and data for the United States are obtained from the Federal Reserve Bank of St. Louis. Data is obtained monthly frequency. Due to the differences in the start and end dates of the data, the common period Jan 2006–May 2021 is used in the analysis.

3.4.1. Analysis of Purchasing Power Parity Theory

In order to analyze the purchasing power parity theory in our study, the model used in Frenkel (1976) was adopted (Frenkel, 1976). The model is derived from the classical purchasing power parity theory and is shown in model 3.1 (Uçan, 2011, p. 158).

$$LnNER = \beta_0 + \beta_1 \ln\left(P / P^*\right) + \varepsilon \qquad (3.1)$$

In model 3.1, NER is the nominal exchange rate, $\beta 0$ is the constant term, $\beta 1$ is the slope parameter, P is the domestic price level and P^* is the international price level. The ratio of these two variables gives the relative price ratio.

3.4.1.1. Data

For the period Jan. 2003–Oct. 2021, the validity of the purchasing power parity theory in the Turkish economy is tested with the model used in Model 3.1. Monthly frequency data are obtained from the electronic data distribution system of the Central Bank of the Republic of Türkiye and the Federal Reserve Bank of St. Louis. The natural logarithm of the variables is taken and the information on the variables is shown in Table 1.

Table 1: Variables of the SGP model

Variables	Beginning	End	Source
Nominal Exchange Rate	Jan. 2003	Oct. 2021	CBRT
CPI Türkiye	Jan. 2003	Oct. 2021	CBRT (TÜİK)
CPI U.S.	Jan. 2003	Oct. 2021	Federal Reserve Bank of St. Louis

The empirical analyses are based on the Extended Dickey–Fuller (1981) and Phillips–Perron (1988) linear unit root tests, Becker et al. (2006) Fourier unit root test (FKPSS), Banerjee et al. (2017). Fourier lag distributed autoregressive model (FARDL), Enders and Jones (2016), Nazlıoğlu et al. (2016) Fourier domain causality tests are applied.

3.4.1.2. *Extended Dickey–Fuller (1981), Phillips–Perron (1988) and Fourier KPSS Stationarity Tests*

For the analysis, the stationarity of the series should be determined. In other words, by determining the levels at which the series are stationary, it should be ensured that the effects of possible shocks in the series do not give misleading results. Extended Dickey–Fuller (1981) and Phillips–Perron (1988) unit root tests will be conducted to determine the stationarity levels.

$$\Delta y_t = \gamma y_{t-1} + \sum_{i=2}^{p} \beta_i \Delta y_{t-i+1} + \varepsilon_t \tag{3.2}$$

$$\Delta y_t = c + \gamma y_{t-1} + \sum_{i=2}^{p} \beta_i \Delta y_{t-i+1} + \varepsilon_t \tag{3.3}$$

$$\Delta y_t = c + \gamma y_{t-1} + \delta_2 t + \sum_{i=2}^{p} \beta_i \Delta y_{t-i+1} + \varepsilon_t \tag{3.4}$$

According to the Extended Dickey–Fuller (1981) unit root test, the regression in Model 3.2 shows the first model without constant term and trend variable. Model The regression in 3.3 is the model with a constant term and no trend variable; Model The regression in 3.4 shows the model in which both the constant term and the trend variable coexist (Dickey and Fuller, 1979).

Compared to the Extended Dickey–Fuller test, the Phillips–Perron (1988) test is a more flexible test that does not take into account the error terms restriction. The main difference between the two tests is that the lag values of the dependent variable are not available in alternative forms (Aktaş and Yılmaz, 2008, p. 96). The autoregressive model of the Philips–Perron test in its plain form is as in model 3.5 with AR(1) process.

$$\begin{aligned} y_t &= \mu + \alpha y_{t-1} + \varepsilon_t \\ (1-\alpha L) y_t &= \mu + \varepsilon_t \end{aligned} \tag{3.5}$$

In the model, $t = 1, 2, \dots, T$, and the unit root for the model is found with $1/\alpha$. Equality of α to one indicates that there is a unit root in the series.

The Phillips–Perron test is T(α-1) distributed. The tested hypotheses are $_{H0}$: There is a unit root (series is non-stationary); $_{H1}$: There is no unit root (series is stationary). The tests are repeated until the level at which the series are stationary is found and the series are continued by taking the difference of the series.

In order to analyze the stationarity of the series more precisely, Becker et al. (2006) introduced a test that detects sudden and slow changes by using Fourier functions (Becker et al., 2006). According to the Fourier KPSS stationarity test developed by Becker et al., the data preparation process is as shown in model 3.6. According to the model εt the stationary error term, ut the variance-independent and similarly distributed error term shows $Zt = [\sin(2\pi kt/T), cos(2\pi kt/T)]'$ where t is the trend term, T denotes the sample size and k denotes the frequency value. Whether yt is stationary at level is expressed as $Xt = [1]$ and whether it is stationary in trend is expressed as $Xt = [1, t]$.

$$\begin{aligned} y_t &= X_t'\beta + Z_t'\gamma + r_t + \varepsilon_t \\ r_t &= r_{t-1} + u_t \end{aligned} \tag{3.6}$$

The test statistic required for the estimation of the stationarity hypothesis is calculated by estimating one of the models in models 3.7 and 3.8 (Yılancı, 2017, p. 56).

$$y_t = \alpha_0 + \gamma_1 sin\left(\frac{2\pi kt}{T}\right) + \gamma_2 cos\left(\frac{2\pi kt}{T}\right) + e_t \tag{3.7}$$

$$y_t = \alpha_0 + \beta t + \gamma_1 sin\left(\frac{2\pi kt}{T}\right) + \gamma_2 cos\left(\frac{2\pi kt}{T}\right) + e_t \tag{3.8}$$

Model 3.7 tests the null hypothesis of stationarity at level and model 3.8 tests the null hypothesis of stationarity in trend. The calculation of the test statistic is as in model 3.9. $\tilde{e}y$ in equation $\tilde{\sigma}$, and proposed to proceed with the selection of l pruning lags from a set of weights wj' $j = 1, 2, 3, \ldots, l$ in the nonparametric estimation of $\tilde{\sigma}^2$.

$$\tau_{\mu}\left(k\right) \text{ or } \tau_{\mu}\left(k\right) = \frac{1}{T^2}\frac{\sum_{t=1}^{T}\tilde{S}_t\left(k\right)^2}{\tilde{\sigma}^2} \tag{3.9}$$

Becker et al. (2006), the residuals from models 3.7 and 3.8 $S_t\left(k\right)=\sum_{j-1}^{\tilde{t}}\tilde{e}_j$ equation $\tilde{\sigma}^2$ and proposed to proceed with the choice of $\tilde{e}_j$ l pruning lags from a set of weights $wj_{,j}=1,2,3,...l$ in the nonparametric estimation of, $\tilde{\sigma}^2$

$$\tilde{\sigma}^2 = \tilde{\gamma}_0 + 2\sum w_j \tilde{\gamma}_{j'} \tag{3.10}$$

In Model 3.10, $\tilde{\gamma}_{j'}$ denotes the autocovariance of sample j in Models 3.7 and 3.8, and the smallest residual sum of squares value is chosen to determine the optimal number of k values. Becker et al. (2006) used the F test statistic as the null hypothesis ($H_0 : \gamma_1 = \gamma_2 = 0$) to show the absence of nonlinear trend (Yılancı, 2017, p. 57).

$$F_i(k) = \frac{(SSR_0 - SSR_1(k))/2}{SSR_1(k)/(T-q)}, \qquad i = \mu, \tau, \tag{3.11}$$

In Model 3.11, SSR_1 (k) denotes the small residual squares value obtained from Models 3.7 and 3.8, SSR_0 denotes the regression small residual squares value where the hypothesis is valid, and q denotes the number of independent variables. The F test is statistically significant when the data are stationary will increase, the test is used when the null hypothesis of stationarity is rejected. Acceptance of the null hypothesis yields the KPSS test statistic, and the table of critical values is presented in Becker et al. (2006).

3.4.1.3. Fourier ARDL Cointegration Test

In this section, the Fourier ARDL method of purchasing power parity theory will be used to analyze whether there is cointegration between variables. The model used in the study of Banerjee et al. (2017) is preferred in the analysis. In their study, Banerjee et al. (2017) changed the model used in Enders and

Lee (2012) to model 3.12 in order to break the effect of possible shocks and breaks in the variables with the Fourier approach of the nonlinear ARDL model dummy variables can be added (Enders and Lee, 2012; Banerjee et al. 2017). In Model 3.12, $\gamma 0$ represents the constant and linear deterministic term, k represents a particular odd frequency, q represents the number of frequencies, and T represents the number of observations. In the absence of a nonlinear trend, the result of the model will be $\gamma 0$ and linear ARDL can be used.

$$d(t) = \gamma_0 + \sum_{k=1}^{q} \gamma_{1,k} sin\left(\frac{2\pi kt}{T}\right) + \sum_{k=1}^{q} \gamma_{2,k} cos\left(\frac{2\pi kt}{T}\right), q \leq T/2 \qquad (3.12)$$

Banerjee et al. (2017) derived model 3.13 by extending the Fourier functions of the ARDL cointegration test used in Banerjee et al. (1998) (Banerjee et al., 1998). In Model 3.13, γ, φ and $y2t$ are the parameters and explanatory variables. $d(t)$ model's nonlinear function, the dependent variable $y1t$ is the univariate process and $\delta 1$ is frequentist (Banerjee et al. 2017, p. 117).

$$\Delta y_{1t} = d(t) + \delta_1 y_{1,t-1} + \gamma' y_{2,t-1} + \varphi' \Delta y_{2t} + \varepsilon_t \qquad (3.13)$$

Basic hypothesis cointegration that you are not, alternative hypothesis indicates the presence of cointegration.

$$_{H0}\!: \delta 1=0 \quad \text{and} \quad _{H1}\!: \delta 1<0$$

In Model 3.13, using t statistic values to test the main hypothesis, F test is possible. Thus, model 3.14 is created with the t-test approach. $\delta 1$ model OLS estimator from 3.13, $s\,e\,(\hat{\delta})$ is the standard error of δ from model 3.13.

$$t^F_{ARDL} = \frac{\widehat{\delta_1}}{se\left(\widehat{\delta_1}\right)} \qquad (3.14)$$

In their study, Banerjee et al. (2017) included trigonometric terms in the model using Fourier functions and developed the Fourier ARDL model that can detect more sensitive changes. The advantage of the model is that it can test the number and duration of structural breaks without the need to know them in advance (Yurtkuran, 2021, p. 68). The test created for this method is as in model 3.15.

$$\Delta y_t = \delta_0 + \delta_1 sin\left(\frac{2\pi kt}{T}\right) + \delta_2 cos\left(\frac{2\pi kt}{T}\right) + \delta_3 y_{t-1} + \delta_4 x_{t-1} + \sum_{i=1}^{p-1} \phi_i' \Delta y_{t-i} + \sum_{i=1}^{p-1} \phi_i' \Delta x_{t-i} + \varepsilon_t \quad (3.15)$$

According to Model 3.15, $\delta 0$ is the constant term, $\delta 1$, $\delta 2$, $\delta 3$, $\delta 4$ coefficients, εt is the error term, k is the odd frequency, T is the total number of observations and t is the trend. After obtaining the optimal frequency, it is checked whether there is cointegration or not, and it is stated that if the coefficient $\delta 3$ is equal to zero, there is no cointegration relationship, and if the value of $\delta 3$ is less than zero, there is a cointegration relationship. The t statistic found is based on Banerjee et al. (2017), the decision is made by comparing the critical table values.

3.4.1.4. Linear and Fourier Causality Tests

The Granger test analyzes causality based on the VAR model and for VAR analysis, the series should be stationary at I(1) level (Granger, 1969). Toda and Yamamoto (1995) developed the Granger causality test due to the reduction of data when the first difference of the series is taken (Toda and Yamamoto, 1995). However, the common disadvantage of these two tests is that they do not take into account shocks and structural breaks. Enders and Jones (2016) developed the Granger causality test and Nazlıoğlu et al. (2016) developed the Toda–Yamamoto causality test by adding Fourier functions to the Granger causality test (Enders and Jones, 2016), (Nazlıoğlu et al., 2016), (Nazlıoğlu et al., 2016). The model derived from Granger causality in Enders and Jones (2016) is as in model 3.16.

$$y_{it} = \alpha_{i1} y_{1t-1} + \alpha_{i2} y_{2t-1} + \sum_{k=1}^{n} \left[\gamma_{ik} sin\left(2\pi kt / T\right) + \delta_{ik} cos\left(2\pi kt / T\right) \right] + \varepsilon_{it} \quad (3.16)$$

In Model 3.16, n is the number of frequencies, k is the frequency, γik and δik are the frequency widths and locations. There are two different types of tests in the model and in the first test, it is determined whether $\alpha ij = 0$ according to the t distribution. According to the Granger causality test, $i \neq j$ is expected to be j. However, according to the model, when there are no breaks, the trigonometric does not know whether the data affect the result. In the second test, according to the F test, values with $\gamma ikk = \delta ikk = 0$ are eliminated, and $n = 1, 2, 3$ values are used as an alternative is repeated once. Enders and Jones (2016) explained the probability values according to sample sizes in a table.

Nazlıoğlu et al. extended the constant term assumption in the VAR model by adding Fourier functions to the Toda–Yamamoto causality test and added structural changes to the new model (Nazlıoğlu et al., 2016). By adding Fourier functions to the model with the assumption that the constant term in the VAR model does not change over time, they derived model 3.17 that takes structural breaks into account.

$$y_t = \alpha_0 + \gamma_1 sin\left(\frac{2\pi kt}{T}\right) + \gamma_2 cos\left(\frac{2\pi kt}{T}\right) + \beta_1 y_{t-1} + \ldots + \beta_{p+d} y_{t-(p+d)} + \varepsilon_t \quad (3.17)$$

In Model 3.17, k denotes the number of frequencies, T denotes the number of observations and t denotes the time term. Nazlıoğlu et al. (2016) suggest using the F test instead of the Wald test due to the weakness of the X^2 distribution in causality tests. The null hypothesis states that there is no causality, while the alternative hypothesis states that there is causality. With the findings obtained in bootstrap simulations, it is determined whether the main hypothesis is accepted or not.

3.4.1.5. Empirical Findings

In this study, which investigates the role of purchasing power parity theory, one of the exchange rate determination models, in exchange rate determination, firstly, the stationarity of the variables is tested with the Extended Dickey–Fuller (1981) and Phillips–Perron (1988) tests. The results are as shown in Table 2.

In ADF (1981) and PP (1988) unit root tests, the null hypothesis is that the variable has a unit root, and the alternative hypothesis is that the variable does not have a unit root. Probability values are taken into account at the decision stage. Accordingly, both variables have unit root at the level value in both the model with constant and the model with constant and trend. Both unit root tests show consistent results. The results of the Fourier KPSS unit root test are presented in Table 3.

Table 2: ADF (1981) and PP (1988) Unit Root Test results

		Variables	ADF	PP		*Variables*	ADF	PP
Level	*Fixed*	**LNER**	2,182 (0,99)	2,199 (0,99)	*First Differences*	**LNER**	−11,267 (0,00) ***	−9,639 (0,00) ***
		LSGP	3,685 (1,00)	3,645 (1,00)		**LSGP**	−11,046 (0,00) ***	−10,851 (0,00) ***
	Fixed+Trend	**LNER**	−1,763 (0,71)	−1,666 (0,76)		**LNER**	−11,951 (0,00) ***	−9,913 (0,00) ***
		LSGP	0,613 (0,99)	0,947 (0,99)		**LSGP**	−9,928 (0,00) ***	−11,289 (0,00) ***

Note: ***, **, * indicate that the alternative hypothesis is accepted at 1%, 5% and 10% significance levels, respectively.

Table 3: Fourier KPSS Unit Root Test results

Models	Variable	Frequenc y	Min SSR	FKPSS	F stat	Hypothes is	Status
Fixed	LNER	1	26,282	0,7442	215,968	H1	Not static
Fixed+ Trend	LNER	1	1,747	0,0903	726,862	H1	Not static
Fixed	LSGP	1	14,767	0,7754	136,793	H1	Not static
Fixed+ Trend	LSGP	1	0,128	0,1063	565,108	H1	Not static

Note: For frequency 1; 10% significance level 0.131, 5% significance level 0.172, 1% significance level 0.269; For Frequency 1, the table critical values for level+Trend are 0.047 at 10% significance level, 0.054 at 5% significance level, and 0.071 at 1% significance level. ***, **, * values indicate that the alternative hypothesis is accepted at 1%, 5% and 10% significance levels, respectively.

In the Fourier KPSS unit root test, unlike other unit root tests, the hypotheses are replaced. In the Fourier KPSS unit root test, the null hypothesis is that there is no unit root in the variable and the alternative hypothesis is that there is a unit root in the variable. Becker et al. (2006) compare the FKPSS test statistics with the table values at the decision stage. If the test statistics are greater than the table values, the alternative hypothesis is accepted. According to the results obtained, both variables have Fourier unit root at the level value in fixed and fixed-trend models.

The results of both ADF and PP conventional unit root tests and Fourier KPSS unit root analysis show that the series have unit roots and become stationary when first differences are taken.

According to Güloğlu et al. (2011), according to the purchasing power hypothesis, the real exchange rate should be trend stationary at the level or the nominal exchange rate and prices, which are components of the real exchange rate, should be cointegrated. In the light of these explanations, when the data of the Turkish economy for the period 2003– 2021 are analyzed, it can be concluded that the variables have unit roots and therefore purchasing power parity is not valid. The fact that both traditional unit root tests and Fourier unit root tests support this result gives strong support that the hypothesis is not valid. However, in order to clarify whether purchasing power parity is valid or not, it is necessary to conduct cointegration tests. The Fourier ARDL cointegration results are presented in Table 4.

Table 4: Fourier ARDL cointegration results

	Test Statistics	**90%**	**95%**	**99%**
FA	10.67357	7.800806	9.054997	10.67469
t	−4.212668	−3.836588	−4.014920	−4.362108
FB	0.189293	−1.606188	−1.285760	−0.342607

Note: The optimal frequency is 0.60 and the minimum Akaike Information Criterion is −4.110.

In the Fourier cointegration test developed by Banerjee et al. (2017), the null hypothesis states that there is no Fourier cointegration relationship, while the alternative hypothesis states that there is a Fourier cointegration relationship. There are alternative cases at the decision stage. According to (Yılancı et al. 2020):

1. Cointegration exists if $_{FA,}$ FB, t are significant
2. No cointegration if $_{FA,}$ FB, t are insignificant
3. If $_{FA,\ FB}$ are significant and t is insignificant, there is degenerate cointegration unstable
4. No degenerate cointegration if $_{FA}$, t is significant and $_{FB}$ is insignificant.

According to the results obtained, there is a long-run Fourier cointegration relationship between the variables according to $_{FA}$, t and $_{FB}$ statistics. Fourier lagged autoregressive model with nominal exchange rate as the dependent variable and (P/P*) as the independent variable it is set up as in 3.18.

$$\Delta NER_t = \delta_0 + \delta_1 sin\left(\frac{2\pi kt}{T}\right) + \delta_2 cos\left(\frac{2\pi kt}{T}\right) + \delta_3 NER_{t-1} + \delta_4 (P/P^*)_{t-1} + \sum_{i=1}^{p-1}\phi_i' \Delta NER_{t-i} + \sum_{i=1}^{p-1}\phi_i' \Delta (P/P^*)_{t-i} + \varepsilon_t \tag{3.18}$$

In Model 3.18, ծ0 is the constant term, ծ1 and δ 2 are the sine and cosine Fourier functions, ծ3 and ծ4 denote the nominal exchange rate and the coefficients of the (P/P*) expression, respectively. Fourier ARDL coefficients are as in Table 5.

Table 5: Fourier ARDL parameter estimation results

	Coefficient (Probability Value)
Ln(P/P*)	1.030877 (0.00)***
Fixed term	1.102013 (0.00)***
Sine functions ($_{\delta 1}$)	−0.459015 (0.00)***
Cosine functions ($_{\delta 2}$)	−0.058467 (0.1135)

Note: ***, **, * indicate that the alternative hypothesis is accepted at 1%, 5% and 10% significance levels, respectively.

Except for the cosine function, all other parameters are statistically significant at the 1% significance level. Accordingly, a 1% increase in purchasing power parity increased the value of the U.S. dollar by 1.030. Contrary to the unit root tests, the results of the Fourier ARDL cointegration analysis indicate that there is a long-run relationship between purchasing power parity and the U.S. dollar exchange rate and therefore the hypothesis is valid. Finally, the relationship between purchasing power parity and nominal exchange rate is analyzed within the framework of causality analysis. Table 6 presents both conventional and Fourier-based causality analyses. According to the results of the analysis, both the standard Granger, Toda–Yamamoto and bootstrap-based Toda–Yamamoto causality analyses and the Fourier-based different frequency causality analyses show that there is a bidirectional causality between the variables. The bidirectional causality implies that purchasing power parity affects the nominal exchange rate, while the nominal exchange rate affects the general price level ratio between the two countries. The last finding provides evidence for the existence of exchange rate pass-through of the nominal exchange rate on inflation in the Turkish economy offers.

All test results analyzing the validity of purchasing power parity can be summarized as follows. While unit root tests support the conclusion that purchasing power parity is invalid since it does not show stationarity, cointegration and causality tests provide evidence that the parity is valid. Considering the basic logic of purchasing power parity, it can be said that the unit root test results are more valid and it is highly probable that the parity is invalid for the Turkish economy. Indeed, when compared with the applied literature, it can be said that the same results are found in Aslan and Kanbur (2007), Şener et al. (2015), Abumustafa and Feridun (2010), Yıldırım et al. (2013), Zümbül (2020), Çağlayan and Saçaklı (2006), Kum (2012) and Gedik and Karaer (2017), which use similar unit root tests. On the other hand, cointegration and causality analyses are similar to Yıldırım et al. (2019), Bilgin (2018), Güriş et al. (2016), Burgaç Çil and Dülger (2017), Şeker and Now (2018).

3.4.2. Mundell–Fleming Model Test Results

In this study, the model used in Hsing (2009) was preferred to analyze the Mundell– Fleming model (Hsing, 2009). The model is obtained by extending the model used in Romer (2001) and according to the model, money and goods markets are as shown in 3.19 and 3.20. ε denotes the real exchange

Table 6: Linear and Fourier Causality Test results

Ho: SGP is not the Granger cause of NER						
	Wald	**Asymp. p value**	**Boots. p value**	**k**	**p**	**d_{max}**
Standard GC (Granger, 1969)	37,132	0,00***	0,001***	-	12	-
TY and bootstrap TY (Toda and Yamomoto, 1995)	49,123	0,00***	0,00***	-	13	1
Fourier standard GC single frequency (Enders and Jones, 2016)	45,108	0,00***	0,00***	1	12	-
Fourier TY single frequency (Nazliogu et al., 2016)	31,265	0,00***	0,00***	1	9	1
Fourier standard GC cumulative frequency (Enders and Jones, 2016)	52,524	0,00***	0,00***	3	12	-
Fourier TY cumulative frequency (Nazlioglu et al., 2016)	51,032	0,00***	0,00***	3	13	1
Ho: SGP is not the Granger cause of NER						
	Wald	**Asymp. p value**	**Boots. p value**	**k**	**P**	**d_{max}**
Standard GC (Granger, 1969)	93,083	0,00***	0,00***	-	12	-
TY and bootstrap TY (Toda and Yamomoto, 1995)	111,582	0,00***	-	13		1
Fourier standard GC single frequency (Enders and Jones, 2015)	88,894	0,00***	1	12		-
Fourier TY single frequency (Nazlioglu et al., 2016)	80,468	0,00***	1	9		1
Fourier standard GC cumulative frequency (Enders and Jones, 2015)	104,980	0,00***	3	12		-
Fourier TY cumulative frequency (Nazlioglu et al., 2016)	117,529	0,00***	3	13		1

Notes: ***, **, * indicate acceptance of the alternative hypothesis at 1%, 5% and 10% significance levels, respectively. Bootstrap number is 1000. k stands for optimal frequency, p for optimal lag length, $_{dmax}$ for maximum degree of integration, GC for Granger causality, and TY for Toda–Yamamoto causality. Akaike Information Criterion is used to select the optimal lag length. Granger-based causality tests are developed by Enders and Jones (2016), while TY-based causality tests are developed by Nazlıoğlu et al.

rate, G denotes public expenditures, T denotes tax revenues, L denotes money demand and R^* denotes the exchange rate.

$$Y = Z\left(Y, R - \pi^e, G, T, \varepsilon\right) \tag{3.19}$$

$$M / P = L\left(Y, R, R^{*}, \varepsilon\right) \tag{3.20}$$

The real exchange rate equilibrium for the solution of Y and ε is as in model 3.21.

$$\bar{\varepsilon} = f\left(M / P, G, T, R, R^{*}, \pi^{e}\right) \tag{3.21}$$

In his study, Hsing (2009) expresses the effects of real money supply, real government expenditures, domestic interest rate and foreign interest rate as in models 3.22, 3.23, 3.24 and 3.25.

$$\partial\bar{\varepsilon} / \partial\left(M / P\right) = -\left(1 - Z_{y}\right) / \left|J\right| > 0 \tag{3.22}$$

$$\partial\bar{\varepsilon} / \partial\left(G - T\right) = \left(Z_{G} + Z_{T}\right) L_{Y} / \left|J\right| < 0 \tag{3.23}$$

$$\partial\bar{\varepsilon} / \partial R = \left[L_{R}\left(1 - Z_{y}\right) + L_{y} Z_{R}\right] / \left|J\right| > 0 \tag{3.24}$$

$$\begin{aligned} \partial\bar{\varepsilon} / \partial R^{*} &= L_{R^{*}}\left(1 - Z_{y}\right) / \left|J\right| < 0, \\ &\quad \textit{if } L_{R^{*}} > 0 \qquad \textit{or} \\ &\quad > 0 \textit{ if } \; L_{R^{*}} < 0 \end{aligned} \tag{3.25}$$

With the assumption that $_{L\varepsilon}$ is positive, the $|J|$ variable is an endogenous variable with a negative value. The real exchange rate balance is expected to be positively correlated with real money supply and domestic interest rate and negatively correlated with real government expenditures.

Uçan organized the model more simply as in model 3.26 (Uçan, 2011, p. 159). According to Model 3.26, the nominal exchange rate (*ER*) represents the domestic price level (*P*), public expenditures (*G*), tax revenues (*T*), domestic money supply (*M*), domestic short-term interest rate ($_{iS}$) and domestic expected inflation rate (π^{e}). In the analyses, the logarithmized exchange rate is represented *by LNER*, the logarithmized real money supply by *LM2P*, the difference between public expenditures and tax revenues *by LKhVg*, the inflation expectation *by BE* and the interest rate by *TF*.

$$LnER = \beta_{0} + \beta_{1} ln(M / P) + \beta_{2} ln(G - T) + \beta_{3} i_{s} + \beta_{4} \pi^{e} + \varepsilon \tag{3.26}$$

3.4.2.1. *Data*

For the period Jan. 2006–Sept. 2021, the validity of the Mundell–Fleming model in the Turkish economy is tested with the model used in Model 3.26. Fourier ARDL model 4 the linear ARDL model is used to test the Mundell–Fleming model since it allows up to one variable.

Monthly frequency data are obtained from the electronic data distribution system of the Central Bank of the Republic of Türkiye. The logarithms of the nominal exchange rate, money supply and the difference between public expenditures and tax revenues are taken, while expected inflation and interest rate variables are tested with their level values. Information on the variables is presented in Table 7.

Table 7: Variables of the Mundell–Fleming model

Variables	Beginning	End	Source
Nominal exchange rate	Jan. 2006	Sept. 2021	CBRT
M2 money supply	Jan. 2006	Sept. 2021	CBRT
CPI	Jan. 2006	Sept. 2021	CBRT (TÜİK)
Public expenditures	Jan. 2006	Sept. 2021	CBRT (HMB)
Tax revenues	Jan. 2006	Sept. 2021	CBRT (HMB)
2Y bond interest rate	Jan. 2006	Sept. 2021	CBRT
Expected inflation	Jan. 2006	Sept. 2021	CBRT

3.4.2.2. *ADF (1981)—PP (1988) Stationarity Tests*

In order to apply the ARDL method, the variables must be stationary at $I(_0)$ or $I(_1)$ levels. The ARDL method cannot be analyzed with variables that are stationary only at I(2) level. At this point, Extended Dickey–Fuller (1981) and Phillips–Perron (1988) unit root tests will be used to determine the stationarity levels.

3.4.2.3. *ARDL Cointegration Test*

In order to conduct Engle–Granger (1987) and Johansen–Juselius cointegration tests, the variables should be stationary at the same level (Engle and Granger, 1987; Johansen and Juselius, 1990). Pesaran et al. (2001) developed the ARDL test, which allows the estimation of long and short-run relationships between variables without considering the stationarity condition as in the Engle–Granger and Johansen–Juselius cointegration tests (Pesaran et al., 2001). The feature of the test is that it allows cointegration analysis even if the variables are stationary at level, first difference or different levels (Pata et al., 2016, p. 265). In the ARDL test, variables are subjected to tests if they are stationary at $I(_0)$ and $I(_1)$ levels, while they are not subjected to tests if they are stationary at $I(_2)$ level. In the ARDL bounds test, as in model 3.27, y is the dependent variable and k $_{Xj}$'s are defined as independent variables. $_{\varepsilon t}$ is the error term, $_{\theta 0}$ is the constant term, γi, γi, $\delta j,i$, $\alpha 0$, αjj are the coefficients of the variables and p is the lag length.

$$\Delta Y_t = \theta_0 + \sum_{i-1}^{p} \gamma_i \Delta y_{t-1} + \sum_{j-1}^{k} \sum_{i-0}^{p} \delta_{j,i} \Delta X_{j,t-i} + \alpha_0 y_{t-1} + \sum_{i-0}^{p} \alpha_j \Delta X_{j,t-1} + \varepsilon_t \quad (3.27)$$

Model 3.28 is used to find the long-run elasticity coefficients when the variables are cointegrated. $_{\varepsilon t}$ denotes the error term, $_{\theta 0}$ denotes the constant term, $_{\theta i}$, $\rho j_{,i}$ denotes the coefficients of the variables, p denotes the lag length of the dependent and $\rho j_{,i}$ denotes the lag length of the jth independent variables.

$$y_t = \varnothing_0 + \sum_{i=1}^{p} \theta_i y_{t-i} + \sum_{j=1}^{k} \sum_{i=0}^{q_j} \rho_{j,i} X_{j,t-i} + \varepsilon_t \quad (3.28)$$

ARDL error correction equation model including short-run elasticities of variables is as in 3.29. In Model 3.29, EC is the error correction term, π_0 is the constant term, λ_i, ω_i are the coefficients of the variables, ψ is the speed at which the model reaches equilibrium.

$$\Delta y_t = \pi_0 + \sum_{i=1}^{p} \lambda_i \Delta y_{t-1} + \sum_{j=1}^{k} \sum_{i=0}^{q_j} \omega_i \Delta X_{j,t-i} + \psi EC_{t-1} + \varepsilon_t \quad (3.29)$$

The error correction coefficient is calculated from the long-run equation as in model 3.30. The error correction coefficient denoted by KC_t takes a value between (–1) and (0) and is statistically be meaningful (Samut, 2016, p. 41).

$$EC_t = y_t - \alpha - \sum_{j=1}^{k} \beta_j X_{j,t-i} \tag{3.30}$$

3.4.2.4. Bai–Perron (2003) Structural Break Test

Bai and Perron (2003) developed a method to test for multiple structural breaks in time series analysis. Although the method is not a unit root test, it can test the independent variables included in the models by adding them to the model. In the Bai–Perron test, the analysis is performed by minimizing the sum of error squares (Bai and Perron, 2003). The model uses the least squares method for each break based on dynamic programming (Çevik and Erdoğan, 2009, p. 31).

The model where the number of multiple breaks is denoted by m (m+1 different regimes) is as shown in 3.31. In model 3.31, $_{yt}$ is the dependent variable, $_{xt}$ ($px1$) and $_{zt}$ ($qx1$) are the vector of dimensional variables, β and δj (j=1, ... , m+1) are the coefficients, and ut is the error term.

$$y_t = x_t'\beta + z_t'\delta_j + u_t, t = T_{j-1} + 1, \cdots, T_j \tag{3.31}$$

In Model 3.31, $_{T1}$, ... , $_{Tm}$ estimate the predicted break locations and least squares estimates are made for each m value. In order to make least squares estimates for β and δj, the sum of squares error should be minimized. In this case, the estimate of the sum of squares error is as in model 3.32.

$$(Y - X\beta - \bar{Z}\delta)'(Y - X\beta - \bar{Z}\delta) = \sum_{i=1}^{m+1} \sum_{t=T_{i-1}+1}^{T_i} [y_t - x_t'\beta - z_t'\delta_i]^2 \tag{3.32}$$

Bai and Perron (2003) put forward three test conditions for determining the number of breaks (Bai and Perron, 2003, p. 76). These are:

1. Sup Ft(n;k) test: According to the null hypothesis there are no structural breaks, but according to the alternative hypothesis there are k structural breaks.

2. UDMaxFt (M,q) and WDMaxFt (M,q) tests: Also known as the Double Maximum test, the main hypothesis is that there are no structural breaks, while the alternative hypothesis is that there are at most *m* structural breaks ($1 \leq m \leq M$).
3. Sup Ft(l + 1 | l) test: The sequential F test shows that there *are l* breaks according to the null hypothesis and *l+1* breaks according to the alternative hypothesis.

Bai and Perron (2003) suggest that these three tests should be applied together to determine the number of breaks in the series. They stated that if Sup Ft(n;k), UDMaxFt (M,q) and WDMaxFt (M,q) tests yield statistically significant results, there is at least one break. They stated that Sup Ft(l + 1| l) test should be applied to determine whether there are more breaks. They also suggested that Bayesian information criterion (BIC), LWZ, which is a revised version of the Schwarz criterion, should be applied to determine the model size for the multiple break test and sequential model selection criteria for the sequential Sup Ft(l + *1* | l) test.

3.4.2.5. Empirical Findings

In this study, which investigates the role of the Mundell–Fleming model, one of the exchange rate determination models, in exchange rate determination, the stationarity of the variables was first tested with the Extended Dickey–Fuller (1981) and Phillips–Perron (1988) tests. The results are as shown in Table 8.

ADF and PP unit root test results are shown in Table 8. According to the test results, LKhVg does not have a unit root at 1% significance l e v e l in the model with constant at level value, LM2P and LKhVg variables do not have a unit root at 1% significance level in the model with constant and trend at level value and become stationary. On the other hand, when the first difference of all variables is taken, it is observed that all variables get rid of the unit root problem and become stationary. These results will be taken into account when constructing the ARDL model. The statistical values of the ARDL bounds test are as shown in Table 9.

According to the ARDL bounds test results, since the value of 4.892 is to the right of I (1) at 1%, 5% and 10% levels, it can be said that there is a cointegration relationship between the variables. This result shows that there is a long-run

Table 8: ADF (1981) and PP (1988) Unit Root Test results

		Variables	ADF	PP		*Variables*	ADF	PP
Level	*Fixed*	**LNER**	1,305 (0,99)	1,286 (0,99)	*First Differences*	**LNER**	−10,494 (0,00)***	−9,028 (0,00)***
		LM2P	−0,790 (0,81)	−0,789 (0,81)		**LM2P**	−13,452 (0,00)***	−13,669 (0,00)***
		LKhVg	−3,469 (0,01)***	−10,812 (0,00)***		**LKhVg**	−16,383 (0,00)***	−87,242 (0,00)***
		TF	−1,762 (0,39)	−1,941 (0,31)		**TF**	−11,680 (0,00)***	−11,650 (0,00)***
		BE	−2,177 (0,21)	−1,621 (0,46)		**BE**	−6,274 (0,00)***	−6,004 (0,00)***
	Fixed+Trend	**LNER**	−1,736 (0,73)	−1,800 (0,70)		**LNER**	−10,746 (0,00)***	−9,059 (0,00)***
		LM2P	−3,742 (0,02)***	−3,742 (0,02)***		**LM2P**	−13,419 (0,00)***	−13,627 (0,00)***
		LKhVg	−12,984 (0,00)***	−13,000 (0,00)***		**LKhVg**	−16,307 (0,00)***	−86,152 (0,00)***
		TF	−1,697 (0,74)	−1,883 (0,65)		**TF**	−11,663 (0,00)***	−11,631 (0,00)***
		BE	−3,288 (0,07)*	−2,532 (0,31)		**BE**	−6,269 (0,00)***	−5,985 (0,00)***

Note: ***, **, * indicate that the alternative hypothesis is accepted at 1%, 5% and 10% significance levels, respectively.

Table 9: ARDL Cointegration Test results

F Test Statistic	**4.892**	
	I(0)	I(1)
10%	2.2	3.09
5%	2.56	3.49
1%	3.29	4.37

interaction between the variables. This interaction provides evidence for the validity of the Mundell–Flemming model in the long run.

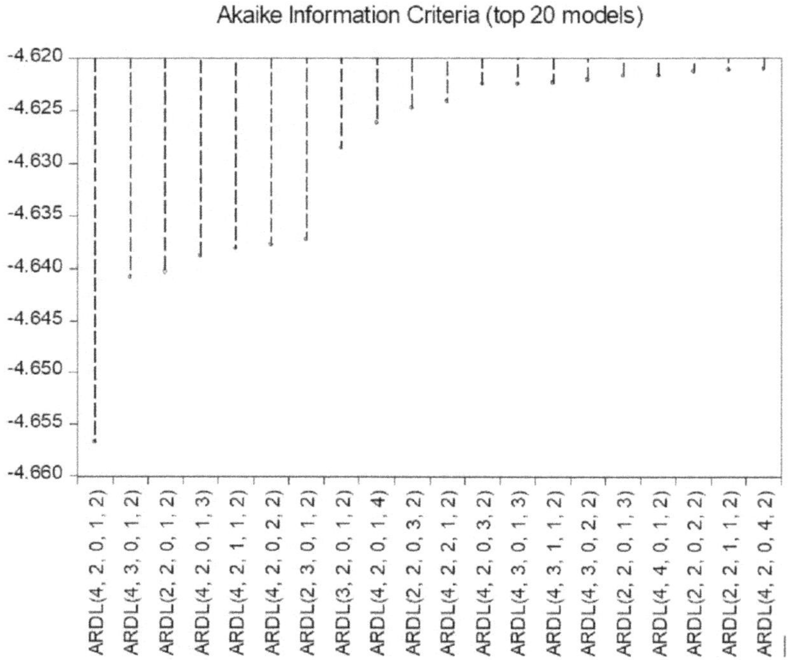

Figure 15: ARDL (4,2,0,1,2) preference according to Akaike Information Criterion

According to the Akaike Information Criterion, the lags of the ARDL model are as shown in Figure 15. In the ARDL model, four lags of the NER variable, 2 lags of the M2 variable, 1 lag of the TF variable and 2 lags of the BE variable are used in the short run. Short-run parameter estimates for the ARDL (4,2,0,1,2) model are presented in the following text. According to the results, the short-run ARDL model should be estimated. The estimation results are summarized in Table 10.

According to the short-run ARDL results, the main determinant of the exchange rate is the value itself. One and two lagged values are statistically significant at 1%, while the third and fourth lagged values are statistically significant at 5% significance levels. The first lag is positive

Table 10: Short-Run ARDL (4,2,0,1,2) model results

Variable	Coefficient	Probability Value
LNER(−1)	1.164891	0.0000***
LNER(−2)	−0.322934	0.0061***
LNER(−3)	0.207874	0.0247**
LNER(−4)	−0.125755	0.0245**
LM2	0.558297	0.0000***
LM2(−1)	0.228717	0.0509*
LM2(−2)	−0.655469	0.0000***
LKHVG	−0.000854	0.5398
TF	0.009293	0.0000***
TF(−1)	−0.007023	0.0000***
BE	0.022399	0.0004***
BE(−1)	−0.038764	0.0000***
BE(−2)	0.019140	0.0019**
C	−1.962885	0.0000**

Note: ***, **, * indicate that the alternative hypothesis is accepted at 1%, 5% and 10% significance levels, respectively.

and has a value of 1.16. In other words, it can be interpreted as a strong stickiness from the previous period. Although the second value is negative, the coefficient is relatively small. The third and fourth values are positive and negative, respectively, and again the coefficients become smaller as the period lengthens.

When interpreted economically, when we talk about stickiness, the change should be in the same direction, that is, it should have the same sign. In this case, while the value in the −1 period is both statistically and economically significant, it does not seem possible to explain the sign changes in other periods economically. The positive and relatively large coefficient in period −1 means that the exchange rate value of the past period determines the exchange rate value of the next period to a large extent in Türkiye. In this case, it can be said that households determine their exchange rate expectations according to the previous period.

Another variable is the real money supply and theoretically, an increase in money supply is expected to raise the exchange rate. Theoretically, an increase in money supply will cause the value of the national currency to fall and the exchange rate to rise. The results obtained are consistent with the theory. When the results are analyzed, it is seen that the coefficients of the variable and the coefficients with –1 period are statistically significant and positive at 1% and 5% significance levels. In other words, an increase in this variable will lead to an increase in the exchange rate. On the other hand, although the 2-period coefficient is statistically significant, it is not economically significant due to the negative value of the coefficient.

When the value of the budget balance is analyzed, it is observed that the coefficient is very small and negative. Since the coefficient is statistically insignificant, there is no need to interpret it.

Another variable that needs to be interpreted is the interest rate. An increase in the interest rate will make the country's financial system more attractive for foreign investors. Therefore, an increase in the interest rate will have a downward effect on the exchange rate (due to foreign capital inflows) effect on the interest rate. In this case, the coefficient of the interest rate is expected to take a negative value. When the results are checked, it is seen that the coefficients of the interest rate in the current period and the –1 period are statistically significant at the 1% level of significance. This is evidence that the Keynesian theory is valid.

On the other hand, it is noteworthy that both coefficients are very small. This implies that whatever happens, the effect on the exchange rate will be quite limited. However, while the coefficient for the current period is positive, the coefficient for the –1 period is negative. In this case, only

The coefficient for the –1 period may be economically significant, while the coefficient for the current period may be significant only in the presence of an exchange rate market that is affected with a lag by the increase in the interest rate due to frictions in capital flows. It can be emphasized that the –1 period can be economically and statistically significant.

Finally, the effectiveness of the inflation expectation variable on the exchange rate is analyzed. Accordingly, current and lagged coefficients are statistically significant at the 1% level. Theoretically, as the expected inflation rate increases, inflation is expected to increase in the following periods according to the inflation rate forecasts of other countries. In this case, as the inflation expectation increases, the exchange rate will also be expected to increase. When we look at the results obtained, as the inflation expectation increases in the current period (the coefficient is positive), the exchange rate will increase. However, the coefficient for the –1 period is negative. This implies that the exchange rate will decrease in case of an increase in inflation expectations, which is economically insignificant.

When all the results are evaluated together, it can be said that the most important determinant of the exchange rate is its past values. In addition, it can be concluded that real money supply, exchange rate and expected inflation, albeit small, influence the exchange rate. In the context of the policies implemented, it can be said that an increase in the money supply may have direct and indirect effects on the exchange rate. This is because when the money supply increases, the exchange rate increases, the increase in the exchange rate increases inflation and puts pressure on the exchange rate. In this case, it can be said that an increase in the money supply exerts pressure on the exchange rate through two different channels, which can be interpreted as both direct and indirect pressure through inflation.

Table 11: Long-Run ARDL model results

Variable	Coefficient	Probability Value
LM2	1.732590	0.0000***
LKHVG	−0.011248	0.5399
TF	0.029888	0.0001****
BE	0.036561	0.0736*
C	−25.853265	0.0000***
ECT(−1)	−0.076425	0.0000***
Breusch–Godfrey Serial Correlation LM Test	0.013	0.9093
Heteroskedasticity Test: Breusch–Pagan–Godfrey	1.641	0.079*
Ramsey Reset Test	0.348	0.727

Note: ***, **, * indicate that the alternative hypothesis is accepted at 1%, 5% and 10% significance levels, respectively.

When the long-run ARDL test results in Table 11 are analyzed, it can be said that the results are consistent with the short-run analysis. The coefficient of real money supply is positive and large and statistically significant at the 1% level. This implies that an increase in money supply leads to an increase in exchange rate. As expected, the results indicate an increase in money supply.

This will lead to an abundance and depreciation of the national currency. This will lead to a decrease in the value of the national currency against foreign currencies and an increase in the exchange rate.

The coefficient of the budget balance variable is negative and statistically insignificant. Although the coefficient is theoretically expected to be negative, its statistical insignificance does not require any interpretation.

The coefficient of the interest rate variable is statistically significant and has a small positive value. This situation yielded similar results with the short-run analysis. Theoretically, an increase in the interest rate is expected to have a downward effect on the exchange rate. However, the positive coefficient is contrary to this. In this case, the fact that the coefficient is insignificant according to Keynesian economics means that capital mobility is restricted for some reason. Therefore, it means that an increase in interest rates will not have a depreciating effect on the exchange rate since it will not attract foreign capital to the country. Although there are no restrictions on capital movements in the Turkish financial system through taxes or any other official channel, there may be restrictions for different reasons. Therefore, it can be said that the coefficient of the interest rate does not have the expected sign. Another explanation for the positive coefficient of the interest rate is that an increase in the interest rate leads to an increase in the exchange rate by decreasing the demand for national currency. This predicts a positive relationship between exchange rate and interest rate. According to the theory, an increase in the domestic interest rate is expected to decrease the demand for national currency and increase the exchange rate.

It can be said that the coefficient of the expected inflation rate has an increasing effect on the exchange rate, as in the short run. However, unlike the short run, the statistical significance of the coefficient is low. While the statistical significance was 1% in the short run, it decreased to 10% in the long run.

Although the error correction coefficient is –0.076, an imbalance that occurs in the model in the short run rebalances in about 13.08 months. In other words, distortions are recovered in more than a year. In addition, there is no autocorrelation problem in the model. The problem of varying variance is found at the 10% significance level and Newey– West estimator is used to estimate the model. Finally, according to the results of the Ramsey Reset test, the model is correctly constructed.

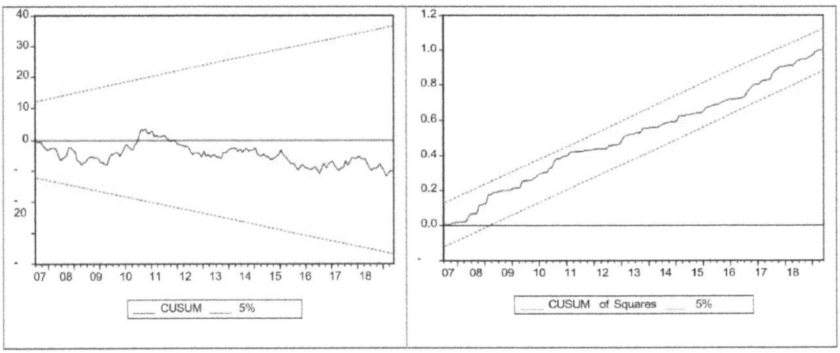

Figure 16: CUSUM and CUSUMQ Tests

According to the CUSUM and CUSUMQ test results in Figure 16, there is an out- of-trend structure in the series between Dec. 2010 (0.37) and Jan. 2012 (0.49). Therefore, cointegration tests that take structural breaks into account should be conducted. In the next stage, the cointegration test developed by Bai and Perron (2003) is applied and up to five structural breaks are taken into account in the model. The statistical values of the structural break dates are as shown in Table 12.

Table 12: Determination of break dates

Number of Fractures	F Statistic	F Critical Value
0 vs. 1	43.71298	18.23
1 vs. 2	37.34806	19.91
2 vs. 3	22.93764	20.99
3 vs. 4	8.047868	21.71

The break dates obtained from the table are June 2008, September 2011, January 2015 and May 2019. The parameters obtained within these periods are presented in Table 13.

First of all, it is useful to analyze each period separately. Because the variables explanatory power may differ across periods. Subsequently, the differences between the periods will be analyzed and the possible effects of possible policy changes on the variables will be interpreted.

Accordingly, the first period covers approximately 2.5 years and is the first years of the transition to explicit inflation targeting. All coefficients of the variables are statistically significant. However, an economic interpretation of the coefficients reveals that the coefficient of the real money supply variable is negative, meaning that the exchange rate decreases when the money supply increases. The reason why this result is theoretically insignificant is that the focus of monetary policies was on the inflation rate due to the adoption of the explicit inflation targeting regime in that period. Another result of this period is related to the budget balance. The coefficient indicating that an increase in the variable obtained by subtracting tax revenues from public expenditures will decrease the exchange rate is statistically significant at the 1% level. However, the coefficient is quite small, and its effect is very weak.

For the first period covering Jan. 2006–May 2008, the effect of expected inflation and interest rate on exchange rate is positive and statistically significant. First of all, the coefficients of the two variables are very small and it is economically significant that an increase in expected inflation increases the exchange rate. However, while an increase in the interest rate is expected to lower the exchange rate, the opposite may occur if international capital flows face a systemic impediment. The break at the end of the period can be explained by the fact that the CBRT raised interest rates by 50 basis points each in May, June and July 2008 to mitigate the effects of the global financial crisis and changed the inflation targets (CBRT, 2009, pp. 47–48).

In the second period covering Jun. 2008–Aug. 2011, it should be emphasized that the disinflation process was successful and at the same time the global financial crisis occurred. Considering these explanations, the coefficients indicate that the effect of real money supply on exchange rate is positive and statistically significant at the 1% level. As the money supply increases, the national currency will become more abundant, and its value will decrease. As a result, an increase in the exchange rate is an economically expected

Table 13: Parameters between break dates

Variable	Coefficient	Probability Value
	Jan. 2006–May 2008	
LM2	−0.844932	0.0000***
LKHVG	−0.007661	0.0080***
TF	0.016650	0.0000***
BE	0.032741	0.0000***
C	12.22119	0.0000***
	Jun. 2008–Aug. 2011	
LM2	0.714146	0.0007***
LKHVG	0.036063	0.0211**
TF	0.014253	0.0199**
BE	−0.077654	0.0105**
C	−10.38337	0.0016***
	Sept. 2011–Dec. 2014	
LM2	0.951016	0.0000***
LKHVG	−0.003202	0.2044
TF	0.002918	0.2995
BE	0.070115	0.0000***
C	−14.15286	0.0000***
	Jan. 2015–Apr. 2019	
LM2	1.444070	0.0000***
LKHVG	0.001556	0.7648
TF	0.013519	0.0000***
BE	0.038109	0.0000***
C	−21.47518	0.0000***
	May 2019–Sept. 2021M09	
LM2	1.350783	0.0000***
LKHVG	−0.003190	0.6221
TF	0.004812	0.0207**
BE	0.014955	0.0062***
C	−19.36513	0.0000***

Note: ***, **, * indicate that the alternative hypothesis is accepted at 1%, 5% and 10% significance levels, respectively.

situation. The coefficient of the budget balance variable is positive and higher than the previous period. The value, which is statistically significant at the 5% level, is theoretically significant. In the event of an increase in the budget deficit, the exchange rate is likely to increase as the public sector will resort to domestic and external borrowing to cover this deficit.

The coefficient of the interest rate variable, which is considered statistically significant at the 5% level of significance, can be considered economically significant if there are obstacles to international capital flows or if there is a political situation with the same effect. However, it can be said that the coefficient is negligibly small. Again, the expected inflation variable is statistically significant at the 5% significance level, although very small. Theoretically, this coefficient is economically insignificant since expected inflation would have an increasing effect on the exchange rate. In this period when the global crisis adversely affected European economies and uncertainties increased, the CBRT aimed to limit short-term capital flows and prevent the exchange rate from overvaluing. The break at the end of the period can be explained by a series of measures taken by the CBRT, such as lowering the policy interest rate from 6.25% to 5.75%, reducing foreign exchange reserve requirement ratios for all maturities and holding foreign exchange selling auctions when deemed necessary to provide liquidity to the market (CBRT, 2012, p. 48).

The third period covering Sept. 2011–Dec. 2014 covers a period of approximately three years. The coefficients of the budget balance and interest rate variables are statistically insignificant. Therefore, there is no need for interpretation. The coefficient for the real money supply variable is statistically and theoretically significant. The coefficient of the expected inflation variable is significant at the 1% level and provides evidence that an increase in inflation expectations increases the exchange rate presents. In this period, the tight monetary policy and macroprudential measures implemented by the CBRT yielded positive results on inflation expectations (CBRT, 2016, p. 37).

In the fourth period covering Jan. 2015–Apr. 2019, the coefficient of the budget balance variable is statistically insignificant and therefore does not need to be interpreted. On the other hand, the coefficients of other variables are statistically significant at the 1% significance level. It is noteworthy that the coefficient of real money supply increased compared to the other periods analyzed. The positive coefficients of interest rate and expected inflation rate can be interpreted as theoretically significant. However, it is noteworthy that the coefficients are very small.

The last period, covering May 2019–Sept. 2021, covers a period of approximately two years and covers the period of the COVID-19 pandemic. We can consider these years as a period in which the focal points of monetary and fiscal policies changed. In this period, the real money supply is the most important variable affecting the exchange rate. Its coefficient is greater than 1 and statistically significant at the 1% level. The coefficients of expected inflation and interest rate are positive and statistically significant. However, the coefficients are smaller than in other periods. Therefore, we can interpret money supply as the only factor affecting the exchange rate.

When all periods are analyzed, it can be generalized that similar results to ARDL short- and long-run analyses are obtained. However, it can be emphasized that the main driver of the exchange rate is the real money supply.

3.4.3. Monetarist Model with Flexible-Price Assumption

In our study, the model used in MacDonald and Taylor (1994) is preferred to analyze the monetarist model with the assumption of constant prices (Hsing, 2009). The model is derived from the models of Bilson (1978), Frenkel (1976) and Hodrick (1978) (Bilson J. F., 1978; Frenkel, 1976; Hodrick, 1978). In the model used by MacDonald and Taylor (1994), nominal exchange rate (*ER*), domestic money supply (*M*), foreign money supply (M^*), domestic gross domestic product (*Y*), foreign gross domestic product (Y^*), domestic short-term interest rate ($_{iS}$), foreign short-term interest rate (^{S}) and the model is expressed as in 3.33. interest rate (i^*_S) model is shown in 3.33.

$$ER = \beta_0 + \beta_1 Ln(M) + \beta_2 Ln(M^*) + \beta_3 Ln(Y) + \beta_4 Ln(Y^*) + \beta_5 i_s + \beta_6 i^* + \varepsilon s \quad (3.33)$$

3.4.3.1. Data

Sept. 2005–May 2021 period monthly data are used to test the validity of the monetarist model with flexible-price assumption in determining the exchange rate in the Turkish economy. Since the Fourier ARDL model allows up to four variables, the linear ARDL model is used to test the monetarist model with flexible-price assumption. According to the monetarist model with flexible-price assumption in Model 3.33, nominal exchange rate (*ER*), domestic money supply (*M*), foreign money supply (*M**), domestic GDP (*Y*), foreign GDP (*Y**), domestic 2-year bond interest rate (*is*), foreign 2-year bond interest rate (*is**) data are used as variables to be used. Since GDP data are quarterly and other data are monthly, industrial production index (IPI) data are preferred in the analysis instead of GDP data in order to harmonize the data. The data used in the analysis are presented in Table 14.

Table 14: Variables of the monetarist model with flexible-price assumption

Variables	Beginning	End	Source
Nominal Exchange Rate	Sept. 2005	May 2021	CBRT
M2 Money Supply—Türkiye	Sept. 2005	May 2021	CBRT
M2 Money Supply—U.S.	Sept. 2005	May 2021	Federal Reserve Bank of St. Louis
Industrial Production Index—Türkiye	Sept. 2005	May 2021	TCMB (TÜİK)
Industrial Production Index—U.S.	Sept. 2005	May 2021	Federal Reserve Bank of St. Louis
2Y Bond Interest Rate—Türkiye	Sept. 2005	May 2021	TCMB
2Y Bond Interest Rate—U.S.	Sept. 2005	May 2021	Federal Reserve Bank of St. Louis

In the analyses, *LNER* stands for the logarithmized exchange rate, *LM2TR* for domestic money supply, *LM2ABD* for foreign money supply, *LIPITR* for domestic industrial production index and *LIPIABD* for foreign industrial production index. Domestic 2-year bond interest rate is defined as *TFTR*, and foreign 2-year bond interest rate is defined as *TFABD*. Sept. 2005–May 2021 period monthly data are used to test the flexible-price assumption model for the Turkish economy. Data on Türkiye are obtained from the CBRT EDS and data on the United States are obtained from the Federal Reserve Bank of St. Louis database.

3.4.3.2. ADF (1981)— PP (1988) Stationarity Tests

In order to apply the ARDL method, the variables must be stationary at $I(_0)$ or $I(_1)$ levels. The ARDL method cannot be analyzed with variables that are stationary only at I(2) level. At this point, Extended Dickey–Fuller (1981) and Phillips–Perron (1988) unit root tests will be conducted to determine the stationarity levels.

3.4.3.3. ARDL Cointegration Test

The ARDL cointegration test will be used in the analysis of the study and the theoretical information about the test is given under the ARDL cointegration test heading 3.3.2.3 under the Mundell–Fleming topic.

3.4.3.4. Empirical Findings

In this section, firstly, the stationarity of the variables is tested with the Extended Dickey–Fuller (1981) and Phillips–Perron (1988) tests. The result is presented in Table 15.

At the level value, the variable does not have a unit root in both ADF (1981) and PP (1988) unit root tests in the model with constant and trend. The LIPITR variable, on the other hand, does not have a unit root according to the PP (1988) unit root test result in the model with constant and trend at the level value. However, when the first difference of the variables is taken, it is seen that the unit root problem is eliminated. The statistical values of the ARDL bounds test are as shown in Table 16.

According to the ARDL bounds test, since the F statistic value of 5.391 is to the right of I(1) at 1%, 5% and 10% levels, there is a cointegration relationship. This result indicates that there is a long-run relationship between the variables. According to the Akaike Information Criterion, the number of lags of the variables in the ARDL model is as shown in Figure 17.

In the ARDL model, four lags of the NER variable, 2 lags of the LM2TR variable, zero lags of the LM2ABD variable, 2 lags of the LIPITR variable, LIPIABD itself, three lags of the TFTR variable and the TFABD variable itself are used in the short run. Short-run parameter estimates for the ARDL (4,2,0,2,0,2,0,3,0) model are presented in Table 17.

The analysis results of the short-run ARDL (4,2,0,0,2,0,0,3,0) model are presented in table summarized in 3.17. Accordingly, the main determinant of the exchange rate is its own lag. The first lag is significant at the 1% level and its coefficient is positive and greater than one. Although the coefficients of other lags are smaller, they are significant at 1%, 5% and 10% levels. Considering the current and lagged values of the money supply variable, it can be said that the current coefficient and the coefficient of the first lag are statistically significant at the 1% level and the coefficient of the second lag at the 5% level. When the magnitudes and signs of the coefficients are analyzed, it is expected that the coefficient of the current period is positive

Table 15: ADF (1981) and PP (1988) Unit Root Test results

Level		*Variables*	ADF	PP	First Differences	*Variables*	ADF	PP
Level	*Fixed+Trend*	**LNER**	1,445 (0,99)	1,515 (0,99)	*First Differences*	**LNER**	−10,502 (0,00)***	−8,987 (0,00)***
		LM2TR	−1,701 (0,42)	−1,730 (0,41)		**LM2TR**	−14,248 (0,00)***	−14,247 (0,00)***
		LM2ABD	1,840 (0,99)	2,023 (0,99)		**LM2ABD**	−6,791 (0,00)***	−6,181 (0,00)***
		LIPITR	−0,205 (0,93)	−2,526 (0,11)		**LIPITR**	−4,982 (0,00)***	−58,120 (0,00)***
		LIPIABD	−2,107 (0,24)	−2,078 (0,25)		**LIPIABD**	−10,426 (0,00)***	−10,743 (0,00)***
		TFTR	−1,775 (0,39)	−1,960 (0,30)		**TFTR**	−11,640 (0,00)***	−11,571 (0,00)***
		TFABD	−1,894 (0,33)	−1,711 (0,42)		**TFABD**	−10,873 (0,00)***	−10,923 (0,00)***
	Fixed	**LNER**	−1,645 (0,77)	−1,605 (0,78)		**LNER**	−10,802 (0,00)***	−9,092 (0,00)***
		LM2TR	−5,971 (0,00)***	−5,962 (0,00)***		**LM2TR**	−14,290 (0,00)***	−14,289 (0,00)***
		LM2ABD	0,037 (0,99)	0,354 (0,99)		**LM2ABD**	−7,080 (0,00)***	−6,305 (0,00)***
		LIPITR	−2,804 (0,19)	−8,535 (0,00)***		**LIPITR**	−4,982 (0,00)***	−57,800 (0,00)***
		LIPIABD	−2,246 (0,46)	−2,153 (0,51)		**LIPIABD**	−10,397 (0,00)***	−10,708 (0,00)***
		TFTR	−1,653 (0,76)	−1,850 (0,67)		**TFTR**	−11,634 (0,00)	−11,564 (0,00)
		TFABD	−1,671 (0,76)	−1,563 (0,80)		**TFABD**	−10,900 (0,00)	−10948 (0,00)

Note: ***, **, * indicate that the alternative hypothesis is accepted at 1%, 5% and 10% significance levels, respectively.

and relatively large, as an increase in the amount of money in Türkiye is expected to increase the exchange rate by decreasing the value of the national currency. When lagged values are controlled, the first and second lags are negative, which is economically insignificant.

Table 16: ARDL cointegration results

F Test Statistic	**5.391**	
	I(0)	I(1)
10%	1.99	2.94
5%	2.27	3.28
1%	2.88	3.99

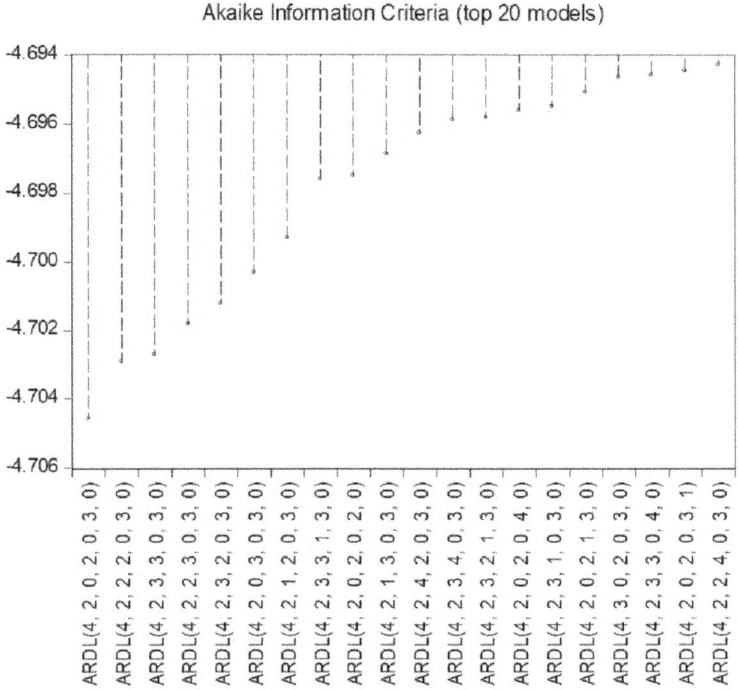

Figure 17: ARDL (4,2,0,0,2,0,0,3,0) preference according to Akaike Information Criterion

Table 17: Short-Run ARDL (4,2,0,0,2,0,3,0) model results

Variable	Coefficient	Probability Value
LNER(−1)	1.262489	0.0000***
LNER(−2)	−0.499520	0.0000***
LNER(−3)	0.252350	0.0269**
LNER(−4)	−0.114853	0.0556*
LM2TR	0.913376	0.0000***
LM2TR(−1)	−0.637960	0.0000***
LM2TR(−2)	−0.188197	0.0250**
LM2ABD	−0.028709	0.6477
LIPITR	0.002879	0.8952
LIPITR(−1)	−0.026105	0.3282
LIPITR(−2)	0.052163	0.0071***
LIPIABD	−0.134849	0.0111**
TFTR	0.008266	0.0000***
TFTR(−1)	−0.002726	0.1786
TFTR(−2)	−0.006083	0.0065***
TFTR(−3)	0.002743	0.0957*
TFABD	0.002721	0.3523
C	−0.992760	0.0256**

Note: ***, **, * indicate that the alternative hypothesis is accepted at 1%, 5% and 10% significance levels, respectively.

An analysis of the coefficient of the money supply variable for the United States reveals that the coefficient is statistically insignificant. Therefore, although the sign of the coefficient is theoretically expected, there is no need to interpret it.

The industrial production index is used to measure the real size of the Turkish economy. An increase in this value means that the country's economy is growing, and the country's currency will appreciate. However, since the current and lagged coefficients of this variable are statistically insignificant, there is no need to interpret them.

The coefficient of the U.S. industrial production index is statistically significant. The coefficient is significant at the 5% level and the coefficient is relatively small and negative. This implies that the value of the U.S. dollar decreases against the Turkish lira in the case of an increase in the production of the United States. This result is contrary to the fact that theoretically, money should appreciate as the economy grows.

When the coefficients of the Turkish interest rate are analyzed, it is observed that the coefficients for the current period and the second lag are statistically significant at the 1% level, while the coefficient for the third lag is statistically significant at the 10% level. When the coefficient for the current period is evaluated in terms of magnitude and sign, it is observed that the coefficient is low and the sign is positive. This situation can be explained in two ways. First, the increase in interest rates in the country accelerates capital inflows and prevents the appreciation of the national currency due to the abundant foreign exchange. The second explanation is that, as a result of the flexible-price monetary model, an increase in interest rates reduces the demand for national currency and increases the exchange rate (De Jong, 1991). Looking at the lagged coefficients, the coefficient of the first lag is negative, indicating that an increase in interest rates after one period leads to appreciation of the national currency through capital inflows. The third lag has a positive coefficient, but it is very small and the significance level is very low. Therefore, it is considered unnecessary to interpret it.

Finally, we examine how a change in the U.S. interest rate affects the value of the Turkish lira against the dollar. The coefficient is statistically insignificant and therefore does not need to be interpreted.

When the short-run analyses are analyzed as a whole, it is understood that the most important variable in determining the exchange rate is the exchange rate itself. This result is similar to that of the Mundell–Flemming model. However, money supply causes the exchange rate to increase in the short run and this result is explained as a consequence of the flexible-price monetary model. This result is similar to the results of the short-run analysis of the Mundell–Flemming model. The coefficients of the industrial production indices of both countries are statistically and theoretically insignificant. Finally, the coefficients of interest rates of both countries are statistically insignificant. An increase in interest rates in Türkiye has a downward effect on the exchange rate with a one-period lag. The long-run ARDL results are as shown in Table 18.

Table 18: Long-Run ARDL model results

Variables	Coefficient	Probability Value
LM2TR	0.876264	0.0006***
LM2US	−0.288433	0.6564
LIPITR	0.290719	0.4194
LIPIUSA	−1.354791	0.0100**
TFTR	0.022107	0.0023***
TFUS	0.027340	0.3295
C	−9.973973	0.0008***
ECT(−1)	−0.100368	0.0000***
Breusch–Godfrey Serial Correlation LM Test	11.094	0.00***
Heteroskedasticity Test: Breusch–Pagan–Godfrey	2.325	0.00***
Ramsey Reset Test	1.376	0.170

Note: ***, **, * indicate that the alternative hypothesis is accepted at 1%, 5% and 10% significance levels, respectively.

In order to analyze the relationship between the variables in the long run, a long-run ARDL analysis was conducted. According to the results of the analysis, the effect of the increase in Turkish money supply on the exchange rate is positive. This value, which is statistically significant at the 1% level, is relatively large and close to 1. In this case, it can be said that every attempt to increase the money supply in the long run will increase the exchange rate. On the other hand, the long-run effect of an increase in the U.S. dollar supply on the U.S. dollar exchange rate is statistically insignificant. Although the coefficient is negative and theoretically expected, it does not need to be interpreted.

When the effect of a change in the industrial production indices of both countries on the exchange rate is analyzed, the coefficient of the variable for Türkiye is statistically insignificant. Therefore, there is no need for interpretation. On the other hand, the coefficient of industrial production in the

United States is statistically significant at the 1% level. The negative sign of the coefficient means that a development in the U.S. economy will lead to a decline in the value of the U.S. dollar against the Turkish lira, which is theoretically insignificant.

When the effect of the change in the interest rates of the two countries on the exchange rate is analyzed, it is seen that the coefficient of the Turkish interest rate is statistically significant at the 1% level in the long run. According to this coefficient, it means that an increase in interest rates in Türkiye will increase the exchange rate. This result can be interpreted from two perspectives. First, it can be interpreted from two perspectives is the existence of a constraint for any reason. Second, as a consequence of the flexible-price monetary model, increases in exchange rates occur when an increase in interest rates reduces the demand for the national currency. On the other hand, it would be wrong in the long run to expect an increase in interest rates to lower the exchange rate.

In the second stage of the long-run analysis, the error correction coefficient is obtained. According to the results of the analysis, although the error correction coefficient is −0.1, an imbalance that occurs in the model in the short run rebalances within approximately 9.96 months. There is an autocorrelation problem in the model. Although the problem of varying variance is found at the 1% significance level, this problem is eliminated by using the Newey–West estimator when estimating the model. Finally, the Ramsey Reset test results show that the analyzed model is correctly constructed.

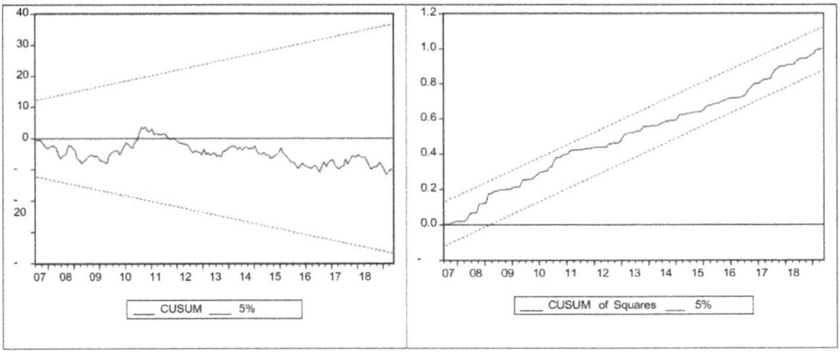

Figure 18: CUSUM and CUSUMQ tests

As showns in Figure 18, according to CUSUM and CUSUMQ tests, there are no structural breaks in the model. Therefore, there is no need to include structural break analysis.

When short-run and long-run ARDL analyses are evaluated together, short-run and long-run analyses are similar. It can be said that the fundamental determinants of money supply and interest rate in Türkiye are similar in both maturity types. The difference between the long-run analysis of the fundamental determinants and the short-run analysis is that the United States interest rate is also effective in the long run.

3.4.4. Monetarist Hybrid Model (Real Interest Rate Differentials Model)

Frankel stated that the monetarist model with the fixed-price assumption is valid only for countries with low and non-volatile inflation. In addition, they stated that the monetarist model with flexible-price assumption is valid for countries with high inflation rates and high volatility (Dornbusch, 1976; Frankel, 1979). For this reason, they constructed a model known as the monetarist hybrid or real interest rate differential model for economies with more moderate inflation. In the model, the assumption of persistence of purchasing power parity is ignored and expectations are added to the model. In this context, variables were added to the model to see the effect of money supply on interest rates and inflation (Uçan, 2011, p. 64).

In order to analyze the monetarist hybrid model (real interest rate differentials model), Pilbeam (2006) model, which improves the model in Frankel (1979), is preferred in our study (Pilbeam, 2006, p. 165). The Pilbeam (2006) model is shown in 3.34.

$$\begin{aligned} ER = \beta_0 + \beta_1 (M / M^*) + \beta_2 (Y / Y^*) + \beta_3 (i_s - i_s^*) \\ + \beta_4 (\pi^e - \pi^{e^*}) + \varepsilon \end{aligned} \tag{3.34}$$

In Model 3.34, nominal exchange rate (*ER*), domestic money supply (*iM*), foreign money supply (M^*), domestic gross domestic product (*Y*), foreign gross domestic product (Y^*), domestic *short-term interest rate ($_{iS}$), foreign short-term interest rate (*S*), domestic expected inflation rate (π^e) and foreign expected inflation rate (π^{e^*}).

3.4.4.1. *Data*

This section tests the validity of the monetarist hybrid model in determining the exchange rate in the Turkish economy with monthly data for the period Jan. 2006–May 2021. Since the Fourier ARDL model allows up to four variables, the linear ARDL model is used to test the monetarist hybrid model. The variables to be used according to the monetarist hybrid model in Model 3.34 are nominal exchange rate (*ER*), domestic money supply (*M*), foreign money supply (M^*), domestic GDP (*Y*), foreign GDP (Y^*), domestic 2-year bond interest rate (*is*), foreign 2-year bond interest rate (is^*), domestic expected inflation rate (π^e) and foreign expected inflation rate (π^{e^*}). Since GDP data are quarterly and other data are monthly, industrial production index (IPI) data are used instead of GDP data. Information on the variables used in the monetarist hybrid model is as in Table 19.

Table 19: Variables of the monetarist hybrid model

Variables	Beginning	End	Source
Nominal Exchange Rate	Jan. 2006	May 2021	CBRT
M2 Money Supply—Türkiye	Jan. 2006	May 2021	CBRT
M2 Money Supply—U.S.	Jan. 2006	May 2021	Federal Reserve Bank of St. Louis
Industrial Production Index—Türkiye	Jan. 2006	May 2021	CBRT (TÜİK)
Industrial Production Index—U.S.	Jan. 2006	May 2021	Federal Reserve Bank of St. Louis
2Y Bond Interest Rate—Türkiye	Jan. 2006	May 2021	CBRT
2Y Bond Interest Rate—U.S.	Jan. 2006	May 2021	Federal Reserve Bank of St. Louis
Expected Inflation—Türkiye	Jan. 2006	May 2021	CBRT
Expected Inflation—U.S.	Jan. 2006	May 2021	Federal Reserve Bank of St. Louis

In the analyses, the logarithmized exchange rate is represented by *LNER*, relative money supply by *LM2*, relative industrial production indices by *LIPI*, 2-year bond interest rate spread by *TF*, and inflation expectation *by BE*. The monetarist hybrid model is tested for the Turkish economy with monthly data for the period Jan. 2006–May 2021. Data on Türkiye are obtained from the CBRT EDS and data on the United States are obtained from the Federal Reserve Bank of St. Louis database.

3.4.4.2. ADF–PP Stationarity Tests

In order to apply the ARDL method, the variables must be stationary at $I(_0)$ or $I(_1)$ levels. The ARDL method cannot be analyzed with variables stationary at $I(_2)$ level. At this point, Extended Dickey–Fuller (1981) and Phillips–Perron (1988) unit root tests will be conducted to determine the stationarity levels.

3.4.4.3. ARDL Cointegration Test

The ARDL cointegration test will be used in the analyses of this section and the theoretical information on the test is given in the subheading 3.3.2.3 ARDL Cointegration test under the Mundell–Fleming topic.

3.4.4.4. Bai–Perron (2003) Structural Break Test

In the analysis of this section, the Bai–Perron (2003) structural break test will be used, and the theoretical information on the test is given in section 3.3.2.4 of the Mundell–Fleming chapter under the subheading Bai–Perron (2003) structural break test.

3.4.4.5. Empirical Findings

In this section, where the role of the monetarist hybrid model in exchange rate determination is investigated, the stationarity of the variables is first tested with the Extended Dickey–Fuller (1981) and Phillips–Perron (1988) tests. The results are as shown in Table 20.

According to the results of ADF and PP unit root tests, the variables generally have unit roots at their level values and therefore are not stationary. However, LIPI variable is stationary at level values in the model with constant and trend according to PP (1988) unit root test. Other variables, on the other hand, have unit roots at their level values but become stationary when the first differences are taken. These results will be taken into account when constructing the ARDL model.

In the second stage, ARDL cointegration analysis is performed. The results of the cointegration analysis are shown in Table 21.

Table 20: ADF (1981) and PP (1988) Unit Root Test results

		Variables	ADF	PP		*Variables*	ADF	PP
Level	*Fixed*	LNER	1,353 (0,99)	1,356 (0,99)	*First differences*	LNER	−10,409 (0,00)***	−8,946 (0,00)***
		LM2	−0,548 (0,87)	−0,558 (0,87)		LM2	−13,228 (0,00)***	−13,604 (0,00)***
		LIPI	0,102 (0,96)	−3,152 (0,02)**		LIPI	−4,158 (0,00)***	−58,030 (0,00)***
		TF	−2,025 (0,27)	−2,207 (0,20)		TF	−11,825 (0,00)***	−11,763 (0,00)***
		BE	−2,037 (0,27)	−1,894 (0,33)		BE	−9,403 (0,00)***	−9,377 (0,00)***
	Fixed+Trend	LNER	−1,654 (0,76)	−1,654 (0,76)		LNER	−10,676 (0,00)***	−9,003 (0,00)***
		LM2	−2,900 (0,16)	−2,819 (0,19)		LM2	−13,194 (0,00)***	−13,549 (0,00)***
		LIPI	−2,849 (0,18)	−10,544 (0,00)***		LIPI	−4,173 (0,00)***	−59,667 (0,00)***
		TF	−1,992 (0,60)	−2,176 (0,49)		TF	−11,803 (0,00)***	−11,728 (0,00)***
		BE	−2,672 (0,24)	−2,538 (0,30)		BE	−9,377 (0,00)***	−9,351 (0,00)***

Note: ***, **, * indicate that the alternative hypothesis is accepted at 1%, 5% and 10% significance levels, respectively.

Table 21: ARDL cointegration results

F Test Statistic	7.478	
	I(0)	I(1)
10%	2.2	3.09
5%	2.56	3.49
1%	3.29	4.37

According to the ARDL bounds test presented in Table 21, the F statistic value of 7.478 is significant at 1%, 5% and Since it is to the right of I(1) at 10% levels, there is a cointegration relationship. According to this result, it is possible to say that there is a long-run interaction between the variables included in the model.

In the third stage, an ARDL model should be established to obtain the short-run coefficients. The relevant ARDL model is shown in Figure 19.

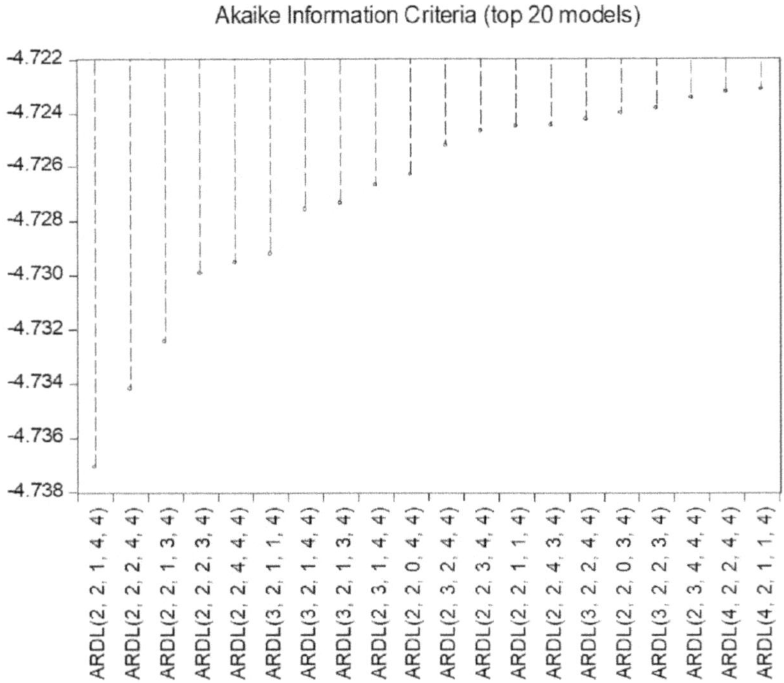

Figure 19: ARDL (2,2,2,1,4,4,4) model according to Akaike Information Criterion

In the ARDL model, 2 lags of the NER variable, 2 lags of the LM2 variable, 1 lag of the LIPI variable, 4 lags of the TF variable and 4 lags of the BE variable are used in the short run. Short-run parameter estimates for the ARDL (2,2,2,1,4,4,4) model are presented in Table 22.

Table 22: Short-Run ARDL (2,2,2,1,4,4) Model results

Variable	Coefficient	Probability Value
LNER(−1)	1.118095	0.0000***
LNER(−2)	−0.168413	0.0040***
LM2	0.872306	0.0000***
LM2(−1)	0.124221	0.4017
LM2(−2)	−0.878686	0.0000***
LIPI	−0.013394	0.5818
LIPI(−1)	−0.040074	0.0748*
TF	0.006768	0.0007***
TF(−1)	−0.004451	0.0105**
TF(−2)	−0.003699	0.1922
TF(−3)	0.001159	0.6365
TF(−4)	0.002404	0.2466
BE	0.002319	0.6633
BE(−1)	−0.003702	0.5987
BE(−2)	0.007914	0.1879
BE(−3)	−0.001795	0.7872
BE(−4)	−0.008804	0.0028***
C	−1.304200	0.0002***

Note: ***, **, * indicate that the alternative hypothesis is accepted at 1%, 5% and 10% significance levels, respectively.

According to the results of ARDL short-run analysis, lagged values of exchange rate are statistically significant at the 1% level. Accordingly, one lagged coefficient of the exchange rate positively affects the current exchange rate. This result is similar to the other models. The coefficient is 1.11, which is quite large. On the other hand, the coefficient with two lags is negative and the coefficient is quite small. Although this result is statistically significant, it is not theoretically significant.

When the coefficients of the relative money supply variable, which shows the ratio of the money supplies of the two countries, are analyzed, the coefficient for the current period is statistically significant at the 1% level. When the coefficient is evaluated, it is positive, and the coefficient is close to one. One lagged value of the relative money supply variable is statistically insignificant, while two lagged values are statistically significant at the 1% level. The coefficient is negative, which is theoretically insignificant.

The current period coefficient of the LIPI variable, which shows the economic growth rate of the two countries, is statistically insignificant. Its one lagged value is significant at the 10% level and its coefficient is negative. This can be interpreted as the appreciation of the Turkish lira against the U.S. dollar as economic growth changes in favor of Türkiye. However, it is noteworthy that the coefficient is quite small.

When the current and lagged coefficients of the relative interest rate variable, which shows the interest rate differentials between the two countries, are analyzed, it is observed that the current coefficient is significant at the 1% level and the coefficient with one lag is significant at the 5% level. The two, three and four lagged coefficients are statistically insignificant. Current period when the coefficient is evaluated economically, it means that the exchange rate increased despite the increase in the interest rate in Türkiye. As in other models, this can be explained through two channels. First, it may be caused by limitations related to international capital flows. Second, it can be explained by the flexible-price monetarist model. The one-lag coefficient is positive, which can be explained by the fact that the relative increase in interest rates and foreign capital inflows increase the supply of foreign exchange and lower the exchange rate.

The last variable is the expected inflation differential between the two countries. When the coefficients of this variable are evaluated, it is understood that the current and lagged coefficients are statistically insignificant. Therefore, there is no need to evaluate it. In the next stage, the long-run analysis was conducted, and the results are as shown in Table 23.

Table 23 presents the long-run ARDL results. In the long run, the relative money supply variable is statistically significant at the 1% level. Accordingly, it is understood that the exchange rate increases when the money supply increases in Türkiye and the coefficient of 2.3 is quite high.

The coefficient of the relative income variable is statistically insignificant. Therefore, there is no need to interpret the coefficient. The coefficient for the relative interest rate variable is significant at the 1% level. The coefficient with

Table 23: Long-Run ARDL Model results

Variables	Coefficient	Probability Value
LM2	2.341905	0.0000***
LIPI	−1.062598	0.1602
TF	0.043358	0.0026***
BE	−0.080838	0.0578*
C	−25.919062	0.0001***
ECT(−1)	−0.050318	0.0000***
Breusch−Godfrey Serial Correlation LM Test	0.399	0.671
Heteroskedasticity Test: Breusch− Pagan−Godfrey	2.470	0.0000***
Ramsey Reset Test	1.223	0.223

Note: ***, **, * indicate that the alternative hypothesis is accepted at 1%, 5% and 10% significance levels, respectively.

a positive sign indicates that while the interest rate in Türkiye rises relative to the U.S. interest rate, the exchange rate is affected upwards. Again, this situation can be explained in two ways. First, it may be due to limitations related to international capital flows. Second, it can be explained by the flexible-price monetarist model.

The long-run coefficient of the expected inflation rate differential between the two countries is statistically significant at the 5% level. When the coefficient is evaluated theoretically, since its sign is negative, it means that an increase in the expected inflation rate difference decreases the exchange rate, albeit slightly. Considering that an increase in expected inflation should have an increasing effect on the exchange rate, this result is theoretically insignificant.

When the short and long-run analyses are compared, it can be said that there are similarities. In addition to the lagged coefficients of the exchange rate itself, interest rate differentials have an increasing effect on the exchange rate in both periods. The significance of the relative income variable is low in the short run and insignificant in the long run. Money supply also has an exchange rate increasing effect. Expected inflation is insignificant in both periods.

The error correction coefficient obtained from the long-run analysis is −0.05. According to this value, an imbalance arising in the model in the short run rebalances within a period of approximately 19.87 months. There is no autocorrelation in the model. Although the problem of heteroscedasticity is found at the 1% significance level, Newey–West estimator is used to estimate the model. Finally, the results of the Ramsey Reset test prove that the model is correctly set up.

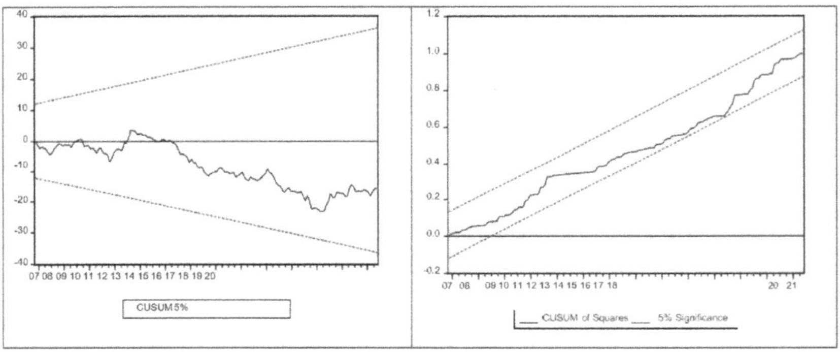

Figure 20: CUSUM and CUSUMQ tests

According to the CUSUM and CUSUMQ tests in Figure 20, there is an out-of-trend structure in the June 2018 period. Since there are structural breaks, a cointegration test with structural breaks developed by Bai and Perron (2003) is required. The results of the structural break dates are presented in Table 24.

According to the results, May 2008, September 2010, May 2013, and June 2017 are the break dates. The parameters obtained within these periods are given in Table 24.

Table 24: Determination of break dates

Number of Fractures	F Statistic	F Critical Value
0 vs. 1	114.1284	18.23
1 vs. 2	23.64206	19.91
2 vs. 3	9.922515	20.99
3 vs. 4	5.267232	21.71

According to these results, the sub-periods to be analyzed are Apr. 2006–Apr. 2008, May 2008–Aug. 2010, Sept. 2010–Apr. 2013, May 2013–May 2017 and Jun. 2017–May 2021 are shaped as follows. The parameters between the break dates are as in Table 25.

The coefficients of the economic growth differentials and expected inflation variables for the first period covering Jan. 2006–Apr. 2008 are insignificant and therefore do not need to be interpreted. On the other hand, the coefficient of the relative interest rate variable is significant at the 1% level and its sign is positive. This means that an increase in the interest rate in Türkiye increases the exchange rate. This situation can be explained in two ways. First, it may be due to limitations related to international capital flows. Second, it can be explained by the flexible-price monetarist theory.

The coefficient of the relative money supply variable in the first period is statistically significant and negative at the 1% level. It can be said that the fact that the coefficient is very close to one is theoretically insignificant. This is because the relative money supply in Türkiye compared to the United States the Turkish lira is expected to depreciate against the U.S. dollar. The break in the first period can be explained by the fact that to mitigate the effects of the 2008 crisis, the CBRT raised interest rates by 50 basis points each in May, June and July 2008, from 15.25 to 16.75 (CBRT, 2009, p. 47).

For the period May 2008–Aug. 2010, only the coefficient of the expected inflation rate difference variable is statistically significant, while the coefficients of the other variables are insignificant. Accordingly, it means that as the expected inflation rate between the two countries increases in favor of Türkiye, the exchange rate increases. However, the coefficient is quite small. The reason for the end-period break is that the annual inflation rate (as the upper bound of uncertainty) exceeds 8.5%.

9.24% (CBRT, 2011, p. 53). One of the reasons why the results are different from the short- and long-term analysis results for the whole period is the effects of the 2008 financial crisis. The 2008 crisis may have affected macroeconomic variables and prevented obtaining significant results.

The third sub-period covers the period Sept. 2010–Apr. 2013. All coefficients of the variables of this period are statistically significant. A positive coefficient indicates that an increase in relative money supply (an increase in Türkiye's money supply) will increase the exchange rate and the coefficient is close to three. Again, an increase in the relative income variable means that

Table 25: Parameters between break dates

Variable	Coefficient	Probability Value
	Jan. 2006–Apr. 2008	
LM2	−0.988430	0.0000***
LIPI	0.198033	0.1472
TF	0.021885	0.0006***
BE	0.013677	0.3060
C	10.53123	0.0000***
	May 2008–Aug. 2010	
LM2	0.049455	0.9368
LIPI	−0.153543	0.4123
TF	−0.011575	0.1433
BE	0.060954	0.0037***
C	−0.324431	0.9623
	Sept. 2010–Apr. 2013	
LM2	2.730735	0.0000***
LIPI	−0.160653	0.0738*
TF	0.015323	0.0152**
BE	0.069301	0.0000***
C	−30.26937	0.0000***
	May 2013–May 2017	
LM2	1.801876	0.0000***
LIPI	−0.033382	0.6020
TF	0.008212	0.0681*
BE	0.010879	0.4795
C	−19.74932	0.0000***
	Jun. 2017–May 2021	
LM2	1.592439	0.0000***
LIPI	0.056187	0.3987
TF	0.007970	0.0046***
BE	0.007700	0.0614*
C	−17.40072	0.0000***

Note: ***, **, * indicate that the alternative hypothesis is accepted at 1%, 5% and 10% significance levels, respectively.

Türkiye grows more. A negative sign of the coefficient indicates that it will decrease the exchange rate and is theoretically significant.

The coefficient of the relative interest rate variable has a positive sign. Although the coefficient is quite small, it implies that an increase in interest rates in Türkiye will increase the exchange rate. This situation can be interpreted in two ways. First, it may be due to limitations related to international capital flows. The second one can be explained by the flexible-price monetarist theory. Finally, a higher expected inflation rate in Türkiye than in the United States will increase the exchange rate. This implies that the exchange rate will change against the Turkish lira as the expected inflation rate increases in Türkiye. Although the coefficient is low, it is theoretically significant. The end-period break can be explained by the negative impact on many financial assets, including exchange rates, and capital outflows due to the increased uncertainty in global financial markets (CBRT, 2014, p. 29).

The fourth sub-period covers the period May 2013–May 2017. In this period covering approximately four years, the coefficients of the expected inflation differential and relative income variables of the two countries are statistically insignificant. Therefore, there is no need for interpretation. The fact that the coefficient of the relative interest rate variable is statistically significant at the 10% level and has a positive sign indicates that as the interest rate increases in favor of Türkiye, the exchange rate increases. Theoretically, this situation can be explained in two ways. First, it may be due to limitations related to international capital flows. Second, it can be explained by the flexible-price monetarist theory. The coefficient is relatively low. Finally, the coefficient of the relative money supply variable is statistically significant at the 1% level and the coefficient is greater than one. This indicates that an increase in money supply increases the exchange rate in Türkiye. In 2017, favorable developments in global activity led portfolio flows to be directed toward emerging economies. The break at the end of the period can be explained by the above-average realization of portfolio flows to Türkiye since May 2017 (CBRT, 2018, p. 19).

The last period covers Jun. 2017–May 2021. The coefficient of the relative income variable for this period is statistically insignificant. On the other hand, the variable for expected inflation rate differences is significant at the 1% level and the coefficient is very small. Therefore, the coefficients of these two variables do not need to be evaluated. On the other hand, the coefficient of the relative money supply variable is statistically significant at the 1% level, has a positive sign and is high. This indicates that money supply is the biggest driver of the exchange rate appreciation and is statistically significant at the 1% level. Finally, the coefficient of the relative interest rate variable is statistically significant at the 1% level. The coefficient is positive and quite small. This can be explained by international capital flow constraints as in the other sub-periods or by the flexible-price monetarist theory.

When all sub-periods are analyzed as a whole, it is observed that the main determinants of exchange rate are relative money supply and relative interest rate variables except for one period. It can be said that an increase in these two variables increases the exchange rate. It can be said that the effect of the difference between expected inflation rates is low and not valid in every sub-period, and the relative income variable is not explanatory.

Conclusion

The exchange rate is defined as the price of the currency of one country in terms of the currency of another country. The exchange rate between the two countries is vital for international economic activity. After the failure of the Bretton Woods Agreement, the International Monetary Fund (IMF) declared that each country is free to choose its own exchange rate strategy, ranging from free floating to fixed. It is worth noting that there are many alternative exchange rate strategies between free floating and fixed exchange rate strategies. Economic managers choose alternative exchange rate strategies according to their economic policy strategy. Which exchange rate strategy to choose depends on the implications of national and international economic policies. The exchange rate affects the relationship between a country and the rest of the world in terms of both goods and capital markets. The value of the exchange rate affects the quantity of exports and imports, by influencing goods market, capital movements with financial markets. At the same time, exchange rates also affect the external borrowing strategy of countries as they determine their external debt in terms of the national currency. The applied exchange rate regime has positive and negative effects on the main macroeconomic variables of a country.

The choice of exchange rate regime has always been one of the most important issues in international macroeconomics. With Robert Mundell's "A Theory of Optimum Currency Area," many studies analyzing the choice of exchange rate regime for countries have been introduced to the literature (Mundell, 1961). According to the optimal currency area theory, the choice of exchange rate regime is determined by some structural and macroeconomic factors such as the size of the country, the degree of openness or the level of economic development.

A diverse literature has emerged linking political and institutional factors, such as political instability, central bank independence or the government's propensity to raise the exchange rate, as influential criteria for choosing an exchange rate regime. The choice between fixed and flexible exchange rate regimes becomes a political decision depending on the credibility of policy-makers. For example, the choice of a credible fixed exchange rate is driven by the prejudice that stable and low inflation in the reserve country will lead to price stability in the home country. In the mid-nineties, there were several financial crises that shook the international monetary system. In the aftermath of these crises, researchers have argued that the choice of exchange rate regime is determined by a country's level of financial integration into international financial markets and the degree of capital account openness.

An analysis of the chronological development of Türkiye's exchange rate regime reveals that Türkiye adopted a fixed exchange rate regime until the 1980s. In this regime type, the Central Bank of the Republic of Türkiye determined the exchange rate. Changes in the value of the Turkish lira were eliminated by adjustments to be made by the CBRT. These changes were usually in the form of depreciation of the Turkish lira and the CBRT's intervention is defined as devaluation. The devaluation in the late 1940s, just before the membership of the International Monetary Fund, intensified with the end of the Bretton Woods System. It increased even more during periods of economic deterioration. In 1973, the Bretton Woods System collapsed, although a fixed exchange rate regime was applied until 1980. Although many member countries adopted a floating exchange rate strategy, Türkiye continued to adopt a fixed exchange rate regime. Within the scope of this easing, devaluation decisions were minimized. After this change, Türkiye's exports increased, and foreign trade surplus was realized.

By the 1980s, import-substitution growth policies were abandoned and an export-led growth strategy was adopted. This development led to the development of the Turkish commodity and financial markets. As a result of this adaptation, the exchange rate strategy changed. The floating exchange rate regime, which allowed the exchange rate to be determined under free market conditions, was adopted and a regime in which the CBRT constantly intervened in the exchange rate was put into practice. In the 2000s, the exchange rate strategy underwent another change. Until the 2001 economic crisis, the floating exchange rate strategy was implemented within a band. After the economic crisis, the floating exchange rate strategy was abandoned, and the managed exchange rate strategy was adopted.

The current exchange rate strategy of the Central Bank of the Republic of Türkiye is the managed floating exchange rate strategy. In case of excessive volatility in the exchange rate, the CBRT intervenes in the market through foreign exchange buying and selling auctions to balance the supply and demand for foreign exchange. The current exchange rate strategy is referred to as managed or interventionist. Although the target exchange rate is not clearly defined, the CBRT intervenes in the market based on the value of a basket composed of the U.S. dollar and the euro.

It is worth mentioning the changes in the Turkish economy after 2000 and 2001. After the February 2001 crisis, an inflation targeting regime was introduced with the stabilization policy. With the implementation of inflation targeting, the stability of exchange rates became more important. To ensure a stable exchange rate after 2002, the CBRT does not only make evaluations based on past data. It also organized foreign exchange buying and selling auctions considering potential developments. After 2009, the Central Bank of the Republic of Türkiye started to hold "foreign exchange buying auctions for reserve accumulation" in the context of global liquidity developments. Although the central bank was not obliged to accumulate reserves as in the fixed exchange rate strategy, it adopted this policy due to the need to hold reserves against external shocks that developing countries might experience. In the second half of the 2010s, the central bank used these reserves to prevent upward movements in the exchange rate.

As can be seen, determining the exchange rate strategy is a critical decision for the Turkish economy. The validity of this situation for every country has contributed to the transition of other countries to floating exchange rates with globalization. This process has led to an increase in the openness of developing countries, a higher share of capital flows and the development/deepening of their financial markets. From this perspective, it can be said that the floating exchange rate strategy has a positive impact on economies.

It can be said that the transition to floating exchange rates, especially in developing countries, is a different area of research. The research area is especially about the factors that determine/influence the exchange rate.

The floating exchange rate system that started with the collapse of Bretton Woods in the 1970s has led researchers to construct different models on the subject. The modeling and determination of exchange rate behavior is one of the unfinished research areas of the century. The problem of exchange rate determination has been at the center of academic debate. Although many models of exchange rate determination have been developed, scholars/researchers still do not agree on which model best describes exchange rate behavior.

Economists have tried to unravel the factors affecting exchange rate movements by examining the behavior of the exchange rate. The first model in this area is the purchasing power parity hypothesis. According to this hypothesis, there is a relationship between the nominal exchange rate between two countries and their price levels. According to this hypothesis, national currencies of different countries should have similar purchasing power in terms of the same currency. This can also be defined as the absolute purchasing power hypothesis. Relative purchasing power parity is defined as the percentage change in the exchange rate in a given period and the percentage change in the general level of prices in two countries.

Another approach is the Mundell–Flemming model. This model combines a simple Keynesian model of goods and money markets for open economies with net international capital flows influenced by domestic interest rates. The analysis focuses on the domestic money supply or interest rate as the monetary policy instrument, treating foreign prices and interest rates as exogenous factors.

In the flexible-price monetarist approach based on the elasticity of prices, money demand, interest rate and relative income variables of the two countries are used to determine the exchange rate. The fixed-price monetarist approach is also called the "high-flying model." In this model, it is emphasized that real factors and financial factors should be used together in determining exchange rates. The model suggests that there may be deviations in purchasing power parities due to sticky prices in the short run. The model claims that real and nominal exchange rates may deviate from equilibrium in the long run due to exogenous shocks. It is argued that the reason for this is the disruption of commodity arbitrage due to the different international flows of different goods.

Finally, it is accepted that the constant price assumption model is valid in low and stable economies, while the constant price assumption model is valid in economies with higher inflation. It is aimed to have an alternative approach to explain the exchange rate movements of moderate inflation economies. For this reason, the Hybrid Monetarist approach was developed as a model in which neither the fixed price nor the monetarist approach is valid.

In this study, the factors affecting the determination of the exchange rate, which shows the value of the Turkish lira against the U.S. dollar in the post-2001 period when the Turkish economy adopted the floating exchange rate strategy, are analyzed within the framework of different models. In this context, purchasing power parity model, Mundell–Flemming model, monetarist model with flexible-price assumption and monetarist hybrid model are tested for the Turkish economy. The analysis periods for each model are as follows: Jan. 2003–Oct. 2021 for purchasing power parity, Jan. 2006–Sept. 2021 for the Mundell–Flemming model, Sept. 2005–May 2021 for the monetarist model with flexible-price assumption and Jan. 2006–May 2021 for the monetarist hybrid model.

The frequency of the data used is monthly for all models, and the reason for the difference between the start and end dates of the data is the different data release schedules of different variables in each model. It can be said that the tests are carried out by using the logarithmic values of the series included in the models in general. Some variables are obtained from the difference or ratio of two-country indicators.

The series of the variables were tested with Augmented Dickey–Fuller (1981) and Phillips–Perron (1989), Becker et al. (2006) Fourier unit root test (FKPSS). ARDL cointegration tests were conducted according to the stationarity results obtained. In the third stage, ARDL short-run and ARDL error correction tests are used to obtain short and long-run coefficients. In the last stage, CUSUM and CUSUMQ tests are used to test whether there are deviations from the trend in the series. If there is a deviation, the possibility of structural break is emphasized. To test for structural breaks, the cointegration test with structural breaks developed by Bai–Perron (2003) is used. Separate tests are performed for each sub-period between the break dates and coefficients are obtained. These sub-periods are compared with the results for the whole period.

To test the purchasing power parity model, unit root tests were first applied. Unit root tests can be categorized into two groups. The first group is the conventional unit root tests ADF and PP, while the second group is the Fourier KPSS unit root tests. When the results of both ADF and PP conventional unit root tests and Fourier KPSS unit root analysis are analyzed, it is seen that the related series have unit roots and become stationary when first differences are taken. As emphasized in the literature, the purchasing power hypothesis for the real exchange rate to be valid, the real exchange rate must be trend stationary at the level or the nominal exchange rate and prices, which are components of the real exchange rate, must be cointegrated. In the light of these explanations, when the data of the Turkish economy for the period 2003–2021 are analyzed, it can be concluded that the variables have unit roots and therefore purchasing power parity is not valid.

The fact that both traditional unit root tests and Fourier unit root tests support this result provides strong support that the hypothesis is not valid. On the other hand, the results obtained from cointegration, and causality analyses indicate that there is cointegration between the variables. This means that there is an interaction between the variables in the long run and is one of the indicators supporting purchasing power parity. Moreover, the existence of causality between variables supports the validity of purchasing power parity. When the results are evaluated together with the reviewed literature, it is concluded that purchasing power parity is not fully sufficient to explain exchange rates in the Turkish economy and alternative models should be evaluated.

In the second stage, the Mundell–Flemming model was tested for the years 2006 and 2021. After unit root and ARDL cointegration tests, short- and long-run ARDL tests were conducted. The results show that the most important determinant of the value of the Turkish lira against the U.S. dollar in the short run is the past exchange rate. The coefficient is above one with 1.16. On the other hand, current and past values of the money supply variable cause the exchange rate to increase. The coefficient is 0.55. It is an interesting result from the short-run analysis that an increase in interest rates has an increasing effect on the exchange rate in Türkiye. Considering that there are no restrictions on capital movements, this can be explained either by the existence of indirect restrictions or by the fact that as the interest rate increases, the demand for national currency decreases and the exchange rate increases. The monetarist approach with the fixed-price assumption explains this as follows. If domestic interest rates rise faster than foreign interest rates or if domestic interest rates fall more slowly than foreign interest rates, the exchange rate will rise, and the national currency will depreciate.

The budget balance has no effect on the exchange rate. Finally, it should be noted that the increase in the expected inflation rate has an increasing effect on the exchange rate in the Turkish economy. It can be concluded that in the short run, apart from the budget balance, other variables affect the exchange rate.

The long-run ARDL analysis shows that all variables except the budget balance are effective, and their signs are the same as the short-run analysis. This indicates that exchange rate behavior is the same in the short and long run.

When the results of the sub-periodized analysis, where structural breaks are considered, it is found that the interest rate and money supply are the determinants of the exchange rate except for one sub-period. It is observed that the budget balance is not a determinant of the exchange rate in any period and expected inflation is not always a good explanatory factor.

The validity of the Mundell–Flemming model can be summarized as follows with the short- and long-term results and sub-period analyses. With the result that the budget balance has no effect on the exchange rate, it can be said that this model is not fully sufficient to explain the movements in the exchange rate. The most important finding here is that the exchange rate itself is the main exchange rate explanator.

In the third stage, the monetarist approach is tested by assuming flexible prices. After unit root and cointegration analyses, ARDL short- and long-run coefficients are obtained. According to the results of the short-run analysis, the main determinant of the exchange rate, which shows the value of the Turkish lira against the U.S. dollar, is the exchange rate itself. As in the Mundell–Flemming model, the lagged coefficients of the exchange rate are quite high. In addition, the money supply coefficient of the U.S. Federal Reserve, the money supply coefficient of the Central Bank of the Republic of Türkiye money supply coefficient and lagged values of the Turkish interest rate are determinants of the exchange rate. It is noteworthy that real economy variables are not effective on the exchange rate.

The results of the long-run ARDL analysis indicate that the money supply coefficient of the Central Bank of the Republic of Türkiye, the interest rate in Türkiye and the income coefficient in the United States are among the determinants of the exchange rate. Although there are some differences between the short- and long-run analyses, it can be said that the interest rate and money supply are effective at different levels of significance in both the short and long run. Due to the absence of structural breaks, no analysis was conducted in the sub-periods.

In the last stage, the monetarist hybrid model is tested. After the unit root test and cointegration tests, the coefficients of the variables are calculated for the short and long run using the ARDL method. According to the results of the short-run analysis, as in the other two models, the exchange rate itself is the main explanatory factor for exchange rate changes. The relative money supply, which is the ratio of the money supply variables of the United States and Türkiye, and the relative interest rate, which is the ratio of the interest rate variables, are the determinants of the exchange rate. On the other hand, it can be said that the expected inflation rate differential and relative income variables do not have determinant abilities.

When the long-run coefficients are analyzed, it is possible to say that relative interest rate and relative money supply variables are the determinants of exchange rate. Although the expected inflation differential is effective at low significance level, the sign of the coefficient is theoretically insignificant.

In the last analysis, it was observed that there were structural breaks and therefore coefficients should be estimated for sub-periods. According to the results of the analysis, except for the period of the global financial crisis, the relative money supply affects the exchange rate, and the increase in Türkiye's money supply has a very large effect on the exchange rate. The relative interest rate determines the exchange rate except for the period of the global financial crisis, and the exchange rate increases as Türkiye's interest rate increases. It can be said that the expected inflation differential has a very limited explanatory role. The relative income variable has no effect in determining the exchange rate in any period. In this case, it can be said that real variables have no effect on the exchange rate in Türkiye.

The first conclusion that can be drawn from the findings of all these econometric analyses is that real variables have very little effect on the exchange rate. Especially monetarist models have not been effective. It can be said that the main factors affecting the exchange rate in Türkiye belong mostly to the financial system. Money supply affects the exchange rate both in nominal and relative terms. Again, the interest rate affects the exchange rate both nominally and relatively.

Another point to be emphasized is related to expectations of the inflation rate and relative prices. While inflation expectations have a limited effect in monetarist models, they have no effect in the Mundell–Flemming model. When this situation is compared with the purchasing power parity model, the ratio of the level of foreign and domestic prices is included in the model. Its effect on the exchange rate is not clear. It is possible to interpret this rate as a relative inflation expectation. In this case, the analysis of purchasing power parity does not provide clear information about its validity. Since other analyses on expectations have not yielded strong results, it is necessary to use the results of the unit root test for the validity of purchasing power parity.

We need to compare the explanatory power of the models analyzing the determinants of the exchange rate in Türkiye in the post-2001 period. Accordingly, it is possible to say that purchasing power parity is not valid. Similarly, it can be said that the explanatory power of the Mundel–Flemming model is low. The budget balance in this model is significant. Thus, real and financial variables in the same model, the model that says that the real sector or public sector variables should be evaluated is not appropriate. Because the real sector or public sector variables are insignificant.

When monetarist approaches are analyzed, it can be said that they are more explanatory. On the other hand, the monetarist hybrid model has the highest explanatory power. These results suggest that the exchange rate is affected by monetary variables and the financial system. Different forms of these variables are included in the equations of the models.

Another conclusion from the analysis is that the exchange rate is affected by past exchange rate values. Except for the purchasing power parity model, the exchange rate was strongly affected by past exchange rate values in the short run in all three models. This can be explained by stickiness. This is because the developments in the exchange rate in the past period determine the exchange rate expectations in the current period and market players adjust the demand and supply of foreign exchange accordingly. This result also implies that individuals are adaptive in forming their expectations, that is, they use past experiences. Considering the adaptive expectations hypothesis of the monetarist approach and the workers' error model, it can be said that the results obtained strengthen the validity of the monetarist approach.

Another reason why interest rate and money supply variables stand out among the determinants of the exchange rate is the intervention of the Central Bank of the Republic of Türkiye in the exchange rate. Historically, the CBRT has pulled the exchange rate up and down through foreign exchange buying and selling auctions. Thus, it has become a determinant of the exchange rate in a sense. Especially until the 2010s, the CBRT tried to affect the exchange rate upwards by buying foreign exchange, and since the second half of the 2010s, it has tried to affect the exchange rate downwards through foreign exchange selling auctions. While conducting buying and selling auctions, in other words, it changed the money supply. The change in money supply, in turn, changed market interest rates. Thus, the determinants of the exchange rate have become interest rates and money supply.

Regarding the interest rate variable, the fact that the exchange rate also increases in the event of a nominal and relative increase in the interest rate is related to the earlier explanations. In Türkiye, an increase in the interest rate decreases the demand for the Turkish lira and leads to an increase in the exchange rate. If an increase in the interest rate creates an expectation that exchange rates will increase, it would be expected to increase the exchange rate by increasing the demand for foreign exchange. An increase in the nominal and relative value of money supply also increases the exchange rate as it causes a decrease in the relative value of money in the market.

Finally, sub-period analyses reveal that global crises, pandemics and similar unusual events have made macroeconomic relations unpredictable. It was observed that some expected interactions disappeared during the global financial crisis. Factors that were effective in these periods disappeared. Again, in the period covering the pandemic, the determinant of the interest rate on the exchange rate decreased. This may have occurred because individuals changed their forward-looking expectations. During the global financial crisis period, it can be said that financial investors sought safe harbor rather than real returns while evaluating their investments in international financial markets, and in this context, the instruments they evaluated their investments changed. This situation brings to the fore the failure of the interest rate hike in attracting capital and thus increasing the supply of foreign exchange and planning to lower the exchange rate.

As a result of all these explanations and interpretations, it can be concluded that the exchange rate can be better explained by monetary variables and that Monetarist models are more explanatory. Moreover, in terms of relative values, the explanatory power of the Monetarist Hybrid model is higher than other Monetarist models. In this respect, it can be said that exchange rate stickiness should be considered when designing exchange rate policies. This result is consistent with the fixed and flexible-price assumption models.

To eliminate this stickiness, importance should be given to transparency in the policies implemented, and it should be ensured that the implemented policies are well understood by individuals. When all these are done, it can be said that the central bank can be successful in its policies, especially in its inflation-targeting strategy, by increasing its credibility and reliability regarding the exchange rate. For further studies, it may be recommended to expand the analysis by including stickiness in other variables in the model. In this way, the behavior of variables can be examined with a model closer to real life.

Bibliography

Abumustafa, N. I., and Feridun, M. (2010). Explaining The Long-term Real Equilibrium Exchange Rates Through Purchasing Power Parity (PPP): An Empirical Investigation on Egypt, Jordan and Türkiye. African Journal of Business Management, 4(7), 1260–1265.

Aghazade, S. (2014). Investigating the Purchasing Power Parity Hypothesis for Russia with Nonlinear Unit Root Tests. Anadolu University Journal of Social Sciences, 14(4), 15–24.

Akbay, O. S. (2009). Social and Philosophical Foundations of Hume's Automatic Flow Mechanism Approach in International Trade. Dumlupınar University Journal of Social Sciences (23), 1–6.

Akçaba, S., and Şafaklı, O. V. (2019). An Analysis on Inflation Tax: TRNC Case. Anemon Muş Alparslan University Journal of Social Sciences, 7, 19–25.

Akçay, A. Ö., and Ertaş, F. (2015). The Validity of the Purchasing Power Parity Theory: The Case of G7. Istanbul Gelisim University Journal of Social Sciences, 2(1), 81–100.

Aktaş, C., and Yılmaz, V. (2008). Estimation of Türkiye's Export Function after the Customs Union. Istanbul Commerce University Journal of Social Sciences (13), 89–104.

Aliyeva, B., & Hüseynov, A. (2017). Analysis of the Validity of Purchasing Power Parity for the Republic of Azerbaijan. Journal of Management, Economics, Literature, Islamic and Political Sciences, 2(1), 73–86.

Alp, İ. A. (2013). Economic Effects of Terrorism. Journal of International Security and Terrorism, 4(1), 1–19.

Alper, A. E. (2016). History of Exchange Regimes. *Çukurova University Journal of Institute of Social Sciences*, *25*(2), 139–150.

Apel, E. (2003). Central Banking Systems Compared: The ECB, The Pre-Euro Bundesbank and the Federal Reserve System. London: Routledge.

Aslan, N., and Kanbur, A. N. (2007). Purchasing Power Parity Approach in Türkiye after 1980. Marmara University Journal of Economics and Administrative Economics, 23(2), 9–43.

Aydın, M. (2018). Gazi University Institute of Social Sciences Master's Thesis. Testing Purchasing Power Parity for OECD Countries. Ankara: Gazi University Institute of Social Sciences.

Aydin, Y. (2014). Trilemma in Open Economy. Istanbul University Journal of Social Sciences (1)1–15.

Aytemiz, S., Coşkun, N., & Tuncer, İ. (2021). Testing the Purchasing Power Parity Hypothesis when Error Terms are Not Normally Distributed: Rals-Lm and Rals-Adf Unit Root Test. Journal of Dicle University Faculty of Economics and Administrative Sciences, 11(21), 57–72.

Bai, J., and Perron, P. (2003). Critical Values for Multiple Structural Change Tests. Econometrics Journal, 6, 72–78.

Baillie, R. T., and McMahon, P. C. (1990). The Foreign Exchange Market: Theory and Econometric Evidence. Cambridge: Cambridge University Press.

Banerjee, A., Dolado, J., and Mestre, R. (1998). Error-correction Mechanism Tests for Cointegration in a Single-Equation Framework. Journal of Time Series Analysis, 19(3), 267–283.

Banerjee, P., Arčabić, V., and Lee, H. (2017). Fourier ADL Cointegration Test to Approximate Smooth Breaks with New Evidence from Crude Oil Market. Economic Modeling (67), 114–124.

Bank for International Settlements. (2019). Bank for International Settlements Statistics.BIS:<https://www.bis.org/statistics/rpfx19.htm?m=6%7C381%7C677> (February 20, 2021)

Bank for International Settlements. (2021, April 27). BIS International Banking Statistics and Global Liquidity Indicators Report for End-December 2020. BIS: Retrieved from <www.bis.org/statistics/rppb2104.pdf>

Barışık, S. (2001). The Monetary Board System, Its Advantages and Weaknesses. Gazi University Journal of Economics and Administrative Economics, 3(2), 51–68.

Barışık, S., and Demircioğlu, E. (2006). Exchange Rate Regime, Convertibility, Export-Import Relationship in Türkiye (1980–2001). ZKÜ Journal of Social Sciences, 2(3), 71–84.

Becker, R., Enders, W., and Lee, J. (2006). A Stationary Test in The Presence of an Unknown Number of Smooth Breaks. Journal of Time Series Analysis, 27(3), 381–409.

Berke, B. (2014). Microstructure Approach to Exchange Rates: A Literature Review. Hacettepe University Journal of Economics and Administrative Sciences, 32(2), 27–56.

Biçici, F. (2016). Chaos Theory, Determinism and Its Importance for Social Sciences and Tourism Research in the Process of New Science Paradigm. Tourism Academic Journal, 3(1), 29–38.

Bilgin, C. (2018). The Problem of the Validity of Purchasing Power Parity in International Trade: A Time Series Analysis for Türkiye. Munich Personal RePEc Archive (87630), 1–14.

Bilson, J. F. (1978). Rational Expectations and The Exchange Rate. The Economics of Exchange Rates, 75–96.

Bilson, J. F. (1978). The Monetary Approach to The Exchange Rate: Some Empirical Evidence. IMF Staff Papers, 25(1), 48–75.

Bitlo.com, (2021). Bitlo Teknoloji AŞ. Bitlo.com: <https://www.bitlo.com/rehber/kripto- para-nedir> (March 24, 2021)

Bonser-Neal, C. (1996). Does Central Bank Intervention Stabilize Foreign Exchange Rates? Economic & Financial Review, 34(3), 797–800.

Bordo, M. D., and Schwartz, A. J. (1997). Monetary Policy Regimes and Economic Performance: The Historical Record. National Bureau of Economic Research (6201), 1–113.

Bozdağlıoğlu, E. Y., and Yılmaz, M. (2017). Inflation and Exchange Rate Relationship in Türkiye: An Analysis between 1994–2014. Bitlis Eren University Faculty of Economics and Administrative Sciences of Academic Projection, 2(3), 1–20.

Bulut, E. (2005). Exchange Rate Determination Models and Micro Structure of the Foreign Exchange Market: The Case of Türkiye. Doctoral Thesis. Ankara: Gazi University Institute of Social Sciences, Department of Economics.

Bulut, E., & Demirel, B. (2015). International Monetary Economics. Ankara: Pelikan Publishing.

Burgaç Çil, A., & Dülger, F. (2017). Testing the Purchasing Parity Hypothesis with Stability and Cointegration Tests for the Turkish Economy. Gazi University Journal of Faculty of Economics and Administrative Sciences, 19(3), 998- 1020.

Büyükkantarcı Tolgay, S. (2019, March). Exchange Rate Theories: An Application on Purchasing Power Parity. Erciyes University SBE Department of Economics Doctoral Dissertation. Kayseri: Erciyes University SBE.

Calvo, G. A., Reinhart, C. M., and Vegh, C. A. (1995). Targeting The Real Exchange Rate: Theory and Evidence. Journal of Development Economics, 47(1), 97–133.

CBRT. (1996). 1995 Report of the Board of Auditors. Ankara: CBRT.

CBRT. (2003). 2002 Annual Report. Ankara: CBRT.

CBRT. (2009). 2008 Annual Report. Ankara: CBRT.

CBRT. (2011). 2010 Annual Report. Ankara: CBRT

CBRT. (2012). 2011 Annual Report. Ankara: CBRT.

CBRT. (2014). Annual Report. Ankara: CBRT.

CBRT. (2016). 2015 Annual Report. Ankara: CBRT.

CBRT. (2018). 2017 Annual Report. Ankara: CBRT

CBRT. (2019). 2018 Annual Report. Ankara: CBRT.

CBRT. (2020). 2019 Annual Report. Ankara: CBRT.

CBRT. (2021). CBRT 2020 Annual Report. Ankara: CBRT.

CBRT. (2022). CBRT 2021 Annual Report. Ankara: CBRT.

Chionis, D., and MacDonald, R. (1997). Some Tests of Market Microstructure Hypotheses in The Foreign Exchange Market. Journal of Multinational Financial Management (7), 203–229.

Chown, J. (2003). A History of Monetary Unions. London: Routledge.

Civcir, I. (2004). The Long-Run Validity of the Monetary Exchange Rate Model for a High Inflation Country and Misalignment: The Case of Türkiye. Emerging Markets Finance and Trade, 40(4), 84–100.

Claassen, E.-M. (1996). Global Monetary Economics. Oxford University Press.

Copeland. L. (2014). Exchange Rates and International Finance (6th ed.). London: Pearson Education Limited.

Cömert, H. (2016). From the Impossible Trinity to the Impossible Dilemma: Bretton Woods and Post-Bretton Woods Monetary Policy. Hacettepe University Journal of the Faculty of Economics and Administrative Sciences, 34(1), 115–136.

Çağlayan, E., and Saçaklı, İ.(2006). Investigation of the Validity of Purchasing Power Parity with Unit Root Tests Based on Spectrum

Estimator at Zero Frequency. Atatürk University Journal of Economics and Administrative Sciences, 20(1), 121–137.

Çevik, E. İ., and Erdoğan, S. (2009). Efficiency of the Banking Sector Stock Market: Structural Break and Strong Memory. Journal of Doğuş University, 10(1), 26–40.

Çeviş, İ., & Ceylan, R. (2015). Test the Purchasing Power Parity Hypothesis in the Fragile Five. Journal of Yaşar University, 10(37), 6381–6393.

De Grauwe, P. (2005). Heterogeneity of Agents and the Exchange Rate: A Nonlinear Approach. In P. De Grauwe, & C. S. Series (Eds.), Exchange Rate Economics: Where Do We Stand? (pp. 125–167). London: The MIT Press.

De Grauwe, P., Dewatcher, H., and Embrechts, M. (1995). Exchange Rate Theory: Chaotic Models of Foreign Exchange Markets. Blackwell.

De Vries, M. G. (1986). The IMF in a Changing World, 1945–1985. Washington: IMF.

Delice, G. (2015). CBRT: Recording 85 Years of History from the Frontiers of an 85-Year History. Journal of Economics Business Politics and Relations, 1(2), 21–55.

Demiray, D. B. (1998). Exchange Rate Determination Methods and an Evaluation for the Turkish Economy in the Post-1980 Period. Unpublished Doctoral Dissertation. Izmir: Dokuz Eylül University Institute of Social Sciences.

Demirel, B. (2011). Optimal Monetary Areas Theory and Analysis of Türkiye's Participation in the EU Monetary System. Doctoral Thesis. Ankara: Gazi University Institute of Social Sciences.

Destek, M. A., and Okumuş, İ. (2016). Investigation of the Validity of Purchasing Power Parity Hypothesis with Fourier Unit Root Tests: The Case of OECD Countries. Gaziantep University Journal of Social Sciences, 15(1), 73–87.

Dickey, D. A., and Fuller, W. A. (1979). Distribution of the Estimators for Autoregressive Time Series with a Unit Root. Journal of the American Statistical Association, 74(366), 427–431.

Dornbusch, R. (1976). Expectations and Exchange Rate Dynamics. Journal of Political Economy, 84(6), 1161–1176.

Dornbusch, R. (1980). Open Economy Macroeconomics. USA: Basic Books Inc.

Dornbusch, R., Fischer, S., and Startz, R. (2017). Macroeconomics (13th ed.). New York: McGraw- Hill Education.

Dülger, F., and Cin, M. F. (2002). Income Velocity of Money (M2): The Case of Türkiye, 1986–2000. Istanbul Stock Exchange Review, 6(22), 33–48.

Edwards, S., and Savastano, M. A. (1999). Exchange Rates in Emerging Economies: What Do We Know? What Do We Need to Know? NBER Working Paper Series, 1–74. National Bureau of Economic Research.

Eğilmez, M. (2013). Writings to Myself retrieved from <https://www.mahfiegilmez.com/2013/07/kur-faiz-dibs-bist-reyting-cds-all.html> (July 10, 2020)

Eğilmez, M. (2013). Writings to Myself retrieved from <https://www.mahfiegilmez.com/2013/03/imkansz-ucleme-ya-da-uclu- acmaz.html> (July 10, 2020)

Eğilmez, M. (2015). Writings to Myself retrieved from <https://www.mahfiegilmez.com/2015/12/triffin-celiskisi-ve-fedin-durumu.html> (July 22, 2020)

Eichengreen, B. (1994). International Monetary Arrangements for the 21st Century. Washington: Brookings Institution Press.

Eichengreen, B., and Flandreau, M. (1997). The Gold Standard in Theory and History (2th ed.). New York: Routledge.

Eichengreen, B., Tobin, J., and Wyplosz, C. (1995). Two Cases for Sand in the Wheels of International Finance. The Economic Journal, 105(428), 162–172.

Enders, W. (1987). Unit Roots and The Real Exchange Rate Before World War I: The Case of Britain and the USA. (198706010700001169), 1–23.

Enders, W., and Jones, P. (2016). Grain Prices, Oil Prices, and Multiple Smooth Breaks in a VAR. Studies in Nonlinear Dynamics & Econometrics, 20(4), 399–419.

Enders, W., and Lee, J. (2012). The flexible Fourier form and Dickey-Fuller type unit root tests. Economics Letters, 117(1), 196–199.

Engle, R. F., and Granger, C. W. (1987). Co-integration and Error Correction: Representation, Estimation and Testing. Econometrica: Journal of the Econometric Society, 55(2), 251–276.

Ergün Tatar, H. (2021). Testing the Validity of Purchasing Power Parity Theory in Selected Integration Organizations with Fractional Unit Roots Using Fourier Function. Socioeconomics, 29(49), 373–388.

Erhan, Ç. (1996). Emergence and Implementation of the Marshall Plan. Ankara University SBF Journal, 51(01), 275–287.

Ersöz, E. (2006). Istanbul University Institute of Social Sciences Master's Thesis. Floating Exchange Rate System and Floating Exchange Rate Application in Türkiye. Istanbul University Institute of Social Sciences.

Evans, M. D., and Lyons, R. K. (1999). Order Flow and Exchange Rate Dynamics. National Bureau of Economic Research Working Paper Series, 1–43.

Fagan, G., and Gaspar, V. (2007). Adjusting to the Euro. Frankfurt: ECB.

Fleming, J. M. (1971). On Exchange Rate Unification. The Economic Journal, 81(323), 467- 488.

Flood, R. P., and Taylor, M. P. (1996). Exchange Rate Economics: What's Wrong with the Conventional Macro Approach? In J. A. Frankel, G. Galli, & A. Giovannini (Eds.) in the Microstructure of Foreign Exchange Markets (pp. 261–294). Chicago: University of Chicago Press.

Frankel, J. A. (1979). On the Mark: A Theory of Floating Exchange Rates Based on Real Interest Differentials. The American Economic Review, 69(4), 610–622.

Frankel, J. A. (1993). On Exchange Rates. MIT Press.

Frankel, J. A., and Froot, K. A. (1990). Chartists, Fundamentalists, and Trading in the Foreign Exchange Market. The American Economic Review, 80(2), 181–185.

Frenkel, J. A. (1976). A Monetary Approach to the Exchange Rate: Doctrinal Aspects and Empirical Evidence. The Scandinavian Journal of Economics, 200–224.

Frenkel, J. A. (1976). Purchasing Power Parity: Doctrinal Perspectives and Evidence from the 1920s. Journal of International Economics (78), 200–224.

Frenkel, J. A., and Mussa, M. L. (1984). Asset Markets, Exchange Rates and the Balance of Payments. NBER Working Paper Series (w1287), 1–117.

Friedman, M. (1990). Bimetallism Revisited. Journal of Economic Perspectives, 4(4), 85–104.

Froot, K. A., and Obstfeld, M. (1989). Exchange Rate Dynamics Under Stochastic Regime Shifts: A Unified Approach. NBER Working Paper Series (2835), 1–26.

Galac, T., Buric, A., and Huljak, I. (2006). Microstructure of Foreign Exchange Marketing Croatia. Croatian National Bank Working Paper (15), 1–41.

Gedik, A., and Karaer, M. (2017). Analysis of Trade Data with Purchasing Power Parity. Journal of Academic Social Research (61), 433–457.

Ghosh, A. R., Gulde, A.-M., and Wolf, H. C. (2002). Exchange Rate Regimes: Choices and Consequences. Massachusetts: The MIT Press.

Girton, L., and Roper, D. (1981). Theory and Implications of Currency Substitution. Journal of Money, Credit and Banking, 13(1), 12–30.

Gleick, J. (2000). Chaos: A New Theory of Science (9th ed.). (F. Üçkan, Trans.) Ankara: Tübitak Popüler Bilim Kitapları.

Goodhart, C. (1990). News and The Foreign Exchange Market. LSE Financial Market Group Discussion Paper (71).

Gözen, M. Ç. (2018). Major Exchange Rate Determination Approaches and the Test of the Effectiveness of Selected Approaches in the Case of Türkiye. Kocaeli University SBE Doctoral Dissertation. Kocaeli University Institute of Social Sciences.

Gözen, M. Ç. (2018). Kocaeli University SBE of Economics Doctoral Thesis. Major Approaches to Exchange Rate Determination and Testing the Effectiveness of Selected Approaches in the Case of Türkiye. Kocaeli University SBE.

Granger, C. W. (1969). Investigating Causal Relations by Econometric Models and Cross-spectral Methods. Econometrica: Journal of the Econometric Society, 37(3), 424- 438.

Grauwe, P. D., and Dewatcher, H. (1993). A Chaotic Model of The Exchange Rate: The Role of Fundamentalists and Chartists. Open Economies Review(4), 351–379.

Grubel, H. G. (2000). The Merit of a Canada-US Monetary Union. The North American Jornal of Economics and Finance, 11(1), 19–40. doi:10.1016/S1062- 9408(00)00030-9

Gül, E., and Ekinci, A. (2006). The Causality Relationship between Real Exchange Rate and Exports and Imports in Türkiye: 1990–2006. Dumlupınar University Journal of Social Sciences, 165–190.

Güriş, B., Yıldırım *Tıraşoğlu, B. and Tıraşoğlu, M. (2016). Purchasing Power Parity Valid in Türkiye? Nonlinear Unit Root Tests. Social Sciences Research Journal, 5(4), 30–42.*

Güven, S., and Ekmen Özçelik, S. (2020). Exchange Rate and Foreign Trade: The Case of Firms in Ankara. Ankara: Gazi Bookstore.

Haji-Othman, Y., and Yahaya, S. (2015). Purchasing Power Parity: Evidence from Selected High and Low Inflation Countries. International Business Research, 8(1), 50–59.

Hatipoglu, M. (2019). A Study on the Validity of Purchasing Power Parity for Selected Islamic Countries. Optimum Journal of Economics and Management Sciences, 6(1), 53–62.

He, Y., and Sharma, S. C. (1997). Currency Substitution and Exchange Rate Determination. Applied Financial Economics, 7(4), 327–336.

Hepaktan, C. E., Çınar, S., and Dündar, Ö. (2011). The Relationship of Exchange Rate Systems Applied in Türkiye with Foreign Trade. Journal of Academic Research and Studies, 3(5), 62–82.

Hodrick, R. J. (1978). An Empirical Analysis of The Monetary Approach to The Determination of The Exchange Rate. The Economics of Exchange Rates, Addison-Wesley. 91- 116.

Hossain, A. A., and Chowdhury, A. (1998). Open-Economy Macroeconomics for Developing Countries. Edward Elgar Publishing.

Hsieh, D. A. (1982). The Determination of The Real Exchange Rate: The Productivity Approach. Journal of International Economics, 12(3–4), 355–362.

Hsing, Y. (2009). The Determination of The Costa Rica Colon/USD Exchange Rate. The International Journal of Business and Finance Research, 3(1), 79–87.

Husted, S., and Melvin, M. (2013). International Economics (9th ed.). Pearson.

IMF. (2019). Annual Report. IMF.

IMF. (2021). International Monetary Fund. IMF Web Site: <https://www.imf.org/en/About/Factsheets/IMF-at-a-Glance> (April 22, 2022)

Ishiyama, Y. (1975). The Theory of Optimum Currency Areas: A Survey. IMF Staff Papers, 22(2), 344–383.

Johansen, S., and Juselius, K. (1990). Likelihood Estimation and Inference on Cointegration with Applications to The Demand for Money. Oxford Bulletin of Economics and Statistics, 52(2), 169–210.

Kalyoncu, H., Kula, F., and Aslan, A. (2010). The Validity of Purchasing Power Parity Hypothesis in Middle East and Northern Africa Countries. Romanian Journal of Economic Forecasting, 4(13), 125–131.

Karagöz, K., and Saraç, T. B. (2016). Testing the Validity of PPP Theory for Türkiye: Nonlinear Unit Root Testing. Procedia Economics and Finance (38), 458–467.

Kardaşlar, A. (2013). Çukurova University Institute of Social Sciences Master's Thesis. The relationship between exchange rate and macroeconomic aggregates: An application on Türkiye. Çukurova University Institute of Social Sciences

Karfakis, C., and Kim, S.-J. (1995). Exchange Rates, Interest Rates and Current Account News: Some Evidence from Australia. Journal of International Money andFinance, 14(4), 575–595.

Karluk, R. (2013). International Economics Theory-Policy. Istanbul Beta Publishing.

Kaya, H., and Çelik, İ. (2018). The Validity of the Purchasing Power Parity Hypothesis in Türkiye: Evidence from Long Memory Tests. Mehmet Akif Ersoy University Journal of Economics and Business Administration, 5(2), 351–365.

Kenen, P. B. (1969). The Theory of Optimal Currency Areas: An Eclectic View. (R. A. Mundell, and A. Swoboda) Monetary Problems of The International Economy, 41–60.

Kesbiç, C. Y., and Çevik, M. (2007). The Effect of Exchange Rate-Based Stabilization Policies on Inflation: A Model Test for the Turkish Economy. Süleyman Demirel University Journal of Economics and Business Administration, 12(1), 95–116.

Keskin, Ş. (2009). The Relationship between Exchange Rate Policies and Terms of Trade: Türkiye Application. Dumlupınar University SBE Institute Master's Thesis. Dumlupınar University SBE Institute.

Krugman, P. R., Obstfeld, M., and Melitz, M. J. (2012). International Economics Theory & Policy (9th ed.). Boston, United State of America: Pearson Education Inc.

Kum, H. (2012). The Impact of Structural Break(s) on The Validity of Purchasing Power Parity in Türkiye: Evidence from Zivot-Andrews and Lagrange Multiplier Unit Root Tests. International Journal of Economics and Financial Issues, 2(3), 241–245.

Kuzuloglu, S. (2020). Paribulog Dictionary. Paribu Teknoloji AŞ: <https://www.paribu.com/blog/sozluk/satoshi-nakamoto-kimdir/?__Cf_Chl_Jschl_Tk__=0f1645470685fa9a47ba6373af ae0621539a65e1-1616681945-0-Aa15H-Jr1pokjfk_Ctyroqnsfd1_ G8wddfkp90ayz1rcqytiqivdbozq_İesde0po1y3g9bdhyau6yn1cji_ K6prjigsanhzgtrozefpum-Ujnkjwc4j8wcis>

Levich, R. M. (1998). International Financial Markets: Prices and Policies. McGraw- Hill/Irwin.

López-Córdova, J. E., and Meissner, C. M. (2003). Exchange-Rate Regimes and International Trade: Evidence from the Classical Gold Standard Era. The American Economic Review, 93(1), 344–353.

Lothian, J. R., and Taylor, M. P. (1996). Real Exchange Rate Behavior: The Recent Float from the Perspective of the Past Two Centuries. Journal of Political Economy, 104(3), 488–509.

MacDonald, R., and Taylor, M. P. (1994). The Monetary Model of The Exchange Rate: Long-run Relationships, Short-run Dynamics and How to Beat a Random Walk. Journal of International Money and Finance, 13(3), 276–290.

McKinnon, R. I. (1963). Optimum Currency Areas. The American Economic Review, 53(4), 717–725.

Meese, R. A., and Rogoff, K. (1983). Empirical Exchange Rate Models of The Seventies. Journal of International Economics, 14, 3–24.

Melvin, M., and Norrbin, S. C. (2013). International Money and Finance. Oxford: Elsevier Inc.

Menkhoff, L. (1998). The Noise Trading Approach-Questionnaire Evidence from Foreign Exchange. Journal of International Money and Finance, 17(3), 547–564.

Mongelli, F. P. (2008). European Economic and Monetary Integration, and the Optimum Currency Area Theory. Brussels: European Commission.

Moss, B. H., and Michie, J. (1998). The Single European Currency in National Perspective: A Community in Crisis? London: Macmillan Press Ltd.

Mundell, R. A. (1961). A Theory of Optimum Currency Areas. The American Economic Review, 51(4), 657–665.

Müslümov, A., Hasanov, M., and Özyıldırım, C. (2002). Exchange Rate Systems and the Effects of Exchange Rate Systems Applied in Türkiye on the Economy. TÜGİAD.

Nakıpoğlu Özsoy, F., and Özpolat, A. (2018). The Relationship Between Consumer Price Index and Purchasing Power Parity: The Case of Mist Countries. Mehmet Akif Ersoy University Journal of Economics and Business Administration, 5(3), 839–848.

Nazlıoğlu, Ş., Görmüş, N. A., and Soytaş, U. (2016). Oil Prices and Real Estate Investment Trusts (REITs): Gradual-shift Causality and Volatility Transmission Analysis. Energy Economics (60), 168–175.

Obstfeld, M., and Rogoff, K. (1995). The Mirage of Fixed Exchange Rates. Journal of Economic Perspectives, 9(4), 73–96.

Obstfeld, M., and Taylor, A. M. (2003). Sovereign Risk, Credibility and The Gold Standard: 1870–1913 Versus 1925–31. The Economic Journal (113), 241–275.

Obstfeld, M., Shambaugh, J. C., and Taylor, A. M. (2004). Monetary Sovereignty, Exchange Rates, and Capital Controls: The Trilemma in the Interwar Period. IMF Staff Papers, 51(Special Issue), 75–108.

Öruç, E. (2016). Monetarist Approach in Determining Exchange Rates: The Case of Türkiye. Kocaeli University Journal of Social Sciences (32), 101–122.

Öz, S. (2009). Crisis and Protectionism: Will History Repeat Itself? Istanbul: TÜSİAD-Koç University Economic Research Forum.

Özdamarlar, D. (2014). Çankaya University Institute of Social Sciences Master's Thesis. Purchasing Power Parity Hypothesis: New Empirical Evidence from Nonlinear Panel Unit Root Tests. Çankaya University Institute of Social Sciences.

Ozer, I. (2007). Optimum Money Areas Theory. Socioeconomics, 5(5), 77–98.

Özkan, F. (2003). Equilibrium Real Exchange Rate Calculation Methods and Measurement of Real Exchange Rate Imbalance: A Study on Turkish Lira. Specialization Qualification Thesis. CBRT General Directorate of Markets.

Özkaya, M. H. (2009). The Changing Role of the IMF: From Bretton Woods to the Present. Uşak University Journal of Social Sciences, 2(2), 102–117.

Özmen, M., and Şanlı, S. (2015). Testing Long-run Validity of Purchasing Power Parity in Developing Countries by Using Seasonal Unit Root Test. Social Sciences Research Journal, 4(2), 195–215.

Öztürk, N., and Bayraktar, Y. (2010). New Approaches to Explain Exchange Rates. Cumhuriyet University Journal of Economics and Administrative Sciences, 11(1), 157–190.

Parasız, İ. (2004). Turkish Economy. Bursa: Ezgi Kitabevi.

Parasız, İ. (2009). Money, Banking and Financial Markets (9th ed.). Bursa: Ezgi Kitabevi.

Pata, U. K., Yurtkuran, S., and Kalça, A. (2016). Energy Consumption and Economic Growth in Türkiye: ARDL Border Test Approach. Marmara University Journal of Economics and Administrative Sciences, 38(2), 255–271.

Pentecost, E. J. (1993). Exchange Rate Dynamics: A Modern Analysis of Exchange Rate Theory and Evidence. Edward Elgar Publishing.

Pesaran, M. H., Shin, Y., and Smith, R. J. (2001). Bounds Testing Approaches to The Analysis of Level Relationships. Journal of Applied Econometrics, 16(3), 289–326.

Philon, D. (1995). Exchange Rates. (M. Bolak, H. Levent, & E. Tokdemir, Trans.) Istanbul Communication Publications: Cep University.

Pilbeam, K. (2006). International Finance (3rd ed.). New York: Palgrave Macmillan.

Rosenberg, M. R. (1996). Currency Forecasting: A Guide to Fundamental and Technical Models of Exchange Rate Determination. Illinois: Irwin Professional Publishing.

Rosenberg, M. R., and Folkerts-Landau, D. (2002). The Deutsche Bank Guide to Exchange Rate Determination. Deutsche Bank.

Sağlam, Y., andErataş Sönmez, F. (2017). Analysis of the Purchasing Power Parity Hypothesis with Panel Multiple Structural Break Tests: BricT Case. EUL Journal of Social Sciences, 8(1), 19–34.

Salvatore, D. (2013). International Economics (11th ed.). John Wiley & Sons.

Samut, S. (2016). KTU SBE Master's Thesis. The Effects of Currency Parity and Volatility on Foreign Trade Sector: The Case of Türkiye. Trabzon: Karadeniz Technical University Institute of Social Sciences.

Sarno, L., and Taylor, M. P. (2003). The Economics of Exchange Rates. Cambridge: Cambridge University Press.

Seki, İ.and Akyıldız A. (2018). The Impact of Terrorist Incidents in Türkiye on the Exchange Rate: An Econometric Approach. Eurasian Journal of Social and Economic Research, 5(8), 76–91.

Seyidoglu, H. (2013). International Finance (5th. ed.) Istanbul Güzem Can Publications.

Seyidoglu, H. (2013). International Economics. Istanbul Güzem Can Publications.

Seyidoglu, H. (2015). International Economics (20th ed.). Istanbul Güzem Can Publications.

Seyrek, İ. (2003). Purchasing Power Parity and The Turkish Exchange Rate. Akdeniz İİBF Journal (6), 151–169.

Şeker, A., and Şimdi, H. (2018). The Validity of Purchasing Power Parity in the Strong Form in the New Era: The Case of Türkiye. Journal of Suleyman Demirel University Institute of Social Sciences, 31(1), 91–104.

Şener, S., Yılancı, V., and Canpolat, E. (2015). Purchasing Power Parity and its Variations Testing for Türkiye. International Journal of Management Economics and Business, 11(25), 53- 63.

Taşkın, F. (1995). Monetary Approach to Exchange Rate Determination: Single Equation Versus Multicointegrating VAR System Estimation for

Exchange Rates in Türkiye. Hacettepe University Journal of the Faculty of Economics and Administrative Sciences, 41–64.

Tavlas, G. (1994). The Theory of Monetary Integration. Open Economies Review, 5(2), 211- 230.

Taylor, M. P. (1995). The Economics of Exchange Rates. Journal of Economic Literature, 13–47.

Tekin, M., Soba, M., and Akıncı, Ö. S. (2018). Factors Hindering IMF's Administrative Reforms and Suggestions for Solutions. Journal of Social Economic Research, 18(36), 147- 171.

Toda, H. Y., and Yamamoto, T. (1995). Statistical inference in vector autoregressions with possibly integrated processes. Journal of Econometrics, 66(1–2), 225–250.

Topal, K. H. (2016). Marmara University Institute of Social Sciences Master's Thesis. Panel Unit Root Tests with Structural Breaks and Cointegration Approach: Validity of Purchasing Power Parity for BRICS Countries. Istanbul Marmara University Institute of Social Sciences.

Toprak, D. (2008). Evaluation of Public Financial Management and Control Law No. 5018 in the Light of January 24, 1980 Decisions. Journal of Süleyman Demirel University, 13(2), 313–333.

Tower, E., and Willet, T. D. (1976). The Theory of Optimum Currency Areas and Exchange Rate Flexibility. Special Papers in International Economics (11), 85–94.

Tradingview.(2021).Tradingview: <https://tr.tradingview.com/symbols/CRYPTOCAP-TOTAL/> (May 2, 2021)

Tunca, Z., and Tunalı, Ç. B. (2007). Monetary Approach to the Balance of Payments. Istanbul University, Faculty of Economics 56(1), 1–12.

Uçan, O. (2011). Exchange Rate Dynamics in Open Economies: The Case of Türkiye. Çukurova University Institute of Social Sciences Department of Economics Doctoral Thesis. Adana: Çukurova University Institute of Social Sciences.

Ulusoy, A., and Karakurt, B. (2004). Causes and Effects of Capital Flows to Developing Countries. Economics, Business and Finance, 19(223), 103–116.

Uz, I. and Dalan Bildir, M. (2009). The Monetary Approach To Exchange Rate Determination: The Case Of Argentina, Brazil, Taiwan And Türkiye. Applied Econometrics and International Development, 9(2), 53–62.

Uz, I., and Ketenci, N. (2009). Exchange Rate Determination: Monetary Approach in The New EU Members and Türkiye. Applied Economics Letters, 17(10), 963- 967.

Ünsal, E. M. (2009). Macro Economics (8th ed.). Ankara: İmaj Publishing.

Woo, W. T. (1985). The Monetary Approach to Exchange Rate Determination Under Rational Expectations. Journal of International Economics (18), 1–16.

Yalçınkaya, Ö. (2016). The Validity of Purchasing Power Parity Theory in G-20 Countries: Evidence from Panel Unit Root Test (1994:Q1–2015:Q4). Bitlis Eren University Journal of Institute of Social Sciences, 5(3), 145–162.

Yılancı, V. (2017). Investigating the Relationship between Oil Prices and Economic Growth: Fourier Approach. Econometrics and Statistics (27), 51–67.

Yılancı, V., Bozoklu, Ş., and Görüş, M. Ş. (2020). Are BRICS countries pollutionhavens? Evidence from a bootstrap ARDL bounds testing approach with a Fourier function. Sustainable Cities and Society, 55, 1–12.

Yıldırım, D. Ç., Yıldırım, S., and Çoltu, S. (2019). An Analysis on the Validity of the Purchasing Power Parity Hypothesis in ASEAN Countries. Balkan Journal of Social Sciences, 8(16), 179–186.

Yıldırım, K., Karaman, D., and Taşdemir, M. (2016). Macro Economics (13th ed.). Ankara: Şeçkin Publishing House.

Yıldırım, K., Mercan, M., and Kostakoğlu, S. F. (2013). Purchasing Power Parity: Time Series and Panel Data Analysis. Journal of Eskisehir Osmangazi University, 8(3), 75–95.

Yıldırım, O. (2002). Anadolu University SBE Department of Economics PhD Thesis. The Effectiveness of Exchange Rate-Based Stabilization Policies 1990–2000 Türkiye Case. Eskisehir: Anadolu University SBE.

Yılmaz, Ş. H., and Özcan, B. (2020). Estimation of Gross Domestic Product Per Capita According to Purchasing Power Parity with Artificial Neural Network and Regression. International Journal of Academy of Social Sciences, 2(3), 57–72.

Yörük, N. (2000). Financial Asset Pricing Models and Testing the Arbitrage Pricing Model in the ISE. Istanbul ISE.

Yurtkuran, S. (2021). the Pollution Refuge Hypothesis Valid in Türkiye? Evidence from Fourier Cointegration and Causality Methods. Journal of Academic Research and Studies, 13(24), 61–77.

Zümbül, G. (2020). Tekirdağ Namık Kemal University Institute of Social Sciences Master's Thesis. An Econometric Study on the Validity of Purchasing Power Parity. Tekirdag: Tekirdağ Namık Kemal University Institute of Social Sciences.

www.ingramcontent.com/pod-product-compliance
Ingram Content Group UK Ltd.
Pitfield, Milton Keynes, MK11 3LW, UK
UKHW021014120926
8556IPUK00040B/1137

9 783631 93383